Contents

Foreword

A TOP World War II ace once said fighter pilots fall into two broad categories: those who go out to shoot and those who secretly, desperately know they are going out to be shot at—the "hunters" and the "hunted."

It didn't take long flying with or against a man to feel out his courage, spirit, skill, and determination. Either he was a hunter or he was the hunted.

Who is better qualified to describe the twisting, churning dogfights that swept across the skies of World War II than a fighter pilot himself? And Edward Sims writes about the "hunters."

His twelve authentic stories sample the heroism, skill, and ingenuity of the men who destroyed the enemy in the air. Because of their achievements, the issue in the air was never in doubt. So will it always be.

And for this reason the fighter pilot occupies a special place in the hearts of his fellow men. He will remain an integral part of the science and technique of warfare for many years to come.

This series of dramatically reconstructed fighter battles contributes a new, informative chapter to the history and the literature of aerial warfare, and will serve as an inspiration to the youth of our country. I found the book absorbing reading.

NATHAN F. TWINING
Chief of Staff, United States Air Force

April 15, 1957
Washington, D.C.

Acknowledgments

IN expressing appreciation for assistance in writing *American Aces,* the first name which must be mentioned is that of General Nathan F. Twining, now Chairman of the Joint Chiefs of Staff.

A gentleman and great airman, General Twining—as Chief of Staff of the Air Force—encouraged the author to set aside other business and compile an account of the most memorable missions of the greatest Army Air Corps aces of World War II.

His support and encouragement were the inspiration and much of the motivation for this work.

My thanks also go to Major General E. J. Timberlake, now in Germany, whose help while commanding general of the Ninth Air Force, at Shaw Air Base, was invaluable.

Major General Bruce K. Holloway, one of the great aces featured in this book, now Deputy Commander of the Eighteenth Air Force, was a source of continuous encouragement and support.

At the Pentagon, Captain James F. Sunderman, Chief of the Book Branch, Department of the Air Force, was of immeasurable aid, in the form of guidance and active support. The contribution of his office was indispensable.

At the Air University, at Maxwell Field, mention must be made of the invaluable job done by Lieutenant Colonel Lawrence Macauley and the historians at the University, Dr. Albert F. Simpson, Dr. Robert F. Futrell, Dr. Maurer Mauer, Dr. Joe G. Taylor, Jr., Mr. Robert T. Finney and Mr. Martin R. Goldman. Without their tireless and prompt response to every request (and there were many), the accuracy and detailed reporting found in this volume would not have been obtained.

Of as much value as anyone else was Mrs. George Zeigler, who, incidentally, lived out World War II in England and was familiar with many of the English airfields encountered in this work, and who spent many long hours on the manuscript.

I should like to mention the valuable counsel and guidance of Mr. Cass Canfield, Chairman of the Editorial Board of Harper & Brothers, without whose co-operation and encouragement this book would not have been possible.

Congressmen John J. Riley and L. Mendel Rivers were invariably ready and willing to lend a helping hand to expedite progress on this project, and were a source of much-needed support.

The public information officers of the Air Force, at so many bases, extended most generous aid. So did some score of Air Force pilots, with whom many memorable flights were made. Space and the fear of leaving out some P.I.O. officer at a faraway base in Europe or Africa, or a pilot who perhaps inconvenienced himself so that a schedule might be met, prevent the listing of names in these categories. I hope each one of these officers will accept my sincere thanks, in this poor form, and know in their hearts of my deep appreciation, as an old Air Force veteran and pilot.

To each of the twelve aces themselves, who did their best to reconstruct their most thrilling battle as a fighter pilot, my thanks are due.

EDWARD H. SIMS

Washington, D.C.
September, 1957

Introduction

THE story of America's highest-scoring fighter aces, as they performed in great fighter battles of World War II, has not yet been adequately told.

This book represents an attempt to re-create the drama of the greatest missions of the top aces so accurately the reader shares the tension and excitement, *goes along* on the flights.

There are several reasons why the reading public does not have a clear mental picture of fighter battles, although their land and sea counterparts have been vividly re-enacted, in minute detail, by the historians.

In the first place, fighters carry no observers, newsmen, photographers, or latter-day historians. To go on a fighter mission, and participate in combat, one must be *the* pilot. In the cockpit are accommodations for only one man.

Secondly, the fighter pilot keeps no written record while carrying out a mission. He is too busily engaged flying, navigating, fighting, and communicating to bother with records.

Finally, a fighter battle is likely to take place over an aerial expanse of fifty or a hundred miles, and the individual exploits of a squadron, group, or wing are next to impossible to follow—even for the commanding officer on the mission.

The goal of this book is to describe the most thrilling fighter battles of the highest-scoring U.S. Army Air Corps aces, in the three principal theaters of World War II—the European, Far East, and China-Burma-India theaters. To accomplish this task the co-operation of each of the aces treated in this work was necessary. Memories were searched and long hours were spent in interrogation—in various places spread over three continents. In addition, because each had forgotten so many details of his combat missions, the memories of others who flew on these missions and the records of the combat actions themselves had to be consulted. In all, some forty thousand miles of travel and two years were required.

The great aces treated in this book include the eight survivors of the twelve highest-scoring Army Air Corps fighter pilots in the European Theater, the two survivors of the six leading aces in the Far East, and the two survivors of the five leading fighter pilot aces in the China-Burma-India Theater.

A chapter is devoted to each of these fighter aces and to his most exciting and unusual mission, with a map and enough introductory background to enable the reader to realize the significance of the action.

The attrition rate among our highest-scoring aces of World War II was tragically high during and after the war. No less than eleven out of the top twenty-three were killed in action or have died in crashes in the line of duty. The choice of pilots to include in this book was therefore made by fate, the twelve who still survive and who could be personally interviewed. While there is no official list of the highest-scoring U.S.A.A.F. pilots, and different procedures were followed in the different theaters in awarding "kills," the unofficial but thought-to-be-reliable totals provided by the Department of the Air Force are the most accurate figures available, and are the figures used here.

The choice of which mission to include of the many flown by all twelve pilots was, generally speaking, made by each man. For one reason or another that is clear to each pilot, and which becomes clear to the reader, the mission described is the most memorable one which he flew. It may not be the flight on which he made the highest number of "kills," and perhaps none of the battles described may properly be called the greatest—opinions and criteria differ widely on this controversial subject—but certain it is that each mission and battle recorded here is fairly representative and typical of the toughest missions flown by our pilots during the war. For each flier involved it was especially memorable, and for the reader all of the missions together provide a wonderfully varied cross section of the different kinds of action our fighter pilots encountered during the war, day and night, in all kinds of weather, on patrol, as escorts, as interceptors, and on tactical offense. In short, it is hoped that the over-all picture provided by these twelve separate incidents gives the reader a good basic understanding of what our U.S.A.A.F. fighter pilots faced as the air war developed between 1942 and 1945.

If inaccuracies are found in this work, as no doubt they will be, they are honest ones. Every effort has been made to verify details of each battle and each chapter has been submitted to the Department of the Air Force's historical division for correction. Whenever there has been any doubt about time, location, altitude, enemy identification or strength, no effort has been spared to obtain the facts—including the examination of German and Japanese accounts.

In reading these exploits, and studying the maps, it should be remembered that conditions under which the twelve aces flew varied immensely. The pilot doing battle with a Zero in 1942 was limited in his choice of tactics because of the superior performance of his foe's aircraft and the restricted capabilities of his own.

Toward the end of the war, however, the United States was producing the finest conventional fighter planes in the world and the situation was exactly reversed, with one exception. That was the Luftwaffe's ME–262 jet, which appeared first in 1944. These jet fighters were too late and two few to turn the tide, though they might have, had they appeared in large numbers a year earlier. (Credit for the fact that they did not lies with Adolf Hitler himself, who delayed the ME–262 program for a year, insisting that these light planes be adapted as bombers.)

When American fighter pilots meeting the Lutfwaffe in the skies over Germany in late 1944 and 1945 encountered the ME–262, as did the author, it was clearly superior in performance to any fighter the Allies had in operation.

In the Far East, the Japanese Zero was a surprise at the beginning of World War II. In range, maneuverability and rate of climb, the Zero (flown exclusively by Japanese Navy pilots in the opening phases of the war) was superior to the Army's P–40 and P–39.

As a result, the "golden rule" of U.S. fighter pilots in those days was to seek an altitude advantage from which a diving pass could be made on the enemy, preferably out of the sun. If our pilots failed to bring down the foe on the initial pass they continued their dives to get away. The heavier U.S. planes had great diving velocity, but couldn't turn and maneuver with the Zero if they tarried at the enemy's altitude.

As the more advanced Army fighters put in their appearance—the P–38's, then the P–47's, and finally the P–51's—the advantage enjoyed by the Zero disappeared. By the time the P–51's were available in quantity, U.S. forces enjoyed both quantitative and qualitative superiority in the air.

In Europe the Germans, like the Japanese, began with the best

The finest fighters of the U.S.A.A.F.: (top to bottom) Lockheed P-38 Lightning; North American P-51 Mustang, Republic P-47 Thunderbolt. (Air Force Photo)

fighters, and stuck with them, partly because they were initially the best and partly because delays necessary for model changeovers were not allowed to interrupt production as the war grew desperate.

In the early days of the war Luftwaffe fighter tactics were designed to take full advantage of more powerful German engines. The ceiling of the ME-109E was greater than that of its opponents, and Luftwaffe tactics usually called for a jump from superior height. When attacking the Spitfire, the Germans often employed the same tactics American pilots in P-40's used in fighting the Zero—a diving pass on and through the more maneuverable foe. The Spitfire, like the Zero, was capable of out-turning its competitors and in a dogfight at most altitudes usually emerged victorious, flying skill and gunnery of the pilots being somewhere near equal.

At the beginning of the war, 1939, the ME-109 was the standard Luftwaffe fighter and probably the best in the world, especially at high altitude. R.A.F. Hurricanes and Spitfires fought magnificently at Dunkirk; and in the Battle of Britain, with superior radar control and the advantage of defense, it was evident that the difference between them and the ME-109 was small. At 20,000 feet or below the Spitfire was, indeed, a match for the 109. But the Germans soon had another fighter superior to the 109. It was the FW-190, and this fighter was clearly superior to the Spitfire until the Spitfire 9 replaced the Spitfire 5, several years later. The highest-scoring British ace of the war, Group Captain J. E. Johnson (thirty-eight accredited victories), frankly admits this inferiority. In his enlightening book, *Wing Leader*, Johnson writes that as late as the spring of 1943 the FW-190's superiority over the Spitfire 5—then in wide use—was considerable.

It was in late 1943 and 1944 that the A.A.F. introduced its late-model fighters, the P-51 and the P-47, which were capable of taking the measure of the FW-190.

Tactics changed, naturally, as one side and then the other acquired an edge in ceiling or speed. But changes in fighter-versus-fighter tactics were not as frequent as during World War I, when new planes put in their appearance so often, and when the advantage shifted back and forth so many times. The general rules remained true throughout the war. The fighter with the greater ceiling enjoyed the advantage. That with greater weight and diving speed could often escape. The more maneuverable fighter, if not surprised from above, had the edge in a dogfight at a given altitude.

Fighter tactics in defending bombers, and in attacking them, also changed during the course of the war. The A.A.F. made the same mistake the Luftwaffe and then the R.A.F. made in Europe—that of tying defending fighters too close to the boxes of bombers they were assigned to defend. This robbed the fighters of necessary maneuverability and flexibility, and prevented them from jumping attacking fighters at a distance from the bombers. When they did intercept the enemy fighters, their own bombers were often already coming under attack.

The Eighth U.S. Air Force changed its fighter escort tactics in 1944, and bomber losses were reduced. Other American air forces had similar experiences.

Japanese escort fighters also seem to have flown too close to their big friends, in the light of lessons learned in the war.

Tactics used by fighters attacking bombers changed relatively little. In the Battle of Britain, R.A.F. fighters usually sought a tail position. Japanese bombers were most often shot down from the six o'clock position, and since they burned rather easily could be brought down more easily. The Luftwaffe experimented with various gunnery approaches in the climactic stages of the Battle of Germany.

German fighters attacking U.S. heavy bombers tried everything from dropping bombs into tight-flying formations to heavy rockets. When the Flying Fortress was first used in numbers over Europe, Luftwaffe pilots found its defensive armament quite awesome. They sometimes substituted head-on, barrel-rolling attacks in place of attacks from six o'clock or elsewhere. German fighters on some occasions purposely rammed U.S. bombers in close formation and the resulting collision often brought down one or two adjacent bombers. The tactics of Japanese fighter pilots were somewhat similar.

In the later days of the Battle of Germany, the ME–262 jets almost invariably obtained an altitude Allied fighters could not reach, remaining there until they spotted a bomber box out of position, or without its fighter escort, and then plunged down vertically on the bombers—at such speed successful pursuit was almost impossible.

The Germans are usually given credit for introducing the "finger-four" fighter formation, also adopted by both the British and Americans. During the first part of the war the R.A.F. employed either the V or string formation.

But R.A.F. aces Douglas Bader and Hugh Dundas were among the first to recognize the merits of "finger-four," and led the changeover to this new formation—which placed a flight of fighters in the same position as the tips of the four fingers. In this formation—still used today—each pilot can glance to his side and clear the tail of one or more of his comrades.

Not only flights (four planes) but squadrons (four flights) assumed this combat formation almost exclusively in the last years of the war.

And finally, in speaking of tactics, planes and formations, it should be recorded that teamwork was the key to the one-sided victory totals U.S. fighters began to rack up in the final months and years of war. The Japanese particularly suffered from a lack of teamwork in fighter combat, as their great fighter pilots readily admit.

The Germans, especially in the later years, suffered greatly because of poor teamwork and a tendency to assemble in large, unwieldy gaggles, logical results of hurried and inadequate training. U.S. fighter pilots seemed especially well adapted to close co-ordination and teamwork in fighter battles, a characteristic vividly demonstrated in several chapters of this book.

It is ironical, as Quentin Reynolds observes in his recent book on World War I fighter pilots—*They Fought for the Sky*—that the great aces of World War II are still less familiar names than the great American aces of World War I—such as Rickenbacker, Luke, Springs, Vaughn, Kindley, Hartney, and others. Perhaps this is because the actions of World War I were a bit easier to follow. Or perhaps it is because there were so many more great aces in World War II. In any event, from this book the reader will get a clearer insight than he had before into actual combat conditions in World War II, and the tactics and triumphs of the greatest American aces.

To become a fighter pilot in the first place is no mean achievement, and of those young Americans who threw themselves wholeheartedly into the effort in World War II, many gave their lives in the process of training, before reaching a combat zone.

Back in the never-to-be-forgotten thirties the young men who would become their country's greatest fighter aces were teen-agers. In those days the thoughts of young men, soon to be flying the fastest and latest fighting instruments science could build, centered on fraternity parties, that new jalopy, the high-school football game, or the Major League pennant races. The world was at peace and the United States was steering clear of war if it came. Life went on, and a dollar bought a good dinner and a ticket to the movies.

But in spite of our national nonchalance, the holocaust was creeping closer and closer, and one was beginning to see more and more posters at the post office advising young men to "Join the Aviation Cadets!" To young men everywhere the fighter pilot was the last relic of the age of chivalry—individual combat in the modern version of knighthood. And in every country the posters were answered.

To the young men of the thirties, the Red Knight of Germany, "Mick" Mannock, Georges Guynemer, Eddie Rickenbacker and Billy Bishop were legendary figures of the "Great War." To the red-blooded American boy who had read of their exploits, and the admiration which existed among them even in combat, the choice of jobs, if there was to be a war, was that of a pursuit pilot, as it was called then. Nothing quite compared with the romantic thrill of flying and fighting alone, on one's own ability and initiative, as a fighter pilot.

In these days the fighter pilot was looked upon as the glamour boy of the service. With dashing manner, white silk scarf and crumpled cap, he followed in the best tradition of the undisciplined soldier. Here was a pilot and officer who flew the fastest thing in the world, all by himself, ready to take on his foe at 30,000 feet in the blue. There was nothing quite like him. The teen-age coeds were convinced of that.

But the youthful American who swaggered down the street behind a pair of silver (or gold) wings had survived a rugged course of academic, flying and officer training. He had seen a considerable percentage of his carefully-screened classmates fall along the wayside, on the road to graduation, some of them paying for mistakes with their lives. Gradually the country woke up to the fact that these cocky young officers (some of whom were colonels in their twenties) were not just glamour boys. Like the Marine Corps, they had esprit de corps. They were convinced they were the best in the world, and had the finest planes—a far cry from World War I, when U.S. industry failed to provide a first-class fighter.

That the cream of the crop of the nation's youth volunteered for flying duty was vitally important. For it was air power that was to prove decisive in so many of the war's campaigns.

The Luftwaffe demonstrated the vital importance of aerial supremacy in conquering Poland in 1939, Norway and France in 1940, and in capturing Crete the next year. And Nazi leaders were prepared to undertake the invasion of England when the Luftwaffe had knocked out the Royal Air Force, in spite of the existence of the Royal Navy. In turning back the aerial onslaught of the Germans that year it was the R.A.F. fighter pilot who earned from Churchill the famous tribute: "Never had so many owed so much to so few."

In the Pacific, the Japanese Navy's Zero fighter, along with a powerful surface fleet, was largely responsible for the rapid Japanese advance in the first half of 1942. And it was a carrier disaster at Midway (and a lesser one the month before) in June, 1942, crippling Japanese naval air power, that finally checked the enemy's advance in this theater. It was well, then, that America had the flower of its youth in the air. These airmen were to meet accomplished foes in outstanding fighters and represent their country well. In a few short years they were to dominate the skies in every theater.

Some may ask why the highest-scoring American ace, the late Major Richard I. Bong (40 victories), came nowhere close to the top scores of leading enemy aces. The Germans claim more than a hundred victories for Hans Marseille, the "Pilot of Africa," and even more for their top ace, and the Japanese credit their greatest living ace, Saburo Sakai, with 64, and others with even more.

The answer lies largely in different operational and awards procedures followed by the air forces of various countries. In the U.S. Army Air Forces, fighter pilots were expected to fly a tour of duty, after which they were withdrawn from combat. Some requested extensions and flew more than a single tour, but this was the exception. Moreover, it was the tendency of American fighter commands to withdraw top-ranking aces from combat when their records and demonstrated abilities made them too valuable to lose.

The Germans and Japanese, on the other hand, were forced to keep their best pilots in combat indefinitely. This allowed a few to achieve remarkable victory totals, but most of them met death in the end, flying on long after having contributed more than their share to prosecution of the war. The Germans, moreover, followed a most complicated and constantly-changing procedure in awarding points for kills, and certain kills were worth more points than others. U.S. fighter pilots were required to produce actual films of their kills, or confirmations from other pilots, which sometimes deprived them of credits for certain victories.

The United States had the manpower to operate under the rotation system, but aside from that, the system provided an incentive and a boost to morale—invariably high among American fighter pilots. Few failures to carry out a mission due to opposition were ever encountered among American fighter pilots in World War II.

The sight of a great American aerial armada, under anti-aircraft fire and beset with hostile fighters, boring on into the enemy homeland, is one of the great spectacles of courage and determination in war. In the Eighth Air Force's offensive against Germany, not once did a major American bomber and fighter armada turn back from its mission because of enemy opposition, although on one tragic occasion the Luftwaffe shot down 60 and damaged 138 of the 291 bombers dispatched—in addition to losses inflicted on American fighters. This was a loss of more than 600 American airmen in a space of a few hours! But the target, Schweinfurt, was bombed, and fighters and bombers carried out their orders. On one mission to Berlin, described in this book, 69 bombers and 11 fighters—80 aircraft and 701 men—were lost in an equally short time.

At the time of the mission to Schweinfurt, in October, 1943, the Eighth Air Force wasn't equipped with the long-range fighters to provide its bombers adequate protection. As longer-ranged "little friends" became available, they were able to escort the bombers all the way in and out, even on the deepest penetrations of Germany, and thereby assure the success of the bomber offensive. U.S. fighters, then, were decisive in proving the theory that strategic bombing can be carried out in daylight without prohibitive losses—a type of bombing both the Luftwaffe and the R.A.F. attempted and called off because of high losses. That was but one of the achievements of our fighters.

The unofficial list of top-scoring U.S. Army Air Corps aces of World War II, which may possibly omit a name which rightly belongs there, but which is utilized in this work as the best and most accurate tabulation in existence, follows. It should be pointed out, in presenting the list to the reader, that the various theaters followed different customs in awarding victories. The greatest variation is found in the award of victories for ground kills—a practice followed in Europe but not adopted in the Far East or in the China-Burma-India Theater.

As a result, the scores of many fighter pilots in the latter two theaters are lower than they would have been had they been credited with ground kills. This statement is not intended to minimize the accomplishment of destroying a Luftwaffe aircraft on the ground—which sometimes constituted a highly dangerous or fatal undertaking. Nevertheless, the difference in scoring should be kept in mind by the reader, and a separate accounting of the aerial scores of the E.T.O. pilots will be found to the right of the combined ground and air totals attributed to them.

HIGHEST-SCORING AMERICAN ACES OF WORLD WAR II AND CONFIRMED VICTORIES*

EUROPEAN THEATER OF OPERATIONS

Air & Ground		*Air*	
John C. Meyer	37	Francis S. Gabreski	31
John T. Godfrey	36	Robert S. Johnson	28
Elwyn G. Righetti **	34.5	George E. Preddy **	26
Francis S. Gabreski	33.5	John C. Meyer	24
David C. Shilling **	33	David C. Shilling **	22.5
Henry W. Brown	32	John T. Godfrey	18
George E. Preddy **	31	Henry W. Brown	17
Ralph Hofer **	30.5	Ralph Hofer **	16.5
John D. Landers	28.5	James A. Goodson	15
Robert S. Johnson	28	John D. Landers	8.5
James A. Goodson	28	Elwyn G. Righetti **	7.5
Joseph L. Thury	28	Joseph L. Thury	2.5

FAR EAST

	Air
Richard I. Bong **	40
Thomas B. McGuire **	38
Charles MacDonald	27
Neal E. Kearby **	22
Jay T. Robbins	22
Gerald R. Johnson **	22

CHINA-BURMA-INDIA

	Air
John C. Herbst **	21
John F. Hampshire **	17
Edward O. McComas **	14
Bruce K. Holloway	13
John R. Alison	10

* To the nearest half aircraft.
** Deceased.

If this volume gives the reader a better picture of aerial combat as described by a combat pilot, creates an appreciation of courageous performances rendered, and helps in some slight way to establish for these American aces their rightful place in the history of World War II, the primary purpose of the effort will have been attained.

EDWARD H. SIMS

GLOSSARY

(The following words or initials are a few that appear in the chapters of American Aces. The brief explanations given will acquaint the reader with their meaning in advance.)

ABORT: To turn back before reaching the target.

ACE: Fighter pilot with five or more victories.

ANGELS: Altitude. "Angels thirteen" is 13,000 feet.

BANDITS: Enemy aircraft.

BARREL ROLL: Medium-speed roll, course remaining constant.

BIG FRIENDS: Friendly bombers.

BOGIES: Unidentified aircraft.

C.O.: Commanding officer.

CHANDELLE: Reversal of course by climbing turn.

CONTRAILS: Visible trails of high-flying aircraft.

DEFLECTION SHOT: Firing from side angle.

ELEMENT: Formation of two fighters.

FLAK: German anti-aircraft fire.

FLAT-OUT: Attaining maximum speed.

FLIGHT: Formation of four fighters (two Elements).

GAGGLE: Assemblage of loose-flying enemy fighters.

GROUP: Three or four Squadrons.

IMMELMAN: A reversal of course by half loop and roll out.

JINXING: To take evasive, erratic action to dodge flak.

LITTLE FRIENDS: Friendly fighters.

LUFBERRY: A circle of fighters in a tight turn.

MAGS: Magnetos.

MAY DAY: Radio distress call, from the French "m'aidez."

MUSH: Sluggish flying performance (in thin air or at low speed).

OPS: Operations.

REVETMENT: Parking area for aircraft.

S.O.P.: Standard Operating Procedure.

SECTION: Half a Squadron, usually eight aircraft.

SPLIT-S: To half-roll and dive vertically.

SQUADRON: Formation of several Flights, usually three or four.

TRIM: To adjust control tabs for proper flying attitude.

TWELVE O'CLOCK: Straight ahead (hours of clock used to denote direction).

VAPOR TRAILS: Visible trails left by high-flying aircraft.

PART *1*

THE ODDS
ARE AGAINST US

1 *Night Scramble at Hengyang*

JULY 30, 1942:

Major JOHN R. ALISON

THE war between Japan and China had begun long before Hitler's armies marched into Poland, September 1, 1939, touching off World War II in Europe. On July 7, 1937, fighting between Chinese and Japanese troops broke out at the Marco Polo bridge near Peiping, and despite United States efforts, and those of other nations, the "incident" (as the Japanese called it) deteriorated into general war between the two countries.

The United States Ambassador to Japan, Joseph C. Grew, recording these events in *Ten Years in Japan*, reports that China sought earnestly (and in vain) to place the dispute before an international tribunal. In August Japanese marines landed at Shanghai, and a bitter struggle for that prize port began between the best-equipped and best-trained Chinese divisions and Japanese forces.

The elite Chinese divisions gave a good account of themselves, holding the city against a superior enemy until November 8. But four months to the day after the outbreak of fighting near Peiping Japanese troops occupied the great seaport and thereafter advanced deeper and deeper into China.

3

Nor was the United States to wait until December 7, 1941, to feel
the hand of Japanese military extremists. On December 12, 1937,
Japanese Army artillery and Navy bombers attacked and sank the U.S.
gunboat *Panay* (retiring before the Jap advance up the Yangtze River),
killing two Americans aboard, and another American ship captain,
whose oil carrier was among other U.S. craft sunk that day.

The Japanese Government in Tokyo made amends and readily paid
indemnities, but the fact that Japanese Army motor launches machine-
gunned *Panay* survivors, that both Navy and Army orders were to
destroy all shipping on the river, despite knowledge furnished by the
U.S. Embassy prior to the event that *Panay* was there, was an ominous
prelude of things to come. The American flag, prominently displayed
atop *Panay*, was thus deliberately fired on in 1937 by the same power
which would sink so many warships flying the same colors December
7, 1941.

Japanese armies controlled much of China until 1945—eight long
years after the Marco Polo bridge "incident," and four years after the
United States had become a belligerent. While the tide on the sea was
turned at Coral Sea and Midway, in 1942, the high tide of the Japanese ground advance into China was reached in 1944, only a year
before Japan surrendered. Thus the campaign in China was a grim
one for eight years.

Because so many of the good airfields were captured early by the
enemy, the task of building up U.S. air strength in China, after December, 1941, was enormous. Equipment had to be flown in, for the most
part, over the towering mountains between India and western China,
under primitive conditions. In the first months of U.S. participation,
little could be done for China, and the American Volunteer Group
(Flying Tigers) carried the ball in the sky. On July 4, 1942, the Flying Tigers were disbanded.

On that day a Fighter Group, the 23rd, replaced the civilian pilots
of Flying Tiger fame, who had been under contract to the Chinese
Government. Some of these veterans remained in China and became
part of the Army and some returned to the United States. The 23rd
U.S.A.A.F. Fighter Group became a part of the Tenth Army Air Force.

The Tenth Air Force was to have the distinction of being the first
U.S. Air Force to send its fighter units into sustained action against
enemy fighters. Because China had practically no air force, the Tenth
—beginning in July of 1942 with a nucleus of former Flying Tiger

pilots—was practically the total Allied fighter strength employed against the Japanese in China.

Headquarters and reception terminal for U.S. supplies in Nationalist China was Kunming. Located in southwest China, 150 miles north of the Indochina border, Kunming is 500 miles east of the mountainous Indian boundary.

One day early in July, 1942, four U.S. fighters—P–40's—roared off an Indian airfield and set course for Kunming on their way to the front-line airfields of central China. In this modest reinforcement was a U.S. Army Air Corps major destined to emerge from the war one of the great aces of the China-Burma-India Theater, John R. Alison, of Micanopy, Florida (now a resident of Los Angeles, California).

The four Curtiss Warhawk fighters crossed the treacherous mountains of eastern India, northern Burma and western China to reach Kunming, with Alison leading the flight. For him it was the successful culmination of a long struggle to get out of Russia, where he had been training Russian pilots.

Originally sent to England in the spring of 1941 to train British pilots in the P–40, Alison and some of the fighters found themselves in Russia in October. Hitler had turned toward the east, dissipating the threat of an invasion of England, and Russia desperately needed U.S. aid. There followed some eight months of irksome duty for Alison, in Moscow and in Basra, before he was able to get clearance to a combat area via India.

Therefore, when Alison landed his P–40 fighter on a dusty field at Kunming in the summer of 1942, he was exhilarated at the prospect of at last seeing action with a U.S. fighter squadron in a combat area.

It was at Kunming that Alison met General Claire Chennault, head of all U.S. air forces in China, and other high-ranking American and Chinese officers, and was briefed on the military situation in China. Total U.S. fighter strength consisted of three squadrons of P–40's, each at a different field, and one flight of four P–40's at another. This force was comparable to the strength of one fully equipped fighter group back in the States. The squadrons were dispersed so one successful Japanese bombing could not knock out all the planes.

The Japanese were attacking airfields on which these fighters operated with a vengeance, and in great strength—often using as many as forty or fifty bombers on a raid, escorted by an equal number of fighters. Since it was highly unlikely that more than one U.S. fighter squadron

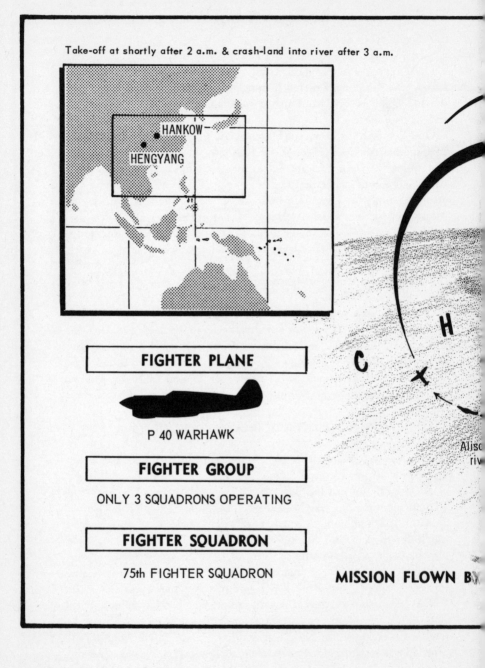

Take-off at shortly after 2 a.m. & crash-land into river after 3 a.m.

HANKOW

HENGYANG

FIGHTER PLANE

P 40 WARHAWK

FIGHTER GROUP

ONLY 3 SQUADRONS OPERATING

FIGHTER SQUADRON

75th FIGHTER SQUADRON

C   H

Aliso
riv

MISSION FLOWN B

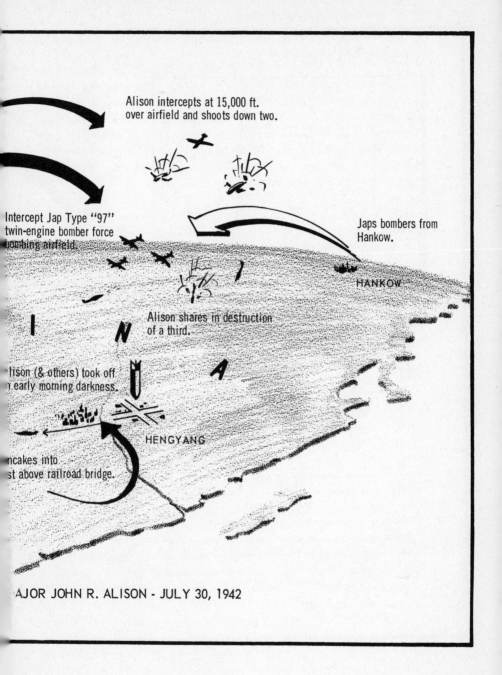

Alison intercepts at 15,000 ft.
over airfield and shoots down two.

Intercept Jap Type "97"
twin-engine bomber force
bombing airfield.

Japs bombers from
Hankow.

HANKOW

Alison shares in destruction
of a third.

lison (& others) took off
early morning darkness.

HENGYANG

ncakes into
st above railroad bridge.

AJOR JOHN R. ALISON - JULY 30, 1942

would intercept the enemy, odds were usually ten to fifteen U.S. fighters against fifty or more enemy planes.

It was a grim picture Kunming officials outlined for Alison. The most vital information of all, for him, was an order assigning him to the 75th Fighter Squadron at Hengyang, as deputy to the commanding officer, Major David L. ("Tex") Hill. He stayed only a short while in Kunming, long enough to learn where Hengyang was, and how to get there. Then, having bade good-by to the three P–40 pilots who had flown into Kunming with him, Alison took off for the Hengyang fighter strip, six hundred miles to the east.

Late in July, 1942, Alison set his new fighter down on a dusty gravel airstrip across the Siang River from the walled city of Hengyang. The airstrip was located in low, rolling red-clay terrain with rice paddies at the foot of the hills and green mountains as background in all directions.

The airstrip itself was hand-built with Chinese labor, 2,700 feet long, running north-south. A small thatched-roof hut to the left of the southern end of the runway served as the operations building. North of it was a stone Chinese guard building. The hostel where U.S. pilots lived was a mile north of the strip, on the bank of the Siang, and was a two-story, cadet-type gray building, with a row of porches on each floor.

In a few days Alison had met base personnel, studied the maps available and been assigned a room on the second floor of the hostel. There was not much to become acquainted with, though the culinary schedule was a bit unusual—five breaks a day—with breakfast at 4 A.M., coffee at 9:30, lunch at 12, tea and cakes at 4 P.M., and supper after 8 P.M. On the first few days after his arrival, nothing happened in the way of aerial warfare. The lull was short-lived.

On the night of July 28, a hot and sticky Chinese summer night, Alison and his roommate climbed into their mosquito-net-protected beds as usual. Flies and mosquitoes, present in clouds in China, buzzed through the night. By midnight they—and most of the other American pilots at the airbase—were asleep. A cloudless July sky, lit by the moon, arched over southwest China.

The sound of Chinese boys running through the hostel woke Alison. It was 2 A.M., and the boys were shouting an air raid was on the way. A Chinese-operated telephone network, which spread over practically all of occupied China, had called in a warning. It was the first time since Alison had arrived at Hengyang that the Japanese had been so discourteous, and he slipped on some clothes and hot-footed it outside, not to go up and intercept the enemy, for the P–40 was not a night fighter, but to look up Colonel Hill, whom he soon found.

Alison, Hill and most of the American pilots stood in the open, looking into the sky and listening. A shelter was nearby. For fifteen minutes they heard nothing. They continued waiting . . . and listening.

The warning network, featuring a Chinese listener, or watcher, on almost every major hill for hundreds of miles, some with field telephones, reported enemy bombers headed toward Hengyang. They might by-pass the airstrip or turn off before they reached it, but they might continue on course and give Hengyang a plastering.

A distant hum became audible. The bombers were headed for Hengyang! Eyes strained. In a few minutes the enemy would arrive over the field. The sound of engines grew louder and louder. Soon it was ominously loud, in the still night—then it came from straight overhead. Someone spotted the dark outlines, and the fire from the exhausts. The bombers were passing above, and though everyone was supposed to be in a shelter, some preferred to watch from outside, among them Alison.

Bombs fell and exploded, and some hit the field, but damage was light. Dummy P–40's out on the field attracted some of the enemy's bombs. The real fighters were well camouflaged. Since no U.S. fighters rose to intercept the bombers, the drop should have been more accurate. As the bombs exploded in flashes on and off the field, Alison's thoughts turned to the possibility of providing opposition to the unopposed enemy bombers. He could clearly see the fire jetting out of the exhausts of the enemy bombers' engines. Why couldn't some of the P–40's go up to meet these intruders as soon as the first warning came in over the telephone network? The idea excited him.

He turned his short, slight frame toward Hill, and with a jaw full of determination, said: "If they come over again tomorrow night, I'm going up after 'em." His words impressed others standing nearby. Another P–40 pilot, Captain Albert T. ("Ajax") Baumler, had similar sentiments: "I'll go with you," Baumler said. Baumler had been an ace in the Spanish Civil War, having fought with the Loyalists, and he, too, thought night interception possible.

But as the P–40's were not equipped as night fighters, Alison and Baumler had elaborate preparations to make if they were to carry air war to the enemy at night.

Next day—July 29—they spent considerable time on the problem. Other pilots prepared to join them in their night interception. They guessed the Japanese bombers had come in over the field at about 8,000 feet. That meant they would have to be at least ten minutes airborne, after take-off, if they were to be ready for the enemy when he reached Hengyang.

Since they wanted an altitude advantage, they would climb to 10,000 or 12,000 feet and circle over the field waiting for the bombers. When they spotted the enemy, they hoped to attack from above, undetected.

July 29 passed slowly. By late afternoon Alison and Baumler had parked their P-40E's at the northern end of the runway. They had left parachutes in the cockpits and made all possible preparations to get airborne as fast as possible on short notice.

That night the sky was again clear. Shortly after eight o'clock the fifth and final meal of the day was served. Pilots lounged and talked. Alison and Baumler, and a number of other pilots, laid out clothes and made special preparations for a race to the runway. They had no way of knowing whether they would be flying that night or not. Around midnight they went to bed, and to sleep.

One A.M. came and passed. Two A.M. Nothing happened. Pilots slept and Chinese hill watchers kept watch, and listened. A near-full moon outside brightened the summer sky. Alison, on the second story of the gray hostel, slept soundly.

Clink! Clink! Clink! Was he dreaming or was that . . . Clink! Clink! Clink! Instantly he was awake, sitting up inside the mosquito netting surrounding him. He wasn't dreaming. A Chinese boy dashed down the porch hallway, shouting, "Air laid—get up please!"

The clink, clink, clink came from a tin can he beat rapidly. Alison didn't take a second look. He grabbed his shoes and dressed as fast as he could move. He rushed out on the porch and headed for the end of the building and the stairway leading to the ground. Somewhere along the corridor, Baumler fell in with him, dressing as he ran, other pilots following. Alison wore only light khaki pants and shirt. They jumped into a tan Ford station wagon, in which a driver waited. He had been instructed to sleep with one foot in the vehicle.

They roared away from the hostel toward the northern end of the runway. The tan station wagon had long since lost its springs and each bump was a crash in itself.

The distance from hostel to aircraft was short. Take-off was to be from north to south, regardless of the wind. The station wagon raced up to Alison's darkened fighter (in daylight a dark green with white and red teeth painted behind the air scoop) and screeched to a dust-cloud stop.

Alison leaped out one side and the wagon raced off toward Baumler's fighter, not far away. Alison bolted a few steps, jumped on the wing, pulled back the canopy and lowered himself into the cockpit. There was just enough light to hook up belts and straps. The question racing through his mind was whether he could get high enough to be in position to attack when the bombers came over—if they were actually headed for Hengyang again.

Shortly after Alison reached his aircraft, Baumler scampered into his. Alison flipped on generator and battery switches. On came dim cockpit lights designed for emergency use. But they didn't furnish enough light for Alison to see most of the gauges, switches, and levers.

He cracked throttle, opened cowl flaps, and pushed the mixture handle to "rich." Making last-minute checks, he pressed the energizer button, starting a high whine. He pushed the "engage" switch.

The long, inline engine coughed a couple of times, the propeller turned slowly and then more rapidly . . . steadily. Smoke from the stacks thinned out and the engine ran smoothly. The 1,100-horse-power plant created a roar heard for ten miles.

Alison was ready to start out to the runway. He closed the canopy and lifted both feet off the brakes. The fighter rolled. There were no lights on the field, but he could make out the northern end of the runway ahead. He turned into it, facing south, and without hesitating shoved his left hand forward, opening the throttle full.

The P-40 rolled faster and faster as the engine gave its all. The air-speed needle began to turn. He kicked one rudder pedal and then the other, to keep the straining fighter in the center of the runway. Mercury and r.p.m. needles lapped at red lines. The green-painted fighter started to bounce. Alison hauled back on the stick. He was doing better than a hundred miles an hour. His wheels left the ground.

As soon as he knew he was off, he pulled the landing-gear lever, retracting wheels. He felt a mush, as they folded and reduced drag, and then speed jumped. He was cutting through the night at about 155 m.p.h., climbing steadily. He circled left and tried to make out the outline of the field below, and separate the earth from the sky.

Not long after Alison took off, Baumler's P–40 surged down the runway and lifted into the night. Other P–40's were also scrambling into the night sky.

Alison noticed considerable haze as he climbed. Because everything below was blacked out, it was difficult—in the haze—to keep the horizon in view. Instruments alone kept him upright. On and on he climbed . . . 7,000 feet, 8,000, 8,500. Below him Baumler and the other pilots also pointed their fighters toward the stars.

According to prearranged plan, all pilots circled constantly to the left as they went higher and higher. They were in touch with the radio shack on the field below; the operator reported the enemy bombers headed straight for Hengyang.

Alison continued to climb . . . 9,000 feet, 9,500, 10,000. He listened to tense words from the radio operator below. The Japs were definitely headed for Hengyang! Then silence. Beetle-beep, beetle-beep, beetle-beep! A whining sound drowned out the operator on the field, who seemed to be talking excitedly. Beetle-beep, beetle-beep, beetle-beep! Alison tried desperately to receive the radio shack. The strange interference continued. It was louder than the signal of the field operator. He couldn't make out his words. Japanese radio operators had jammed Hengyang's radio communications.

Alison reached 12,000 feet and leveled off, circling left. Visibility was still reduced by haze. Only the steady roar of his engine and the Japanese jamming in his earphones broke the peacefulness of the summer night. He couldn't spot Baumler below and continued to circle, constantly looking around.

Alison's right forefinger rested on the stick below the gun trigger, ready to be moved up that final inch in an instant. His six fifty-calibre guns were each loaded with three hundred rounds of mixed tracer and armor-piercing ammunition. Minutes seemed long as the fighters circled slowly in the night sky and waited.

Suddenly, in a break in the Japanese jamming, Alison heard the radio shack below: "Three twin-engine bandits just went over the field . . . from north to south. Looks like they're making a turn and coming back!"

Alison rubbernecked wildly, taking in the entire sky. He was crossing the field from east to west, and since the enemy bombers were turning at the south end, he should have seen them to his left. But he couldn't spot them. At 12,000 feet, he had expected them below. As

a last resort, he began to look above. A small light! Two, three, four—
six!

Six small bluish-white lights . . . exhaust fire! The Japanese bombers were almost directly above him, crossing from his left to his right.
Three twin-engined 97 enemy bombers! The identification charged
him with excitement. Alison kept his eyes on the small white lights
and added power. He pulled back on the stick, began a climbing right
turn that would put him behind the enemy bombers.

He screamed into the mike, to airborne comrades and the radio shack
below: "I see 'em! They're above me! I'm climbing into position behind
them! Watch the fireworks." Baumler was nearby. So was Lieutenant
E. W. Richardson. Both men heard Alison's call.

Alison's P–40 banked right and up through the night sky, pulling
in below and behind the enemy bombers now headed north. The P–40
was closing the distance fast and every few feet closer made it easier
for Alison to make out the bluish-white fire from the enemy's exhaust
stacks. He had climbed from 12,000 to 15,000 feet and was now on the
bombers' level, closing quietly from behind. He could see the dark
silhouettes of the bombers as they continued north.

He snapped on gun switches two hundred yards behind the bomber
to the left. The three enemy planes were in a triangle or V with the
point of the V forward. He noticed the moon was off to the right and
that he was slightly left of the left-most enemy aircraft, in good position to open fire on him.

The bomber was almost in range. Its left wing went up . . . it was
turning. All three were turning. It took Alison by surprise. He was on
the outside of the turn, banked right, following. The bombers completely reversed course. Now they headed south again, to pass over
the field for the third time. Since they had released no bombs, obviously this was the bomb run.

Alison now found himself on the moon side of the bombers, still
behind the enemy pilot flying his leader's left wing. He had lost distance when the bombers suddenly turned, and now closed again. He
pulled in directly behind the bomber on the left, which was slightly
ahead of the bomber off the enemy leader's right wing.

Suddenly, flashes of light off to the right. Thump! Thump! Thump!
It takes a while to register. Thump! Thump! Thump! He is hit! The
enemy bomber to the right has caught him, clearly outlined by the
moon, closing his comrade from behind, and opened up fast. It is alert

and accurate gunnery. Shells rip through the cockpit, destroying instruments, tear into the engine . . . a crashing deluge!

In the crisis, deadly determined, Alison makes a split-second decision. He presses the trigger to his six guns as he takes hits. The enemy ahead is squarely in his sight ring. The P–40 spits fire. It shudders and takes more hits. A shell crashes into the fighter's cockpit. Alison knocks a piece of burning phosphorus off his lap. The enemy bomber to his right rakes his fuselage. Disregarding it, he keeps up his fire on the bomber ahead. Now his shells begin to find the mark.

It's a grim battle. Alison is gambling he can knock out the bomber ahead before being fatally damaged, or killed. His guns throw out almost a hundred fifty-calibre shells a second. He has a firepower advantage. Keeping the enemy ahead focused in the orange ring of his gunsight, ignoring the thud of hits on his own fighter, he piles up hits on the enemy ahead. Black smoke and oil stream back from his victim. Then the enemy pilot suddenly veers wildly left, out of formation. Baumler, coming up fast from below, gets him in his sight and closes from behind.

Not losing a second, Alison banks his stricken fighter into a sharp right turn, into the teeth of the enemy bomber firing on him, and allows the bomber to pull ahead, to his left. It is time for revenge. He turns back sharply, to his left, in behind the 97. His engine beginning to trail smoke, cockpit and controls partly shot up, Alison eases into firing position on the bomber which nearly finished him.

The bomber, seeking to make its bomb run, holds course, and opens fire rearward. Alison, in return, opens with all guns. This time his fire is more accurate. Sparks and disintegration reveal a heavy concentration of fire hitting the enemy's wing. For several seconds the burst continues. Suddenly a wing tank in the enemy bomber explodes in a spectacular yellow ball. The bomber plunges earthward, out of control. No chutes. By now Baumler has the first 97 in flames, so this is victory number two.

The blazing sight is so awesome Alison almost forgets the third bomber, ahead. He sees the burning bomber's frame and tail skeleton clearly outlined as the fabric burns away and lights up the sky. He glances ahead. The lead enemy bomber is dropping bombs! He opens the throttle of his smoking engine to close, and sees one bomb explode on the runway below, on which he hopes to land.

The lead bomber holds course on its run, flying a straight and level southerly heading. Alison's P–40 is straining. The engine is knocking and smoking but the distance between the two aircraft isn't great. In seconds the wounded American fighter is on the bomber's tail. As soon as the 97 fills the sight ring, Alison opens fire for the third time that night.

The supply of ammunition remaining is limited. A few hundred shells will have to do the job. Alison aims at the wing tanks, sees his shells striking home. The P-40 vibrates amid the roar from its guns. The enemy bomber returns a feeble fire. These are crucial seconds, and he holds in there behind the bomber, engine now beginning to cut out, smoking, low on ammunition.

With his last rounds, Alison rips a hole in the right wing root of the lead bomber. Other shells rip into the trapped enemy. Pieces fly off. Then a bright orange flash. Ruptured gasoline lines, and the tank, go up in flame! The third victim rolls over, out of control, and starts down, its right wing streaming fire. Crew members bail out—some trail fire in the night sky, others fall beneath open or partially-opened and burning chutes. Soon the entire aircraft is a ball of orange flame. Victory number three. For a fleeting moment Alison grimly watches his third victim plunging earthward. He notices far below a dying ball of fire, his second victim about to hit the ground. His last two victories are burning at the same time.

The knocking engine catches his attention and ends the satisfaction of seeing the bombers falling. The stomach-weakening realization that his engine is failing and threatening to catch fire grips him through and through. He knows a forced landing at night, in a strange area, is to be avoided at all costs.

He pulls throttle back, but the dying engine runs rougher and rougher. He must get down fast! He sticks nose down and heads for the field below. The engine is missing badly. Going down he notices another burning bomber—Baumler's second victim of the night. He can't watch. The engine sounds finished. Steeper and steeper he dives on the field, circling to stay above it at all times.

About 3,000 feet above the field, the engine quits. Everything is unnaturally quiet. Alison keeps spiraling down. It's to be a dead-stick landing at night—highly dangerous. He had thought of jumping, but now—down to a couple of thousand feet—he'll stick it out. The moon offers just enough light to give him a fair chance to land and walk away.

The altimeter registers a steady loss of altitude . . . 1,500, 1,300, 1,100, 900 feet above the field. Alison looks at airspeed, strains his eyes to make out the field, its landmarks and boundaries. He must maintain over 100 m.p.h. to avoid spinning. He turns the damaged fighter sharply to the left and starts an approach to bring him in on the northern edge of the field. His head bobs up and down as he tries to adjust airspeed and altitude, watching the instruments, maneuvering the fighter into the right position to come over the edge of the field. He slides the canopy back to see better.

He is approaching the northern edge of the field. He comes up on it fast . . . too fast. The field is flashing by, underneath his wing. The fighter won't sit down. Alison has too much airspeed! He realizes it too late. He'll never make it. He pulls back on the stick and pushes the throttle forward, by instinct, even though the engine had cut out minutes earlier.

The engine coughs and seems to catch. Then a bright flash—the engine streaks flame! Alison is just up over the trees on the edge of the field near the river. He doesn't have power to go around, or even to make a complete turn and go back in from the opposite direction. He has to crash-land the fighter in a matter of seconds, or burn alive, possibly explode in the air.

But nothing ahead offers encouragement. He is approaching the river, and Hengyang is on the opposite bank. He can't crash into the town. The river is now only a few hundred feet ahead. He instinctively turns left to avoid the town. At that moment he knows he will have to crash-land in the Siang River.

He is losing altitude. It is hard to see ahead, fire and smoke streaming back from the engine. He glides down toward the water. Suddenly a dark object looms ahead. Bridge! Can he pull up over it? Closely-placed support pylons leave no space to go under it.

Alison tugs back on the stick. The burning fighter shudders. He gets the nose up over the onrushing bridge, pops the stick forward to avoid a spin. He has lost flying speed and settles fast. The shudder had been a spin warning. Using rudder pedals and stick to keep the aircraft in the middle of the dark stream, Alison quickly mushes down into the water, hard. He had dropped fast after pulling up over the bridge.

The impact throws him forward and his head strikes the gunsight in the front of the cockpit. Blood oozes from his forehead but he remains conscious. The fighter skims along on the water for a short distance, begins to settle and comes to a halt, settling more and more.

Sinking fast, Alison cranks the canopy open the rest of the way. He loosens his flying gear and harness and steps up and out of the cockpit.

As he climbs out, water begins to pour over the side. He splashes into the river, which is quite cold, and is instantly swimming.

Alison ditched at a spot where the Siang River is two hundred feet wide. When he plunged into the cold water he was about sixty feet from a log raft tied to the right bank. The light from the moon was enough to outline the raft. He swam for it, heavily weighted down with clothing soaking up water.

He was swimming for the right bank of the river, the town side. It was all he could do to make the raft. A Chinese boy came out and helped pull him up, helped him across the raft to the bank. There he saw three Chinese soldiers waiting for him, their bayonets pointed his way.

They didn't know he was American. Alison grabbed at his shirt pocket and pulled out a small Chinese flag. He yelled, in the few Chinese words he knew, that he was an American. But the soldiers pointing guns at him, and others crowded around, didn't trust him, even with the flag. The boy helped him up the long, steep bank. It was fifty feet high, sloped at a forty-degree angle. As they slowly ascended the bank in dim moonlight, the three soldiers backed up the bank ahead of him, keeping their guns aimed straight at him.

He continued to wave the Chinese flag. Finally, when he was almost to the top, the soldiers lowered their guns. They looked him over curiously. Alison sighed with relief. To have been shot by his allies, after surviving the crash in the Siang, and the aerial battles, would have been an ironical ending to the night.

At the top of the bank the Chinese, jabbering constantly, led him to a small house. Inside they sat him on a wooden bench. Alison relaxed. The Chinese looked him over in the flickering light of tung oil lamps. There were only the bench and a table in the room. Alison, dead tired, flopped on the table. For forty-five minutes he sat there, exhausted and releasing tension. It was a welcome rest. The Chinese sat silently on the floor and watched, or talked, and pointed his way.

Then some of the Chinese who had escorted him to the house came back. They motioned for him to follow, talking all the while to the others. Alison pulled himself up off the bench and followed. They led him down a pathway, back to the river. They had secured a boat.

The first glimmers of light were visible in the eastern sky. Weary and wondering about his injured head, Alison sat down in the boat and the Chinese began to paddle. The Chinese boat pilot made for a dock across the river from the hostel, shortly landing him there. Alison bade his rescuers good-by with a tired smile and started up the road to the hostel.

He had gone two-thirds of the way to the hostel when he heard a whistle . . . and hit the ground. A falling bomb! Close. Alison looked up and saw three Japanese bombers and their yellow Rising Suns. The bomb struck the dock where he had been minutes before, wrecking it, and killing one of the Chinese.

Now he could hear his comrades taking off—going up after the enemy. He got up and walked a little faster. In the dim early-morning light he made out the hostel, beside which several pilots were standing, watching the enemy attack. Alison's appearance took them by surprise.

They had seen him on fire several hours earlier, had heard his plane hit the river after he missed his landing pass at the field, and had given him up as lost. Now they examined his head and offered congratulations and compliments. He needed stitches in his forehead—but there was no doctor at the airfield.

One pilot suggested he try the missionary doctor in town. Once again, after a short rest, Alison set out on foot. A Chinese houseboy took him by footpath to the trestle going across the river and into the town and to the doctor, who looked at the cuts. They had to be sewed up. The doctor's lone suture needle was dull and the sewing was a rugged ordeal.

He was told to get some rest, and the doctor put him in his own bed. He had hardly stretched out when he heard the town alert for another air raid. The Japs were really going after Hengyang. Disregarding the advice of his host, Alison jumped out of bed and dressed again.

In the sky above, now a bright blue, he saw ten P–40's headed straight for some forty Zeros, strung out in wide formation. "Tex" Hill was leading the Americans and Alison saw him make a head-on pass at one of the enemy fighters, both firing until they flashed by one another.

The Zero began to trail smoke and went into a spiral directly over the town. Alison stood motionless watching the spectacular show. Hill and the Jap pilot had completed their head-on pass at 17,000 feet. When the stricken enemy pilot reached 12,000 his Zero suddenly straightened out into a vertical dive.

The enemy pilot was still alive, obviously aware his aircraft had suffered fatal damage. The Zero screamed down toward the field, leaving a trail of smoke behind and dived straight into the field, near one of the dummy P–40's. The code of the *Samurai!* It was the first kami-

Curtiss P-40 Warhawks based at Chengkung Airbase in China fly across mountain ranges en route to their target. Note the painted shark mouth. (Air Force Photo)

kaze attack the Americans had seen—one of the first of its kind in the war. But the enemy pilot missed.

"I'm going back," Alison told his protesting host. Soon he was approaching the field again, on foot. He met Hill as the C.O. was parking his P–40. Hill had thought Alison lost the night before, and Alison's unexpected appearance cheered him up. The victories registered over the Japs cheered him even more. They exchanged congratulations.

Alison and Baumler had accounted for four of six Japanese bombers taking part in the night attack. Considering the meager strength of the Americans in China at this stage of the war, and the fact that none of their P–40's were equipped for night fighting, their interception must be rated one of the great night-fighter efforts of World War II. For a long time the Japanese did not return at night to bomb Hengyang. Thus the pioneer night interception proved to be a significant American victory.

Headquarters, China Air Task Force, awarded Alison the Distinguished Service Cross for the mission. Captain Baumler also won a D.S.C. for the mission.

The slender, quiet-spoken major from Micanopy, Florida, had done more than shoot down enemy planes. By refusing to bail out of his damaged P–40 he had saved many of its parts for future use. For while the Americans at first believed Alison's fighter could not be successfully raised from the Siang River, the patient, knowing Chinese soon fetched it out of the water and most of its parts saw action again.

The 75th Fighter Squadron, then, had not lost a pilot or a plane. And one was as important as the other in July of 1942, in China.

2 Chase Over New Guinea

DECEMBER 26, 1942:

First Lieutenant JOHN D. LANDERS

THE southernmost Pacific penetration by the Japanese in World War II, on the decisive pathway to Australia, was to the southeastern tip of New Guinea.

After paralyzing much of the U.S. fleet at Pearl Harbor in December, 1941, the Japanese Navy had carried the flag of the Rising Sun southward and eastward at a rapid pace.

In June, 1942, the U.S. Navy and Army Air Force won a critical victory at Midway, checking the Japanese advance across the central Pacific. But in the southwest Pacific, Japan's advance on Australia continued.

The high tide of the Japanese advance in this area came in September. In that month, Australians and Americans stopped five battalions of Japanese troops which had crossed the Owen Stanley Mountains and advanced on the capital city of Port Moresby, on the southeastern tip of New Guinea.

The advancing Japanese had reached a point only thirty-two miles from the capital, and American pilots, cooks, and service troops had been issued weapons to defend the city—only an hour's flight from the Australian coast—when the Japs were halted.

In the same month a Japanese amphibious operation, designed to capture three airfields under construction on the southeastern tip of New Guinea, more than a hundred miles east of Moresby, was defeated after several weeks of heavy fighting near Milne Bay.

On August 7, 1942, the 1st Marine Division was hurriedly landed at Guadalcanal in the Solomon Islands, where Japanese troops had been detected constructing an airfield. Thus began a struggle which lasted until February of the following year and which cost the U.S. Navy two carriers, seven cruisers, and fourteen destroyers sunk, and two carriers, one new battleship, and many cruisers and destroyers damaged.

Guadalcanal is approximately seven hundred miles due east of Port Moresby. In these two South Pacific battle areas, New Guinea and the Solomon Islands, American ground, naval, and air power turned back the Japanese victory tide in costly, hard-fought, and lengthy actions.

Imperial headquarters finally ordered Guadalcanal in the Solomons evacuated in January, 1943, and by February it was entirely in American hands. The struggle for New Guinea, a greater prize, was destined to last longer. It was not until well into 1944 that MacArthur's forces conquered northwestern New Guinea, and finally established firm control over its vast area.

This struggle was marked by two years of bitter jungle fighting, numerous amphibious operations and steadily mounting aerial battles. It is to this campaign that we now turn to record one of many memorable battles which eventually won for the Army Air Forces supremacy in this theater.

Of all the great American fighter aces of World War II, few had a more varied assortment of combat experience than Lieutenant Colonel John D. Landers, of Fort Worth, Texas. Big, blond, and all-Texan, with a ready smile, Landers entered the Army Air Corps as a cadet in the spring of 1940 at the age of nineteen. He had hardly begun training when German armies smashed into the Low Countries and France, which surrendered in June, leaving England to face the might of Germany alone in Europe.

Throughout 1940 and most of 1941 Landers successfully negotiated the pitfalls of flying training, while England held on and Hitler's power reached its zenith. In those dark days aviation cadets were not unaware that the United States was drifting closer and closer to the war. They realized all too well that, in the event of U.S. participation, they were certain to see action early, as the first echelon of Uncle Sam's mobilizing air strength. The first echelon, moreover, was sure to be sent up against numerically stronger forces, for the Axis powers had been mobilizing for years while the United States was just beginning its preparedness program in earnest.

As Landers proceeded through cadet training, then, it was with a sense of urgency. The world was falling apart—the anti-Axis world. After crushing France, Hitler had launched the Battle of Britain, sent his troops into Africa and expanded his power. In June of 1941, he assaulted Russia, and at the very moment Landers was receiving his wings and a second lieutenant's commission, Hitler's troops were approaching the snowy suburbs of Moscow. Six days before Landers' graduation as a pilot the Japanese struck Pearl Harbor and the United States officially entered the war.

Thus, on December 13, 1941, when Landers' class of aviation cadets became flying officers, the military outlook for the Western world was bleak. Little did the 226-pound Texan realize that day that before the war was over he would be leading squadrons (and groups) against the enemy in both the Pacific and European theaters, and would finish the war as one of the country's leading aces.

The Army Air Corp fighter pilot class of December, 1941, was needed immediately on many fronts, and Landers did not have to wait long for overseas orders. In January of 1942 he departed Zone of the Interior (United States) for duty in the Pacific. Not long afterward he found himself in Darwin, Australia, flying the P-40—as Japanese forces steadily advanced nearer and nearer the British dominion.

Landers was transferred to New Guinea after several months' action at Darwin, and with the 49th Fighter Group there played an outstanding role in helping to stem the Japanese tide that moved so relentlessly across the Pacific in the early stages of the war.

He became an ace early, a more difficult feat in this phase of operations than it became later on—when American fighters were superior to Japanese models, and when American fliers usually met the enemy in even numbers, or better.

In the summer of 1943, having completed a combat tour of duty in the Pacific, Landers came back to the United States. He remained for six months, after which he requested reassignment to a combat area. He was ordered to England as combat replacement pilot, and soon was assigned to 357th Fighter Group, Eighth Air Force. In a short time he became the acting leader of 357th.

Take off was at 9:45 a.m., bails out at approximately 11:15.

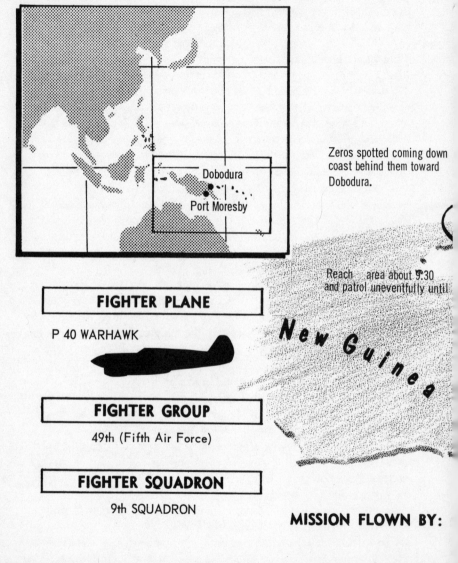

Dobodura

Port Moresby

Zeros spotted coming down
coast behind them toward
Dobodura.

Reach   area about 9:30
and patrol uneventfully until

New Guinea

FIGHTER PLANE

P 40 WARHAWK

FIGHTER GROUP

49th (Fifth Air Force)

FIGHTER SQUADRON

9th SQUADRON

MISSION FLOWN BY:

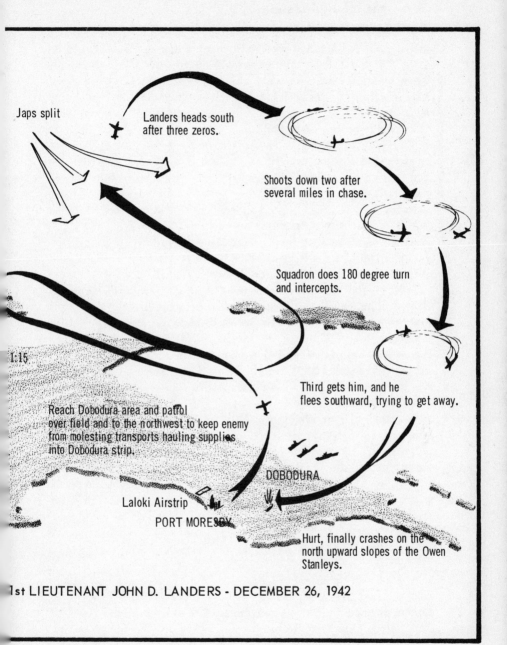

Japs split

Landers heads south
after three zeros.

Shoots down two after
several miles in chase.

Squadron does 180 degree turn
and intercepts.

1:15

Third gets him, and he
flees southward, trying to get away.

Reach Dobodura area and patrol
over field and to the northwest to keep enemy
from molesting transports hauling supplies
into Dobodura strip.

DOBODURA

Laloki Airstrip

PORT MORESBY

Hurt, finally crashes on the
north upward slopes of the Owen
Stanleys.

1st LIEUTENANT JOHN D. LANDERS - DECEMBER 26, 1942

He was next named commanding officer of the 78th Group, stationed at Duxford. Landers flew a complete combat tour in England, and an extension, and had begun another when Germany collapsed. Having flown a Pacific tour, a European tour and extensions, Landers was not long in getting another combat assignment. While still in England he began to train and lead 361st Group, an assemblage of selected pilots scheduled to be sent to the Far East.

The Japanese surrender in August, 1945, finally ended Landers' chances of continuing combat and orders of 361st were canceled. He had been in action against the enemy, except for a six-month interval, since early 1942.

In his years of combat duty Landers flew practically every fighter in the Army Air Corps. He started out (in the Pacific) flying the P–40. After changing over to P–38's, and being transferred to Europe, he wound up piloting the P–47 and then the P–51 Mustang—the latest and longest-ranging American fighter in World War II.

In 1942—the year with which this chapter is concerned—there was no such thing as a P–51 Mustang; its dive-bombing sire, the A–36, was just being acquired by the U.S.A.A.F. Landers was stationed on New Guinea with 49th Group, flying the P–40. American aerial strength in this theater was modest, and U.S. pilots usually went into combat out-numbered. In addition, American pilots suffered the hardships of primitive quarters and the ravages of diseases like malaria, which sometimes grounded half the group.

Surrounding Port Moresby in late 1942 were a number of fighter strips—Moresby being the center of a major build-up of Allied air power in this theater. One of these strips was Laloki, which had been hacked out of the jungle west of Moresby. Often squadrons staged into Laloki the morning of, or the day before, a mission, awaited orders, and took off from Laloki on their assignment. On Christmas Eve, 9th Squadron had been ordered to report at Laloki, near Moresby —for a mission to be flown on the 26th. Home of the 9th was Rorona —not far from Laloki.

At 4:30 A.M. the day after Christmas, First Lieutenant John Landers pushed aside mosquito netting above his box-springed mattress at Rorona (hauled with loving care from a Darwin hotel) and began to dress. When he reached for his shoes he picked up a brand-new pair of high-top G.I.'s. He always flew in low-quarter shoes, never liked the heavier G.I.'s. This morning he would give the G.I.'s a final try. It was an important, spur-of-the-moment decision.

The climate is always mild in New Guinea, so Landers wore no jacket as he stepped into the darkness outside. In his hand he carried an oxygen mask. An old house, serving as squadron mess hall, was 150 yards away, and he stepped off the yardage in businesslike manner. For him there would be no breakfast, but the usual coffee. There was no sugar or cream, but plenty of bully beef, of which Landers had long ago had his fill. Black coffee was breakfast, a contrast with the special Christmas breakfast the day before—ham and real dinkum fresh eggs, biscuits, butter, jam, oranges, and coffee.

Pilots around the tables speculated about the day's mission. Best bets were the squadron would escort mediums to the north coast, or patrol over one of the newly acquired airstrips in the area. Gona, on the northern coast, had fallen to Australian troops December 9, and Buna to the 127th U.S. infantry regiment on the 14th. Installations and fields in these areas were being readied to support a further advance along the coast.

Landers checked in at the squadron's lounge room, next door, where pilots were awaiting the departure of the squadron's green fire truck, which had also been hauled from Darwin as official transportation for 9th Squadron. Piling into the truck in the December darkness, the twelve pilots and driver began the mile and a half trip to olive-green fighters dispersed on the edges of the field.

They were dropped off at the P–40's one by one. Each made a visual check of his aircraft and climbed down into the cockpit. As soon as the squadron leader turned over the rest started engines. It was a few minutes before six. Slowly they taxied to the northern end of the strip. Landers, ready to go, signaled his wing man. The two planes roared off down the runway almost abreast.

The first two Warhawks lifted off the runway and began a slow turn to the left. They were followed by five pairs, and in one large circle of the field the dozen green fighters were joined. Landers pointed the nose of his fighter—*Big Doll*—to the east and Laloki Field. He was Red Leader. The squadron was composed of three four-plane flights, Red, White, and Blue.

The sky began to brighten. The twelve green fighters of 9th Squadron, their rudders painted red as squadron identification, sliced upward into the eastern sky. In a few minutes Laloki came into view and

Landers led his men down. They landed singly at the stage-in strip. Fighters taxied to the end of the runway and then off into the edges of palm trees. There maintenance crewmen busied themselves with camouflage work and checked aircraft. Gas trucks were ordered out to top tanks. Pilots walked to the field's operations tent nearby, where they were to await take-off instructions. Inside, Landers telephoned immediately for instructions. The others played cards or talked.

The 9th was to take off at 9:45 A.M. and proceed northward to the American airstrip at Dobodura, near the coast, patrol that area and to the northwest—in the direction of Japanese positions. Transport planes would be hauling supplies into Dobodura by air and the 9th Squadron was to see that the big, slow aircraft were not molested as they brought in much-needed stores. The 9th was to stay on patrol for two hours, then return home.

Landers put down the phone and explained the job to his squadron. From the looks of it, there wouldn't be much to it. Pilots relaxed—it was some time until take-off—and resumed cards, or reading. Minutes ticked away. Outside the sun was turning the tropical foliage to a bright green. Vision was excellent. (The only cause of canceled mis-

P–38's on line will take off over mountains in New Guinea.

sions in this part of the Pacific Theater was weather—thunderheads, which built up over the Owen Stanley Mountains, to the north.) Landers walked out into the warm sunlight and looked at the sky. The weather man had been right—the sky to the north was relatively free of clouds.

It was 9 A.M. Landers broke up the card game and led the squadron outside to camouflaged fighters. In ten minutes he was starting *Big Doll's* Allison. He taxied to the end of the runway; the other eleven fighters followed. Pushing throttle handle forward, Landers watched the mercury needle climb. The P–40 bounded down the prefab runway. Landers' wing man following just to the right, behind. The two fighters cut upward into the air before they reached the end. They circled to let the others catch up; then Landers set course northward at a steady rate of climb. It was 9:18.

The altimeter registered gains: 5,000, 6,000, 7,000 feet. Landers was heading for the "backbone" of Papua—the mountain range running northwest-southeast. He would cross it at 16,000 feet.

As the P–40's reached 10,000, pilots went on full oxygen and mountains loomed straight ahead. Landers kept *Big Doll's* nose pointed upward. A few clouds hovered above the mountains. They would probably build up during the day, as they did every day. Altitude eased upward . . . 12,000, 13,000, 14,000 feet. Gun switches were now on; the 9th was ready for action if the enemy challenged. Dobodura was not far away. The squadron crossed the mountains near Kokoda Pass. The patrol area was fifteen minutes distant.

Landers spread out flights and stacked them at different altitudes. Red Flight, which he led, was to fly low position, so he nosed down to 9,000 feet. White Flight, behind right, began to ease down to 11,000. Blue Flight, slightly back from White and off Lander's left, remained at 16,000 as top cover. Dobodura neared below. The coast, and the western Solomon Sea, a brilliant blue, came into view ahead. The squadron banked left as it passed over the field, curving to the west, toward Japanese territory.

Eyes in each of the flights searched out the sky for the enemy, but to no avail. The flight up the coast continued. All was quiet and peaceful. Only the steady roar of the engines broke the silence.

Landers leans into a turn and heads back for the airstrip 9th is guarding. The twelve fighters snake gracefully along the coast. The flight is almost monotonous. Time and again the squadron crosses the field and makes its run up and down the shoreline. Minutes, then a half hour, then an hour, go by. By now pilots are relaxing. Many unhook safety belts and parachutes. Nothing seems to be doing today.

An hour passes . . . then another fifteen minutes. It is 11 A.M. Only fifteen more minutes to patrol and the squadron will turn south for home. Over the radio Landers hears his relief squadron call in—they're approaching the pass over Kokoda. In fifteen minutes they'll relieve 9th. The squadron is flying southeast, down the coast, and Landers begins to hook up his chute and safety belt again, in preparation for the return flight.

An excited voice cuts in over the radio: "Zeros—coming down the coast!" Landers whips his head around, knowing the enemy will be coming out of the west, behind. He makes out the forms of ten or eleven bandits, very low. (There were others—twenty in all—he was to discover later.) He presses the mike button: "White Leader will cover at 9,000. Blue Leader come down with me!" At the same time Landers steps on right rudder and yanks stick right, letting his nose drop in the turn. The Japs are only 500 to 1,000 feet high. He calls White Leader again, telling him he can descend from 9,000 feet to 5,000 feet. That will still give him a good altitude advantage in the fight ahead.

The three flights streak down, airspeed races upward . . . 300, 350, 400 m.p.h. Landers is aiming straight; on this course he'll meet the enemy fighters head on, with such speed the P-40's can pull up and come down again. Every pilot in the squadron is gripped in the suspense of imminent combat.

The enemy gaggle spots the onrushing Americans and the Japs break formation. One group of three turns south; another group continues on toward Dobodura. Landers must pick his foe. Since he's leading the squadron, he's slightly ahead of the others; he will go for the Japs heading south. The bandits streaking toward the field can be intercepted by the P-40's behind, between Dobodura and the Zeros.

Down to 1,500 feet, throttle wide open, Landers rolls into a vertical left turn, curving in behind the three bandits. *Big Doll* is easing up on them smartly. Landers doesn't have much time to look around; he keeps the enemy fighters in sight as they grow larger. The Zeros are flying in a V and Landers jockeys his nose into position to close the two Zeros to the right; his wing man can take care of the third, to the left.

The Zeros can't match *Big Doll's* speed. Their low-wing outlines stretch wider and wider in the gunsight glass. Landers steadily comes on from behind. . . . The Zeros fly straight and level. Haven't they seen him? Now the enemy fighter on the right is filling the orange light circle. Landers' finger feels the trigger button on the stick. He presses down. *Big Doll's* six fifties spurt flame and shell. The P-40 shudders and roars; range is so close hits immediately rip up the Zero.

Landers is coming on even closer; he can see strikes all over the enemy plane.

His guns are loaded with seven explosives to two armor-piercing and one tracer and the trapped Zero staggers from the effects of the explosive barrage. The concentrated close-range fire is too much—pieces of the Zero tear off. Suddenly there's a flash; the enemy plane literally explodes in the air with Landers only feet behind. Landers doesn't have time to gloat over the kill. Slamming stick left, he banks into position behind the enemy leader—still flying straight and level. The leader is almost in range, so close was he to his wing man. Maneuvering the P-40 into dead astern firing position, Landers begins to fill the sight ring again. He's closing slightly slower, as his speed gradually falls in level flight. The enemy's picks up. Even so, he's closing the Zero's tail.

Fire! *Big Doll* vibrates again and shells streak out toward the enemy ahead, who at the last second catches on, banks vertically right. The Zero is a second too late. He is already hit. As the enemy's left wing whips high, exposing the yellow Rising Sun insignia, Landers sees a faint trail of smoke. He opened fire just in time.

Hanging on in the right turn, Landers pours fire at the stricken Zero. Another burst! A third! The bandit is hard hit. Range is close and fire accurate. The Zero is doomed. . . . Landers keeps his eye on the enemy ahead, now trailing a long stream of smoke, and losing altitude. He's going down, and there isn't far to go. Now in a steep descent, Landers squarely on his tail, the second victim points his nose at a mountainside ahead and never finishes the right turn: the pilot must be dead at the controls. The Zero dives on and on, straight toward the mountain. The trees loom up ahead but the enemy pilot doesn't pull up. Landers watches him plow straight into the mountain. Burning gasoline and a boil of dark smoke mark the spot where pilot and plane hit.

Landers notices he's only a hundred feet over the trees. He pulls back on the stick and banks right. He looks for his wing man and the other two fighters of Red Flight. He hasn't seen them since he began to concentrate on the three Zeros. His wing man to the left must have caught the third Zero, furthest left.

Big Doll suddenly shudders! Landers looks at his high left wing . . . holes! He feels the shudder again. In a split second he slams left wing down, reverses turn and jams the throttle full forward. He's caught from behind! As he stands on the left wing, pulls it tight, he sees the Zero dead astern, wing guns blinking and spurting shells. He's on the deck, with no speed advantage to get away. The Zero can out-turn him. His position is immediately desperate.

Landers hauls *Big Doll* around the left turn as tight as he can bank; the Zero swishes by overhead and up: The enemy pilot has speed on him, and turns back down and around for another pass. Sweating and already hit, realizing he's trapped, Landers experiences the fear of probable death the two Jap pilots in front of him just felt. Caught by the standard mistake—not clearing his tail! For a few seconds he stays out of the line of fire . . . he twists and turns wildly, hoping to throw the enemy pilot off. He glances back as he continues erratic maneuvering. The Zero is there.

Now the enemy is off to his left. Landers straightens out his flight path, engine wide open. But *Big Doll* isn't getting away. The grim low-wing silhouette behind flies almost like a wing man who sticks by at every turn. The Zero outturned him when he banked left, winding up on his left! The enemy pilot now moves in for another pass. . . . Landers goes hard right, just as the enemy fires again. This time he misses.

Leaning into a reverse turn, back to the left, he sees the enemy calmly lining him for another firing pass . . . the Zero comes in this time from the right rear. Landers maneuvers desperately, kicking rudder to throw the enemy's aim off while banking sharply left. Thump! Thump! Holes open up in a row just in front of the cockpit; the enemy has laid a burst across the nose of *Big Doll*.

Hit again, desperate, Landers tries everything he knows; stick up, down, hard to the left, jinxing rudder and taking every evasive action he knows. In glimpses behind he sees the enemy fighter hanging on. *Big Doll* still runs smoothly, but smoke begins to steam back from the engine—hits in the engine! In the wild maneuvering Landers almost gets on the enemy's tail. For a moment he can see the Zero in his sight, for the first time. He holds the stick back in his stomach with all his strength . . . the P–40 staggers on the verge of a spin . . . he can't come on around . . . the Zero begins to move ahead in the turn, pulling out of view . . . that means he's gaining on Landers in the turn.

Big Doll suddenly stands on right wing and breaks off in that direction. The Zero, a glance behind reveals, is coming on from behind and right. The enemy pilot closes in for another pass despite everything Landers can do. Landers jerks the stick and hits the rudders . . . the

Zero comes on, stays with every turn . . . flashes in off the side and up again. That was a pass. But the enemy pilot didn't fire. Landers managed to keep out of the line of fire on that one.

From the left, behind, the Zero comes on again. This time Landers skids rudder and stands on his right wing . . . the enemy fighter makes another pass . . . again he doesn't fire. Why? Landers wonders if the Jap isn't satisfied with his passes, or whether he might be out of ammunition. In a cold sweat, engine smoking and barely over the trees, Landers doesn't hold a card. Slowly, in the wild battle, he is working his way southward, up the slopes of foothills of the Owen Stanley Range. Ahead he can see clouds over the mountains. If he can make it that far . . .

The Zero moves in with another perfect firing pass, using speed and turning edge to close from the right, behind. Landers banks away as sharply as *Big Doll* can turn . . . the Zero alters course to follow through on the pass . . . Landers hits rudder to evade the line of fire. *Big Doll* shudders, vibrates . . . Landers can hear the shells slamming into him . . . hit again! The enemy isn't out of ammunition! He's cool enough not to waste any.

Big Doll vibrates constantly . . . the engine's losing power . . . dense smoke streams back. The Zero is getting ready for another pass. Landers is almost to the first high ridge ahead . . . clouds hovering above it. He pushes the throttle again; it's all the way. *Big Doll* can do no more. The vibration increases. Landers knows he won't make it home. He glances at the altimeter—6,000 feet! Just over the trees and 6,000 feet! That means the elevation of the ground below is almost 6,000 feet.

Straight ahead now the high ridge draws closer. Landers has one chance—he will aim for the small open space between the tops of the trees and the clouds above—scarcely a hundred feet. Beyond the ridge the clouds come down to cover the tops of mountains on all sides. If the Zero follows him into the valley his chances of coming out won't be good. Landers has nothing to lose. He might sneak up into the clouds or he might find a place to crash-land in the valley. It's his only chance.

The ridge is rushing toward him. The bottom of the clouds is just above it; *Big Doll* steadily loses power. He can just make the ridge . . . can he make it up into the clouds? Does the engine have the power? Out front smoke streams back . . . Landers glances at the instrument panel . . . power is failing . . . *Big Doll* is about through. Suddenly the ridge flashes by beneath . . . a valley dips away below

—the tops of the peaks ahead hidden by the clouds. Landers dips nose and heads down, down into the valley. Even a fully functioning fighter would be on dangerous ground down in the valley, mountains on all sides, tops invisible, obscured by the clouds.

The Zero pilot behind, watching the American fighter skip over the treetops and through the narrow margin between cloud and trees, and then down, has a fearful choice. The P–40 is streaming smoke, apparently finished.

The clouds are building up; they will sock in more, not less. In minutes the gap now open over the ridge top will probably close. The enemy suddenly turns away, as Landers plunges down, over the ridge, into the valley. With the P–40 damaged beyond recovery, heading into a dead-end valley, there's no point in following. The enemy pilot is wily. Though he might not have known, his diagnosis was right.

Landers slopes down the incline toward the valley bottom. His eyes race across the tops of trees and into every corner of the depression, looking for a clearing, a spot to crash-land. Nothing. *Big Doll* is puffing black smoke and power drains out rapidly now; Landers is desperate. Where can he land? He has a little speed left, eases back the stick . . . the P–40 noses upward on momentum alone . . . the engine seizes! Landers takes a last look at the countryside below . . . no salvation for *Big Doll*. He knows he must get out . . . in seconds.

The engine is strangely quiet and the propwash suddenly missing. Landers is only a thousand feet above the trees . . . the airspeed needle winds downward . . . he's still holding the nose up. Instantly he reaches for the canopy handle and jerks it back. He grabs his safety belt and unfastens it with a flip of both hands. All the stories he recalls about not having to jump out when the canopy is opened and safety belt unfastened rush through his mind . . . not true. There is no force pushing him up and out.

He has no time to lose. Looking at his parachute handle for a split second, he lunges upward in his seat and stands straight up; the wind hits him in the face. But the P–40 is flying so slowly even the force of the wind is not too great . . . and it doesn't pull him out. He must literally jump. Without hesitating, he stands up in the seat and leaps up—and back—into the air. He notices *Big Doll's* rudder flash by him; as he does he yanks the parachute handle . . . falling toward the trees below. For a second or two it looks as if he'll fall into the trees before the chute opens. Then a sudden jolt—the silk billows out above him. Landers is hanging beneath the chute at a slight angle. He begins the swing down under, like a human pendulum. One swing. Before he reaches the bottom of the initial swing, green rushes up. His body beats against limbs and branches. Then he stops, hanging. A sharp pain in his right knee makes him wince; the leg is paralyzed. Landers looks up . . . his chute is hooked on the top limbs of the tree—a huge one, 125 feet tall. Hanging from its top he's still a hundred feet from the maze of green below.

Landers wonders how he'll make his way out of the thickness below him with a bad leg. About a hundred yards away he sees a small stream. For a few seconds he hangs there, looks up and around and down. He will have to climb up the shroud lines. He can't cut loose. The fall would be fatal. Feeling begins to come back to his leg. He rubs his knee, where the pain is. He finds he can move it. He must have struck the kneecap a good blow falling into the tree, but he realizes with relief he'll be able to walk when he gets to the ground. Just where he'll walk to he doesn't know. The enemy pilot kept him so busy he had no time to navigate. His exact position is a mystery.

Landers pulls 226 pounds up the shroud lines, into the top of the tree, reaches the limb which caught his chute. He takes stock. He can't go down the trunk. The tree is too large. He begins to pull the chute to him; after working and tugging a while, he has harness, chute and lines on the limb beside him. He reaches for the small jungle kit American pilots carry—it's there! Two .45 pistols are strapped securely under his arms. His belt and jungle kit contain three boxes of ammunition for the .45's. If there are Japs below, he'll be able to provide a noisy reception. Landers also has a machete, which he now uses to cut lines and rig up a rope, which he ties to the limb and to himself. He uses the rope to lower himself to a large vine about fifty feet below, on which he reaches the ground.

He has thrown the jungle kit to the ground. As he reaches the bottom he finds himself in a mass of undergrowth, vines and bushes. For a few minutes he tries to make his way around to find the kit. Impossible! He couldn't clear away the dense growth at the base of the tree—fifteen feet in diameter—in less than a day's work.

Landers remembers the direction of the stream. He will cut his way through to the waterway. With machete he begins to hack at the thick growth barring his path. Progress is unbelievably slow. Five minutes, ten minutes, fifteen pass . . . the stream is only a hundred yards away. He chops away with machete vigorously. Every few steps is an accomplishment. It takes forty minutes to get the first glimpse of the stream.

Finally he breaks out of the growth and to the bank. The water is clear. He's thirsty. He leans down and takes a long drink, sits on the bank.

For some reason he looks at his watch. A few minutes before twelve! A long morning. As he sits there resting, he realizes take-off was only two and a half hours earlier. It seems a long time ago. He's a long way from civilization, in the foothills of mountains he crossed in *Big Doll* so easily time after time, and so quickly. Checking his guns and putting away the machete, Landers stands up and begins to walk upstream.

Sooner or later he will come to a path, a crossing of some kind. The stream is shallow . . . he walks on the edge whenever he can, in the water when the undergrowth reaches both banks. Time passes slowly; the stream is rocky, and Landers gives thanks for the G.I. high-tops. An hour passes, two hours . . . not a sign of life, no sounds, no trails. Landers begins to wonder. It's two o'clock in the afternoon. He sloshes on upstream, getting wearier step by step. He has had no food, other than coffee, all day.

Three hours pass; Landers trudges upstream. Three o'clock. Only the sounds of birds and the ripple of water break the jungle silence. He could have been back to Moresby, returned to Dobodura and landed again back at Moresby in this time—in a fighter. The banks along the side of the stream get higher as he moves upland. He looks at his watch . . . four o'clock! For four hours he has been walking upstream and not a trail, not a path, has he come across.

The right bank of the stream rises up some thirty feet ahead. Landers makes out an outline which could be a path winding up the bank. He takes a long look, and anxiously approaches it. There is no one around, but the path is there, a footpath, one used regularly. Landers starts up the winding pathway on the right, ready to go for his .45's at a moment's notice. He hears soft words and hesitates, then climbs on. He reaches the top. As he tops the crest, in front of him stands a young girl with a baby in her arms. Both are surprised. The native girl screams, begins to run. Landers, speechless, hears a rustle in the brush on the low side of the bank; he whirls around.

All at once nine natives break out of the brush on the low side of the bank, running toward him; they carry axes and knives. Landers has happened on a poor introduction—having frightened the girl. He reaches for his guns. The natives hesitate, then stop, looking him over from the bottom of the bank. It's a tense moment. Then the natives turn and begin to run. Landers wants no hostile natives around him at night. He fires his .45's over their heads, a long-shot chance they'll realize he's not trying to hit them, but stop their flight.

The strategy works. An elderly native halts the others. He turns slowly and looks back at Landers, who stops firing and motions frantically for the brown-skinned, bikini-ed group to come back. The old man walks slowly forward, crosses the stream and approaches, others following at a distance.

Landers tries to explain his plight. The natives jabber. Neither can make out the other. The old man steps forward; around his neck he wears a round disc, and Landers reads the English words: "Native Chieftain of Paupau County." Landers smiles and uses his hands and a few words in an effort to get through. He offers cigarettes, which they accept and light. The natives know only four words of English, which they repeat over and over: "American—Jap—machine gun." That's the vocabulary. Landers doesn't know how much they understand of what he's trying to tell them—that he's an American pilot just shot down, trying to make it back to American lines. The natives become friendly. All of them sit down and smoke. Landers sits among them.

Resting, Landers takes out his handkerchief and begins to field-strip his pistols. The natives watch every move. No one seems to be in a hurry. Tired from the long walk, Landers decides to relax a while, too, not knowing whether the natives understand or not. For half an hour they sit on the bank of the stream. Then a native runs up out of the underbrush. Landers recognizes two fifty-calibre shells . . . from *Big Doll*. The native proudly displays them. The others jabber excitedly as they gather round and look the fifties over. His guns stripped, now impatient to be on his way, Landers gets up and motions to the group to get started. They seem to understand, start down the bank to the stream, signaling him to follow.

They cross the brook, then go about twenty steps along a path leading from the low bank, and come to a path that parallels the stream; they turn left and start following the path downstream. For six hours Landers sloshed up the stream, in the other direction—with a path twenty yards to his left! The natives walk ahead. An hour passes. They are leading him up the side of a mountain, have turned away from the stream. Up and up they walk, Landers behind the bare-backed natives, who wear only scant bikinis. It's six o'clock, and in a few minutes the top is reached. Landers sees a small shack ahead. The natives must plan to spend the night here; they lead him inside, gesture, and start a fire on the dirt floor. They are getting ready to eat.

Since he hasn't had any food all day, and since he can't do anything about it anyhow, Landers sits down wearily and watches preparations. The shack is small, about ten by twelve feet, its sides made of bamboo canes, the top straw. With the fire in the center, the natives and Landers around it, and a couple of the dogs who have joined the group also present, the little shack is packed. The natives go out and bring in green bananas. They also bring in coconuts.

They throw the green bananas into the hot coals, chop the coconuts open and drink the milk. Landers accepts a coconut and enjoys the nourishment. He tries to motion to the natives he prefers ripe bananas, not green ones. No progress. Charcoaled green bananas or nothing. Landers eats a few and drinks more coconut milk. Outside the sun is setting.

A native runs in with a present—his chute! Landers thanks him. The chute will be his cover during the night. The natives, almost entirely unclothed, have no cover, sleep on the ground. More natives come in as darkness settles over New Guinea; finally there are some fourteen natives and half a dozen dogs in the shack. They prepare to sleep. Landers is cold, though clothed and covered with the silk of his chute. The natives sleep soundly on the ground.

During the night, which somehow passes rather quickly, it rains and Landers hears large tropical drops beating muffled tones on the straw roof above. By morning the rain has stopped. The natives rise early and once again go out for bananas and coconuts. Breakfast! Green bananas and coconuts. Again Landers tries to get through on the subject of ripe versus green bananas. Again he fails. Soon all are out on the trail, walking down the mountain in a different direction from that of yesterday's ascent.

The trail is rugged and progress slow. Landers begins to get impatient. Where is he going? The natives know he is an American; he has given them all coins, cigarettes, his lighter. They know his identity. They must be leading him toward the coast—but it doesn't seem so. Up above he sees a transport plane fly over . . . American . . . probably headed for Dobodura from Moresby . . . and he's going in neither direction. He tries to understand the natives . . . he is beginning to get a few words . . . but still they can't tell him where he's going.

For hours they walk down into a valley . . . Landers recognizes nothing. About noon some of the natives ahead become excited, talk rapidly . . . Landers wonders if he's coming to a town, or a road. He looks ahead and steps a little faster, but sees nothing. Then in the jungle up ahead he makes out the cause of the excitement . . . a green wing, scattered parts . . . *Big Doll!* The natives have taken him to his aircraft! Landers goes forward to look it over. The natives think somebody must be inside; Landers convinces them he was the only occupant. *Big Doll* is pretty thoroughly demolished—the engine burned, fuselage blackened and wings and tail broken by the trees she struck. Landers was right in jumping . . . he wouldn't have survived this landing.

Once again it's time to eat bananas and drink coconut milk—dinner. It has taken half a day to reach the plane. Landers is impatient. The natives start a fire and throw the green bananas in. Finally they are ready to go again. To his dismay, Landers sees them start back the way they came. They've been walking all morning in the wrong direction. Now they must go back the way they came—a day wasted!

By nightfall the group reaches the shack. They will spend the night here again. Landers' feet are acquiring blisters and he's tired. He settles down in the shack for the second night. It's December 27.

Early next morning he is greeted by a guide, evidently sent for by the other natives. He recognizes enough native words to get across two points. He wants to be taken to the nearest Americans, and he likes ripe bananas, not green.

The guide seems to understand. They bid the rest of the natives good-by and start off down the mountainside. And while the guide leads, and he follows, there always seems to be someone else behind, following out of curiosity. The guide obliges him with a stalk of ripe bananas and Landers eats several. They walk on for several hours . . . reach a small village . . . the natives have a stalk of ripe bananas waiting for him. How did they know? They halt only a few minutes, and continue on. Another village is reached several hours later. Another stalk of ripe bananas is waiting for him. Landers downs a few more. His feet are sore and he's tired after three days of walking, but eager to continue.

After passing through three villages during the day, Landers and guide stop at the next one for the night. He had noticed during the day they were moving east or north most of the time. He reasons he is heading for the nearest Americans on the north coast. The chief, the guide, and Landers are allowed space around a fire; everyone else retires out of sight, the men in their bikinis, the women in little or nothing at all. They all go to sleep. It's December 28.

Next day Landers reached the Kokoda trail. He and the guide followed it, northeast, toward the northern coast of New Guinea, passing many dead Japanese soldiers, which always excited the guide and other natives who happened to be along. They passed through more villages. In answer to Landers' standard question: "Where are the Americans?" the reply was invariably "Over the next hill." But they never were. So passed the 29th.

On December 30, feet blistered, leeches working on his legs, tired and weak from his banana-coconut diet, Landers and guide reached a village in which a native spoke English. The guide informed him that several villages further along he would at last see the sea. True enough, at the third village, Landers glimpsed the ocean ahead. It took several hours to reach the beach; finally they made it. Landers carefully removed his shoes . . . walked painfully along in the sand . . . the blisters were so bad he couldn't get his shoes back on, nor did he want to . . . he wanted the salt water to clean and soothe his feet. His legs were covered with sores where the blood leeches had fed during the last five days.

An American food dump, so the natives had said, was not far, and Landers and the guide walked the beach in its direction. Stepping lightly on his tender feet, Landers at last saw three G.I.'s guarding the entrance to the U.S. food dump. He approached slowly, introduced himself and explained he had been shot down. The guards had a telephone in their sentry house and offered it to him. He talked to their commanding officer, who agreed to radio Moresby. Landers wanted someone at Moresby to pick him up at a nearby airstrip, formerly Japanese, down the coast a few miles.

Next day, the 31st, an Aussie came to the U.S. dump, where Landers had spent the night, paid the guide the standard five pounds' reward for bringing out an American, and gave him all the food he could carry away. The guide said good-by and promptly left. Then the Aussie sailed Landers in a small boat to the landing strip down the coast. A medical unit stationed here immediately looked him over, a doctor lanced blisters and treated his legs. An A–24 from Morseby landed and picked him up, and a couple of hours later he was back in Morseby. It was December 31. He had been gone since 9:15 A.M. of the 26th. It had been a long mission.

Other pilots in 9th Squadron had witnessed Landers' Japanese victims going down on the 26th . . . he was credited with two kills. The Americans, in the battle, had destroyed seven enemy fighters that morning, preventing an attack on Dobodura. Victories had been scored by Lieutenants William O. Sells, William A. Levitan, James A. Watkins, Robert A. McDaris, and Arthur A. Wenige. The interception, then, had been an important success, and an outstanding victory.

Landers asked why the other three planes in his flight had disappeared that morning as he headed for the three Zeros.

His element leader had attached himself to another flight in the wild battle. And Lieutenant Robert A. McDaris, who dived on the Zeros with him, had shot one down and been jumped himself. That left Landers alone, as he closed in to attack his second victim.

For bravery and aggressive leadership in combat, and two kills, Landers was awarded a second Oak Leaf cluster to the Silver Star. At war's end he had been awarded the Purple Heart, the Silver Star with two clusters, the Distinguished Flying Cross with three clusters, numerous air medals and British and French decorations. He was officially credited with the destruction of 28½ enemy planes, and probably destroyed several more.

For continuous service in combat and over-all record few fighter pilots in World War II surpassed him.

3 Battling Zeros Over Kunming

MAY 15, 1943:

Colonel BRUCE K. HOLLOWAY

CREATION of the Fourteenth Air Force in China (March, 1943) came at a time when Japanese armies almost completely encircled American bases in the western part of that country. The only supply line was that over the mountains to the west (the "Hump" route).

On other battlefields the tide had turned against the Axis. The Russians had swallowed the Sixth Panzer Army at Stalingrad; the Eighth Army in the Middle East had defeated Rommel and the Afrika Korps at El Alamein, and American troops were in action in North Africa. But the Fourteenth U.S. Army Air Force, in China, was at that moment threatened by a large Japanese air concentration bent on the destruction of the Chinese terminal at Kunming.

The Fourteenth contained only one fighter group, the 23rd (formerly part of the Tenth Air Force), for a long time after its birth. The 23rd consisted of three and then four squadrons, which were usually spread out over three or four different fields to minimize the danger of destruction on the ground.

Photo U.S.A.A.F.

42

Each squadron was capable of putting up about twenty fighters on maximum-effort occasions in the first half of 1943, the period with which we are concerned in this chapter. The Japanese Army Air Force was capable of sending eighty or more aircraft on a single bombing mission, and since it was usually possible for only one squadron to intercept, American pilots were consistently outnumbered by the enemy.

In spite of this handicap, U.S. fighter pilots usually shot down more enemy planes than they lost in battle. Nor was it because the Americans were flying fighters vastly superior to the Japanese Zero. Indeed the Zero, used first and most successfully by the Japanese Navy, was superior in performance—in most categories—to American fighters available early in the war.

Japan's opening victories against the United States were largely the result of the Zero's outstanding performance. Japanese pilots entered dogfights in those days confident they could outclimb, outmaneuver, outrange and possibly outrun the P-40. Not until P-38's, and later P-47's and P-51's and the Navy's F4U's and F6F's, entered the struggle did the Americans have a fighter to outperform the Zero.

Japanese industry failed to keep pace with the rapid improvement made in American fighters, and the introduction of newer and better fighters by U.S. builders. And the Japanese fighter pilot found himself flying an obsolete Zero, comparatively, in the latter stages of the war, a summation ably supported by such authorities as Japan's leading living ace, Saburo Sakai, in *Samurai*. In addition, the Japanese were never able to replace their best fighter pilots, lost in the Coral Sea, at Midway, and over Guadalcanal and New Guinea.

The first commander of the 23rd Fighter Group in China, under the Tenth Air Force, was Colonel Robert L. Scott, author of *God Is My Co-Pilot*, who took command when the 23rd was formed, July 4, 1942. In January, 1943, Colonel Bruce Holloway, now Major General Bruce Holloway, replaced Scott. Holloway was a dead-serious, blond, blue-eyed Tennessean not long out of West Point. He was soon to become one of the China-Burma-India Theater's highest-scoring aces.

More than a dozen airfields were available to the Americans at this point in the war; most of them were crude one-runway strips constructed by thousands of Chinese workers who toiled daily to repair bomb damage, regularly inflicted by Japanese bombers. Fields were located at Kunming, Changyi, Yunnanyi, Hengyang, Lingling, Kweilin, Chengkung, Yangkai, Kienow, Kanchow, Suichwan, Chihchiang, and Shaoyang. Three other fields were available, but out of the range of op-

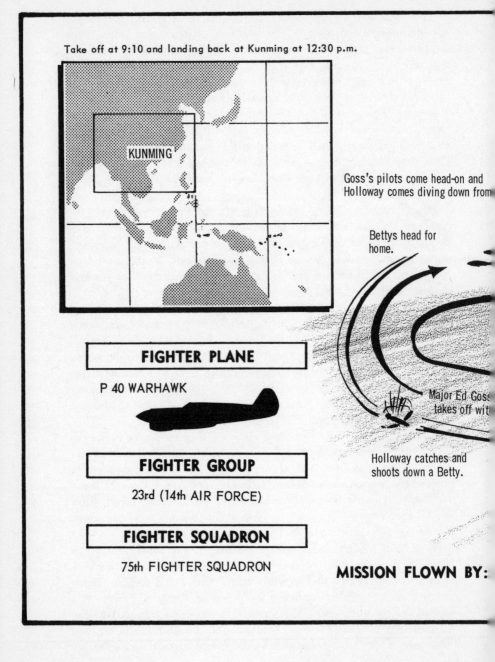

Take off at 9:10 and landing back at Kunming at 12:30 p.m.

KUNMING

Goss's pilots come head-on and
Holloway comes diving down from

Bettys head for
home.

FIGHTER PLANE

P 40 WARHAWK

Major Ed Goss
takes off wit

FIGHTER GROUP

23rd (14th AIR FORCE)

Holloway catches and
shoots down a Betty.

FIGHTER SQUADRON

75th FIGHTER SQUADRON

MISSION FLOWN BY:

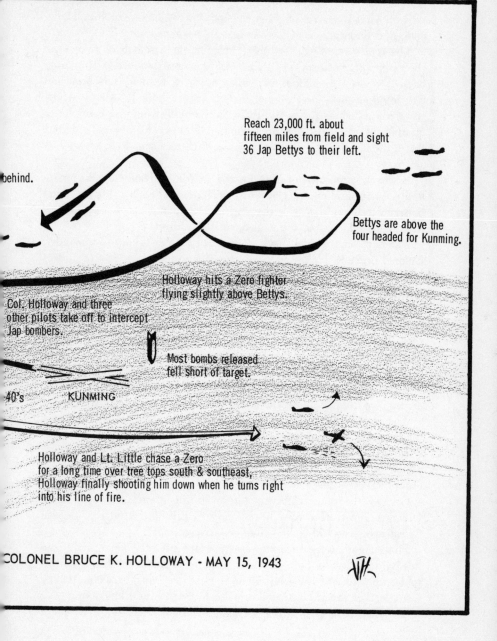

Reach 23,000 ft. about
fifteen miles from field and sight
36 Jap Bettys to their left.

behind.

Bettys are above the
four headed for Kunming.

Holloway hits a Zero fighter
flying slightly above Bettys.

Col. Holloway and three
other pilots take off to intercept
Jap bombers.

Most bombs released
fell short of target.

40's   KUNMING

Holloway and Lt. Little chase a Zero
for a long time over tree tops south & southeast,
Holloway finally shooting him down when he turns right
into his line of fire.

COLONEL BRUCE K. HOLLOWAY - MAY 15, 1943

erations. In 1944, at the high tide of the Japanese Army's advance in western China, several of them fell into enemy hands, such as Heng-yang and Kweilin.

The four squadrons using these fields in the first half of 1943 were the 74th, 75th, 76th and 16th. The 75th was now stationed at Kunming, deep in southwest China, 175 miles north of French Indochina and two hundred miles northeast of Burma. Major John R. Alison, whom we met in Chapter 1, was still flying in the 75th. Kunming being head-quarters of the 23rd Group, Colonel Holloway maintained quarters there, usually flew his combat missions with this squadron.

In the early morning of May 15, 1943, darkness blanketing Kunming and the surrounding red clay hills, a Chinese hostel boy hurries along between the gray shacks of sleeping U.S. fighter pilots. It is 3:30 A.M. in western China, and nippy at 6,200 feet altitude.

The boy comes to the shack of the 23rd Fighter Group Commander, Colonel Bruce K. Holloway, opens the door and steps inside. He nudges Holloway—it is time to get up! The Japs pay their calls early when they visit Kunming, and the C.O. has to be ready. Holloway slips out of bed, turns on the light, and begins to dress.

Lights go on in other shacks in the hostel after the group commander rises. Hostel Two is a mile north of Kunming Airfield. Nestled in hills and crystal-blue lakes, Kunming is the best airfield available in China. Its runway is the prettiest sight of all—6,000 feet! Kunming airfield is also the eastern terminus of the famous over-the-Hump airlift—lifeline of supplies from India for the 23rd Group.

The shark-toothed fighters of 75th Squadron are well spread out over the field. Holloway disperses his aircraft and rotates his four squadrons from field to field in a cat-and-mouse game with Japanese air forces which outnumber him heavily and constantly seek to annihilate his group.

One of the other three squadrons in the group, the 16th, is at Changyi—not too far away to respond to a call of assistance, if needed (a call which would come before the day was out).

Shaved and dressed, Holloway steps out into the clear night and heads for the mess hall. Weather is perfect. Kunming has a tourist-folder climate and the May night is brisk, visibility excellent. Hollo-way's leather jacket feels good over khaki trousers and khaki shirt.

Breakfast consists of tea, eggs, sour bread and marmalade. As pilots of the 75th Squadron down breakfast, at 4 A.M., they wonder if the airfield will experience a "jingbow" today.

A "jingbow" is U.S. slang for the Chinese "Jin-boa" which means "air raid." On April 26th, at Yunnanyi, Japanese fighters surprised one squadron, caught its P-40's on the ground, and destroyed more than a dozen of the priceless fighters. Not an officer or enlisted man sweating out the supply situation in China in 1942–43 failed to appreciate the magnitude of that disaster.

The 23rd Fighter Group's operations were always conducted on a shoestring. Missions were dependent on the supply of gasoline, aircraft, ammunition, etc.—as flown in over the mountain ranges of northern Burma and eastern India. Because one squadron had so recently been badly mauled, Holloway was doing everything possible to conserve strength and outmove and outmaneuver the enemy. These worries flash through his mind at the breakfast table in the mess hall of Hostel Two.

Breakfast finished, 4:30 A.M., Holloway jumps in an old olive-green Chevrolet and heads for Squadron Operations, arriving in five minutes. No orders have arrived for a mission. All is quiet. Next is a check with the engineering officer, whose "status board" will tell how many P-40's are in the "in commission" column. The news is good. Of the squadron's twenty-five aircraft, nineteen are in commission.

Ammunition and fuel supplies have to be checked. Adequate. Inspections completed, Holloway heads for the nerve center of the fighter base—the field operations shack, which contains the key to victory over the enemy, the "warning board" of a vast Chinese listening network.

In a small room where only one U.S. pilot, an interpreter, and a Chinese officer taking telephone calls are allowed, the efforts of thousands of Chinese, in almost every part of China to the east and southeast, culminate.

The warning system, consisting of thousands of sentries posted on the hills of China, listening for the sound of aircraft overhead, worked effectively all through the war. Listeners called in audible reports immediately, over precious telephone wire sometimes stolen each night and replaced next morning.

So accurate was the network that American fighter pilots usually had time to "scramble" into the air and be at good altitude before the Japanese were sighted.

From the dark hours until well after daylight Holloway keeps watch in the small warning board room. Nothing comes in over the wires.

Is it to be quiet today? It's six o'clock, well light, and the Japs usually fly early, but nothing is stirring.

Minutes, then hours, tick by. Holloway decides he can leave the warning board, go to his office in the Headquarters Building, adjacent to the operations shack, and tackle paper work. A group commander has to write commendations, bestow medals, and fulfill a pretty heavy schedule of routine executive duties. This paper work had begun when the 23rd Group came into being, ten months earlier.

As the hours pass, a brilliant sun rises and whitens the teeth painted on the P-40's of the 75th Fighter Squadron.

The telephone on Holloway's desk rings. "This is the pilot duty officer. We're getting some unknowns coming up from near Mengtze." Mengtze is some distance to the south—in the direction of the main concentration of enemy air strength.

"Coming over," Holloway replies. It is after eight o'clock. In three minutes Holloway is at the warning board. Reports are numerous, rapid and consistent. It looks fairly certain that a raid is coming in, and word is passed around.

Now a red ball goes up on the tall warning poles used by the Chinese to signal danger. It is the Chinese method of warning the Chinese populace in and around the airfield. One red ball means caution. Two red balls indicate enemy attack imminent.

Reports now come in telling of heavy engine noise. Calls are coming in right up the line, closer and closer as the enemy passes over Chinese sentries on hill after hill on his way toward Kunming. The U.S. duty pilot and the two Chinese in the warning board room move constantly over the plotting board, placing little red cardboard arrows closer and closer to Kunming.

Sirens on the base now sound and two red balls go up on the warning poles. Time is short. Holloway's fighter pilots are ready. They get the signal to slip into chutes and head for their aircraft.

Crew chiefs are warming up the liquid-cooled engines. The first four U.S. pilots scheduled to take off, Holloway and three others, hurry out to revetments. Their job is to fly out and meet the Japs and send back the enemy's position, strength, course, etc.

As soon as they can get into the cockpit and hook up equipment, while absorbing advice from the crew chief about engine, brakes, or guns worked on overnight, they start engines. At 9:05 the wheels of Holloway's fighter begin to turn.

The P-40 carries 1,500 rounds of fifty-calibre ammunition, gasoline enabling it to stay aloft two to three hours, the length of time depending on performance demanded from its 1,200-horsepower engine.

Holloway reaches the end of the runway at 9:10. He gives Ronnie Wilcox, Ed Chrysler, and Johnny Alison the signal and left hands ease forward on the throttles. The Allison engine roars louder and louder as more and more high octane squirts into the cylinders.

Holloway pulls back the stick at one hundred roaring, bumping miles per hour. Heavily loaded, the P–40 flies only slowly in the thin air at 6,200 feet. Up folds landing gear; it closes into the wings with a thump, reducing drag. The four P–40's start a slow climbing turn to the left.

On the ground, sixteen pilots head for their aircraft, to be ready to take off on the Group Commander's signal.

The four airborne pilots reach 7,500, 8,000, 9,000—10,000 feet. They don oxygen masks, continue the growling climb southeast. The sky is clear, they search it well, but see nothing. Holloway orders Major Ed Goss, leading 75th Squadron, to take off with his planes and circle the field, and climb as quickly as possible.

Meanwhile, the "scouts" reach 20,000 feet; red clay valleys, green mountains and blue lakes grow smaller and smaller far below. (Into the lakes men and aircraft will fall before the day is over.) It's a perfect spring morning.

According to the warning board in the operations shack, the scouts are on an interception course, practically at point of contact. The enemy is making good time. Holloway will see him in a matter of seconds or minutes, or miss him altogether. His head turns constantly, side to side, up and down, ahead and behind.

The shark-nosed P–40's are slicing upward into clear sky . . . 21,000, 21,500, 22,000 . . . compass heading 135 degrees. Eyes strain; victorious fighter pilots see the enemy first. Holloway constantly rubbernecks, behind and around, but mostly ahead to the southeast. Every speck is mysterious, and investigated. But the Japanese armada isn't sighted.

The other sixteen fighters of the 75th are now aloft and climbing at maximum throttle setting behind, to the northwest. Holloway begins to worry about missing the enemy force altogether, letting the bombers slip in over the field without being intercepted.

Twenty-three thousand feet! Still no sighting. A voice pierces radio silence: "Bandits! Twelve o'clock high." In spite of Holloway's long climb, the Japs are above him, after all. He glimpses a gaggle of dots up ahead. The enemy fleet! They are three thousand feet higher than the four P-40's. And the fighter escort, which looks to number thirty to forty Zeros, is another four thousand feet above the bombers! Holloway orders full throttle, eases back on the stick.

The enemy bomber formation is spread out into one big, wide V—thirty-six bombers in all. Bettys! The armada converges with the P-40's surprisingly fast. Holloway realizes he is west of the path being followed by the enemy. The specks grow larger and larger. He orders a slight left turn. The enemy fleet is now almost directly above. Slowly the four P-40's swing around. It soon becomes a climbing chase below and behind the Bettys. He calls to Goss to get as high as possible—quickly.

But time is wasting, and the Japanese are not far from Kunming airfield. The enemy fleet has passed above the four straining, climbing P-40's. The Americans must gain altitude fast. Holloway figures the Japs haven't spotted his four interceptors. Their course doesn't vary. The three roaring P-40's gain the three thousand feet, are closing behind the enemy force at 26,000 feet, still climbing.

With his Allison engine wide open, the frustration of knowing he can't dive into the bombers before they reach Kunming disgruntles Holloway. What a difference a few minutes, or a few thousand feet, would have made!

The Japanese fleet approaches the airfield. Over the field two of Goss's pilots have reached sufficient altitude to make a head-on pass, and aim straight for the oncoming enemy, wings twinkling with gunfire. But the bravery of these two is not enough to turn aside the big enemy force. The bombers return the fire. Zeros 3,000 feet above curiously fail to intercept the Americans. Bomb-bay doors in the belly of the twin-engined Bettys slowly open. The four dauntless American fighters finally arrive above the bombers at six o'clock, ready to start down on their fat opponents. Holloway begins a diving pass.

The field below lights up with several explosions. The daring attack by Goss's two fighters evidently hastened release of enemy bombs. Most of the explosions are south of the field below. But on the southern edge a B-24 goes up in yellow flames and a B-25 is struck. First blood for the Japs. Most of the bombs miss the field, but a small Chinese village south of it is almost completely wiped out from above; fires sweep it from end to end. There is no time for Holloway to watch the carnage below.

His outstretched arm holds the stick forward . . . down, down from behind on the green Jap Bettys . . . their orange suns clearly visible.

A glance to each side . . . wing men in place . . . the rush of air, the roar of the engine . . . louder and louder . . . airspeed—400 m.p.h.

Out in front of the bombers, ahead, Holloway sees half the 75th Squadron, at last high enough to attack, point noses straight for the Bettys.

Unfortunately, the full weight of the 75th's interceptors wasn't brought to bear before "bombs away." High-altitude performance of the P–40 is so limited, even with warning and good weather, only head-quarters flight and one from 75th had reached the enemy's altitude. However, these two flights upset the lead bombardier. Holloway picks out a bomber just ahead, below . . . his target. But something reflects light off one side. His head snaps for a quick look . . . Zero! Jap fighters are finally jumping the P–40's!

Holloway sees others. He suddenly sees a sky full of enemy fighters. The Americans must fight the hard way—fighters against more fighters. Out front a Zero flashes across the blue . . . Holloway sees his chance. Stick and rudder respond . . . he twists and turns to line up behind the Zero.

The Jap pilot doesn't spot him . . . the gray enemy fighter's low-wing silhouette grows larger and larger . . . Holloway is moving up from behind faster than expected . . . he reaches for the gun button . . . almost on top of his opponent. Heavy recoil vibrations shake the P–40 . . . the Zero is hit . . . heavily hit! But Holloway bolts past the stricken enemy, overshooting because of his great speed.

He banks sharply in an evasive turn, to stay clear of the Zero's fire, which he would get should he inadvertently bolt straight out in front of him. In the sharp turn he scans the sky . . . Wilcox, Chrysler, and Alison are in fights . . . he looks around for his victim . . . he looks . . . up and down. He doesn't find him.

He S-turns and searches the sky, but the Zero he hit has disappeared. Unengaged, Holloway catches sight of two of his comrades. Both have locked on behind Zeros and each victim is trailing black smoke. But he has let the enemy slip away: he banks sharply and looks again.

Two columns of black smoke over a lake now mark the fall of his comrades' victims. The numerically superior Zeros have been chased— by twelve U.S. fighters. Disappointed his foe got away, Holloway looks again toward the enemy bombers.

At that moment the bombers execute a left turn, still in perfect formation, a wide-spread V. Some of the Jap fighters, obviously timid, head for home. The enemy is getting a hot reception. Zeros dispersed, many

American fighters fix attention on the slower bombers. Back at 26,000 feet after another climb, Holloway pushes stick forward and heads once again down on the Bettys.

As he roars down on the now-fleeing enemy, he notices two bombers straggling. A shark nose is already going after one. He dives far below to close the other from six o'clock. The twin-engine Betty, slower than the P–40, grows bigger and bigger in the gunsight circle. He is gaining on the bomber fast. The enemy's wingtips reach further and further to the sides of the light circle. Now the green Betty fills the ring. Fire! Aim is good. Pieces fly back. Holloway keeps gun button down, closing nearer and nearer. The American fighter, locked on at six o'clock, pours fifties into the trapped enemy—eighty shells a second. The overwhelming fire is too much for the Jap bomber.

A bright fire leaps out from fuselage and wing. This one won't get away. The Betty wings over, trailing fire and smoke, and begins to spin, vertically. Three times around, burning and spinning, straight down and then a blinding flash. The Betty explodes and disintegrates completely. At the same moment Holloway notices the other straggler, jumped by another P–40, burning fiercely, going down.

Satisfaction relaxes taut nerves an instant; Holloway has his first confirmed kill of the day. And he realizes the P–40's have gained the upper hand, despite the failure of some eight of Goss's fighters to get into the battle. The enemy is being mauled. He hasn't seen a single P–40 go down, though Jap fighters have been dispersed, are heading home, and U.S. fighters are freely attacking the fleeing, unprotected bomber formation. Bombers go down steadily as the 40's dart in and out.

Holloway's thoughts turn instinctively to conserving fuel and ammunition in the battle so he'll be able to direct reserve fighters from the air if a second wave of enemy bombers appears. Turning back toward Kunming in a climbing arc, his thoughts are suddenly · interrupted when he spots a P–40 trying to close a Zero far below. He decides to help. Once more he pushes stick and throttle forward, eyes fixed on the enemy fighter below.

Through the clear sky two American fighters streak down on the bandit. The Zero is going all-out for home and in speed is approximately a match for the P–40. Lower and lower the enemy pilot descends. Holloway and the other P–40 pilot, Lieutenant "Poco" Little, hang in behind, continue the chase.

With an unknown quantity of ammunition, Holloway is gambling he can catch the enemy fighter and shoot him down. He will have little or no ammo left after another fight, and fuel will also be a concern.

The sensational chase continues down and down, two P–40's behind an enemy headed for the treetops. From 15,000 feet Holloway has come . . . building up speed. How can the enemy stay out front? The two Americans have to admire the performance of the Zero.

Throttles are wide open as the three fighters race for the hills and valleys below. Out front the rough sound from the uneven stacks of the Zero echo over the hills, followed immediately by the smooth roar of two even-stack inline P–40 engines. Both Holloway and Little keep their eyes on the silhouette of the gray, low-wing fighter, constantly ask themselves if it's growing larger or smaller.

The Jap fighter flashes over the trees of the countryside below and down into the gap of a valley, heading south, following the contour of the valley, flying as low as possible. The two straining American fighters roar into the valley behind him. Holloway finally realizes he is catching the bandit; his outline is now growing bigger.

Temperature gauges in the fighters inch upward and every ounce of power is coaxed out of engines. Lieutenant Little is behind and to the left of the Zero. Holloway is dead behind. The enemy pilot gamely begins to twist and turn as the Americans ease up slowly, trying to bracket him. Each time he turns Holloway and Little maneuver behind him, staying apart, grimly determined to end the chase.

Holloway watches his gunsight glass as the enemy fighter grows larger and larger. He notices Little fire a few rounds, but the Jap is either too far ahead or aim was off. Holloway, now moving up at last on the enemy, decides to try a pass of his own, swerving out slightly and coming in from the rear quarter. He touches the button, but distance is too great. No hits.

Now Little tries again. The Jap hugs the treetops and flies on, turning with the turns in the valley. Again Holloway tries to line him up in his sight. But the enemy is cunning. Holloway and Little each make another pass. The enemy flies on, getting closer and closer home, Holloway and Little getting further and further from Kunming. Six passes and no hits! Will the battle have to be broken off? Will the wily enemy pilot get home to tell his story of ordeal over the valleys?

Then, up ahead, the answer. The valley comes to an abrupt end a mile ahead. A sheer cliff rises up to wall off the earthly trench through which three fighters have been hurtling. What will the Jap do now?

Little pulls slightly further off the left. If the Jap makes a left turn, to pull up and out, Little can cut him off in the turn and get a good firing pass. Holloway is almost straight behind the enemy, doesn't have the speed or time to get out right.

Down the valley the three planes thunder, the Jap staying low, aimed straight at the cliff ahead. Holloway grimly clutches the stick and firing button and sweats out seconds, occasionally glancing at Little, to the left. The Zero stays down until the last moment, then executes a sharp pull-up. Holloway and Little feel the suspense of wondering which way the Jap will turn. Up the Zero shoots—then . . . right!

It was the Jap pilot's best chance. Little had position for a perfect left-turn pass. Holloway is faced with a deflection shot—the toughest kind—as the enemy breaks right to escape the trap. He hits right stick and rudder, leans into a sharp right turn and tries to cut off the Zero as much as possible. The Zero grows larger in the sight ring; Holloway has gained precious yards. Now he is suddenly in range and the Zero is streaking across in front, from left to right. Banking right, eyes fixed on the gray enemy ahead, whose wings now reach from one side of the sight ring to the other, Holloway pulls the trigger.

Six guns roar, and shake the fighter. Shell casings fly backward and tracers rocket ahead, converging from both wings on the Zero. It is a tough firing pass and excitement chases up and down his spine as he notices shells striking the long-fleeing Zero in perfect sequence. The enemy tries desperately to shake his tormentor with a few violent jerks, but Holloway holds in, spitting shells which have been hauled, the hard way, from the United States.

Little looks on as deflection firing from Holloway's fighter literally shreds the Zero. In a last gasp, the Zero pulls straight up, but the enemy pilot can no longer control his aircraft, or is no longer conscious. The Zero falls off on a wing and noses down, straight down. It hits the ground with a flash of exploding gasoline, which burns brightly as Holloway shoots over, only a few feet above the trees. Holloway eases stick back and looks for Little, sweat covering his face and hands. It was a long chase!

Off to the side, having watched the kill, Little turns in toward his climbing group commander. They reverse course and head back to Kunming. Nowhere can a plane be seen in the sky. The tension begins to drain out, Holloway again takes stock of his fuel and ammo, and suddenly the warning comes from the radio shack: "Second wave of enemy bombers headed toward field!" The warning is like an electric shock. Holloway has to move fast. At that moment Lieutenant Little reports his guns jammed! Bidding him good-by, after ordering him to land, Holloway points the nose of his lone fighter into the sky and continues to climb. It's a long way back to 26,000 feet, but he knows the higher he gets the better his chances in another attack.

He picks up the mike and rattles off orders to the 16th Squadron commander at nearby Changyi, Captain John D. Lombard: "Send three of your flights down to Kunming immediately . . . expecting another enemy attack." Lombard confirms the order. Holloway continues the long climb. It's some time before he sees the field and crosses in over its boundaries, approaching desired altitude. Over the field he notices several 75th fighters milling about, and a few more defenders from group headquarters, who have taken to the air and are awaiting the next Jap assault.

At Changyi the three flights ordered to support the defense of Kunming lose no time. They report being airborne and bearing down on

A P–40 approaches the field for a landing at Kunming,
site of Bruce Holloway's encounter with the enemy.
(Air Force Photo)

Kunming with all possible speed. Tired, wrung-out, and worried about his ammo supply and the problem of landing in the face of an enemy attack, Holloway circles the field and tries to figure the answer. He has won a victory, but now, with another attack coming in, he might well lose it, if the enemy catches his fighters landing.

Anxiously, he looks toward Changyi for the three Red flights on their way as reinforcements. He circles and searches the sky for several minutes. The radio below continues to report Japanese aircraft to the south. Then the relief fighters heave into view as dark specks to the north, a cheerful sight!

Holloway picks up his mike and orders the fighters circling the field —all who had taken off to intercept the first enemy attack—to follow him to nearby Yangkai, where a B–24 bomber squadron is based, for refueling. He orders Lombard to take over defense of the field until his fighters are readied for another mission. With that, Holloway points his P–40 away from Kunming and toward the nearby bomber base, usually not utilized by fighters, but which is needed by "little friends"—running short on fuel—today.

The flight to Yangkai, a short distance, is uneventful, but Holloway keeps an eye on his fuel gauges. At the bomber base traffic is heavy. Other planes have sought refuge here. But fortunately the commanding officer of the base is a hustler who goes all out to provide hospitality and fast service for weary fighter pilots.

As soon as a P–40 lands, it is gassed up. Holloway touches down, taxis to a stop, gets out and walks over to the control tower to keep in touch with the situation at Kunming. The enemy attack has not come in. There are reports the enemy has turned back. Could it be? The three flights from the 16th are in position over the field and waiting to give the enemy another hot reception, and soon Holloway's fighters will be ready again, in case.

But the listening network no longer hears approaching planes. The enemy has apparently decided to call off the second attack. This affords fighter pilots waiting anxiously for take-off grim satisfaction; they know news of the first wave's virtual annihilation has reached the enemy command. But they are also disappointed prospects for another good fight fail to materialize. As the chance of another fight dims, they swap tales about their battle that morning . . . the hits, the misses.

Holloway decides to go home. He orders the 75th to prepare for take-off. Soon the half squadron is airborne, words of appreciation having been expressed for the emergency aid at Yangkai. Kunming comes into view, south, and all is quiet. The radio shack on the field has announced "all clear." The red balls have come down from the poles. The fighters which had been called over from Changyi are released. Holloway noses his fighter down over the runway and touches down at approximately 12:30 P.M. He had lifted off the same strip ten minutes after nine in the morning.

A lot has happened in less than three and a half hours. It seems more like days. Holloway turns off the runway and wearily parks his long-nosed P-40 amid greetings and curious looks from ground crewmen. Yes, he had gotten in some licks—two confirmed kills and one probable, a probable Zero, a confirmed bomber, and a confirmed Zero! The ground crew, elated at the accomplishment, will lose little time in painting the red Rising Suns, signifying kills, on the side of Holloway's plane. Major Alison was credited with a victory during the day also.

As soon as he gets to headquarters, Holloway wants to know the day's score. The claims were fifteen Japanese kills and many damaged. Other Japs failed to return home as a result of damage sustained. How many had gone down on the return flight no one knew.

Holloway asks about losses. One P-40 had been shot up. The pilot brought it down safely. It would be repaired. Not a single American pilot had been shot down or killed. The day's battle, then, had been one of the outstanding victories of the aerial war over China. The bombing, which caused casualties in the small Chinese village, did little military damage.

Pilots were jubilant. They agreed the Jap fighters had done a poor job protecting the slower Bettys. One of the pilots cracked that the few Jap fighters that did get away were shot down by the Japanese bombers on the way home.

Victories like that of May 15, 1943, finally won for the U.S. Army Air Corps mastery of the skies over China. To the glory of the men who suffered the ordeals of primitive living conditions, limited supplies, inferior numbers of aircraft—in addition to the trials of fighter combat —stands the record of the 75th Fighter Group.

The battle of May 15 over Kunming checked the Japanese bombing offensive on that headquarters airfield. So heavy were losses inflicted on attacking aircraft May 15 that Kunming was not molested by the Japanese for months afterward, months used to good advantage by a steadily growing 14th Air Force.

PART 2

THE CONTEST
BECOMES MORE EQUAL

4 Scratch Two of the "Abbeville Boys"

AUGUST 16, 1943:

First Lieutenant JAMES A. GOODSON

THE famed 4th Fighter Group achieved the much envied distinction of scoring more kills than any other group in the U.S. Army Air Force in World War II. The 4th was one of fifteen fighter groups in the mightiest air force ever seen up to its time, the Eighth Air Force. The Eighth could put more than 2,000 heavy bombers and 1,000 fighters in the skies of Germany at its peak strength.

Photo Josef Josuweck

At the end of the war in Europe (the Eighth was based in England with a few groups moving to France late in the war) the Eighth's fifteen fighter groups had destroyed more than 9,000 enemy aircraft. To appreciate its achievements, and the power of this aerial assemblage, one need only scan a list of the highest-scoring American aces of the war.

Twelve of the top fifteen aces served in the Eighth. Three of them came from the 4th Group—one of the first American fighter groups to go into action from England. This group's pilot nucleus came from the Royal Air Force's three Eagle Squadrons, and these pilots had already been credited with more than seventy German victims on September 29, 1942, when they became the 4th Fighter Group, U.S. Army Air Corps, at Debden Airdrome. Debden is near Saffron Walden, in Essex.

There were other Army air forces in Europe—in Italy and later in France, but the Eighth was the giant. It carried out attacks on enemy targets from 1942 until the Nazi surrender, in May, 1945. At peak strength the Eighth contained 185,000 officers and men, three heavy bomber divisions and the aforementioned fifteen fighter groups, which were used for high-altitude escort, strafing, dive bombing or tactical support—as the occasion demanded.

Naturally, there was great rivalry among the various fighter groups. And while the 4th ended the war with a record 1,052½ confirmed victories, just ahead of the famous 56th (985½), there were times when odds favored 56th as the group most likely to win the race for top honors. When the final totals were tabulated immediately after the war, 56th was less than seventy victories behind 4th.

The 56th lost its legendary commanding officer, Colonel Hubert Zemke, when he was transferred to the 479th Fighter Group. He was captured after bailing out over Germany in September, 1944. Colonel J. M. Blakeslee, commander of the 4th, was grounded the same day.

A hot rivalry existed between 4th and 56th. Because 4th was operational first, it assumed an early lead. But the redoubtable Zemke, once he got the Wolfpack into the air, came on fast. Soon 56th was credited with twice as many kills as 4th. It was not until the "Debden Gangsters"—as Radio Berlin referred to 4th—were equipped with P–51 Mustangs that they began the comeback which finally won for them group honors in the Eighth Air Force.

From February 25, 1944, when Mustangs were delivered to the 4th, or shortly thereafter, until the end of the war, it was nip and tuck, often from day to day, whether 4th or 56th led in victories. Colonel Blakeslee remained on operations continuously from 1941, when he was with the R.A.F., until well into 1944—more than three years.

He flew more than four hundred combat missions, the equivalent of several tours of duty, and over 1,000 hours. It was a record among American fighter pilots. He was a hard leader who loved to fly and fight, highly popular with the 1,500 officers and men at Debden.

Blakeslee and Zemke differed on the relative merits of the P–51 Mustang and the P–47 Thunderbolt, a controversial topic when pilots of the two groups got together in London, or elsewhere. Blakeslee and many of the old Eagles of the R.A.F. had been accustomed to the

British Spitfire, a trim, light fighter, with great climbing and turning ability. When the 4th was given Thunderbolts many of its pilots were frankly critical of the "seven-ton milk bottle," capable of only a moderate rate of climb, though endowed with outstanding performance capabilities.

P-47N Thunderbolt (Air Force Photo)

Only after Blakeslee succeeded in getting P-51 Mustangs for his pilots did they begin to reclaim lost laurels—laurels picked up in the meantime by 56th. On the other hand, pilots at Halesworth, home of the Wolfpack, were not formerly wed to the Spit and gave the Thunderbolt undying loyalty and affection. Until the end of the war the argument continued between pilots of the two groups, 56th pilots almost invariably proclaiming the P-47 queen of the sky, those at Debden swearing by the Mustang.

The commanding officers of these two groups, Blakeslee and Zemke, were two of the great combat leaders of the war. This was perhaps the main reason for the records of their groups. Which of the two was the greater, or the greatest of the war, is and was a question still debated by pilots of 56th and 4th, and by pilots from other groups, some of whom have candidates of their own.

The Luftwaffe was fully informed and appropriately appreciative of the exploits of both 4th and 56th Groups. Zemke was to find this out upon capture, and German officers were to tell captured 4th Group pilots they would swap the whole lot of prisoners on hand for the 4th

Group leader. Other indications of the qualities of leadership displayed by Blakeslee, at Debden, are related in Grover C. Hall's *1,000 Destroyed*, an absorbing history of the 4th Fighter Group.

Serving in the 4th during World War II were two of the twelve aces featured in this book—Major John T. Godfrey and Major James A. Goodson, a native of New York, N.Y., with whom this chapter is concerned. Goodson ranks seventh among the living aces of the Army Air Force in World War II, is credited with twenty-eight kills. More about Godfrey, who ranks second, and an account of his most memorable mission, can be found elsewhere in this book.

Goodson, now an executive of a major American rubber company in Europe, got into the war the hard way. The Germans came close to snuffing out his life before he ever flew a fighter, even before he was in service. Had they succeeded in drowning him when one of their U-boats torpedoed and sank the British passenger steamer *Athenia,* taking him to Canada to join the Royal Canadian Air Force, they would have missed some of the zip they later encountered in the skies over Europe. They would not have missed some of their pilots, after they had encountered the American ace in the skies of Europe, in later years.

Goodson had boarded the *Athenia* September 2, not to get out of the war zone, but in order to get into it as a pilot. When the Wehrmacht marched into Poland on the morning of September 1, 1939, igniting World War II, Goodson was a student at the University of Paris, completing a summer course. He hurried to England, to join the Royal Air Force, but was told to go to Canada and enlist in the Empire Training Program.

Determined to become a pilot, Goodson booked passage on *Athenia* and on September 3, one day outbound, she was torpedoed two hundred miles west of Ireland, and sunk, with the loss of 112 lives, including those of women and children, by the U–30. Though *Athenia* was unarmed, U–30 sank her without warning. Goodson lent aid to the ship's medical party, caring for the injured as *Athenia* prepared to take the final plunge, then he splashed into the Atlantic and swam to a nearby lifeboat. A Norwegian tanker rescued survivors, landing them in southern Ireland.

Goodson tried again, undaunted by the sinking, unaware that years later the Germans would dunk him (and his fighter) again, in the North Sea—an adventure he would also survive. This time he signed on as a crew member of a Canadian-bound tanker, and made it. Then, at last, he joined the R.C.A.F. After successfully completing flying training, he arrived back in England more than a year later. Assigned to gliders, he later transferred to the 133rd Eagle Squadron, thence into the 4th Fighter Group.

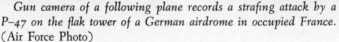

Gun camera of a following plane records a strafing attack by a P-47 on the flak tower of a German airdrome in occupied France. (Air Force Photo)

Goodson had one victory in a Spitfire to his credit when he became a member of the 4th. He flew the first low-level mission of the war by fighters with U.S. star insignia—shooting up trains in the marshaling yards at Brugge, and strafing barges—with the 336th Fighter Squadron. Three squadrons made up the 4th—334th, 335th and 336th.

In these days the Luftwaffe was often more than Allied pilots could handle. German pilots had an edge in experience and also enjoyed the advantage of fighting over their own territory. The ex-R.A.F. pilots of the 4th continued to fly Spitfires for a time after becoming an American fighter group. The Spitfire could outturn an ME-109 or an FW-190, and had a good rate of climb—but was not equal to the 190 above 20,000 feet until Spitfire 9's became available. The ME-109G was a highly capable performer at altitudes of 30,000 feet and better.

Spits sometimes took a licking from Luftwaffe fighters. On September 26, 1942, three days before the Eagle Squadrons transferred to the A.A.F., an entire squadron was wiped out by 190's. The twelve Spitfires had been ordered to escort a small force of Flying Fortresses to a target near Brest. The pilots, navigating through miserable weather, which hid checkpoints below, flew too far south, and because of unexpected winds found themselves running out of gas as they sought to return to England. In this precarious situation, the Spits were jumped by a host of 190's while still over enemy-occupied France. They were also beset by German flak. The squadron disintegrated and eight pilots mysteriously disappeared; three were buried next day by the Germans, and one, who destroyed what is thought to be the second Luftwaffe fighter shot down by an American fighter pilot in Europe, was taken captive after bailing out—his Spit shot up.

Even so, when the 4th switched over to Thunderbolts there were misgivings among Debden pilots. But Goodson was not one of the majority who lacked confidence in the P–47. True, the "Abbeville boys" were sometimes flying circles around the Americans in these days, but they were the Goering Geschwader, the Focke-Wulfs and Messerschmitts whose yellow noses earmarked them as the elite of the Luftwaffe Fighter Command. The difference was more experience than it was technical superiority of the German fighters.

In August, 1943—a year later—the 4th was still flying Thunderbolts. Goodson and other 4th Group pilots had put almost a year of combat under their belts as A.A.F. pilots. The Germans still held the coast of France, but British and American strength was swelling and the resources of the Luftwaffe were being drained away in Russia, Italy and North Africa. Even so, German fighter strength in France was increased steadily as the war continued. Allied raids on the coast of France grew in strength, and penetration of "Festung Europa" grew deeper and deeper. But the Focke-Wulfs and Messerschmitts of St. Omer and Abbeville were still formidable, and growing in numbers, and it would be misleading to give the impression that Luftwaffe fighter forces, as of August, 1943, were waning. The Americans had merely gained confidence, experience and numbers. It was not until much later that a preponderance of Allied power tipped the scales of battle sharply.

On August 15, 4th Fighter Group received orders to provide "general support" for a force of 170 B–17's bombing the aircraft repair depot and airdrome at Le Bourget in the vicinity of Paris. The full group would go out, as well as fighters from three other groups—78th, 56th and 353rd. Colonel Blakeslee would lead 4th. American pilots knew the Luftwaffe's hottest fighters, the familiar squadrons from St. Omer and Abbeville, would not remain idle as Allied fighters swept inland over their bases. Commanding the German fighters of the Luftwaffe's Second Fighter Wing, Richthofen, was the German ace Egon Meyer—who would be quick to engage Allied formations. Thus the morning's mission was an inevitable battle from the very beginning.

The morning of the 16th dawned warm and hazy, visibility adequate for a fighter sweep. Goodson was roused from his slumber by a batman, who informed him briefing would take place in an hour. Pulling on G.I. shirt and pants, and getting into prized R.A.F. flying boots, reinforced with steel to facilitate ground escape in the event of being shot down, Goodson set off for the mess hall and breakfast.

The officers' mess at Debden—a permanent station turned over to the 4th by the R.A.F.—was first class compared to field tents and temporary quarters occupied by many Americans. U.S. pilots stationed at former R.A.F. bases at least enjoyed comfortable quarters, central heating, batmen and a dining room in their living quarters, which were usually brick. Therefore, pilots stationed at bases such as Debden, Wattisham (home of the 479th Fighter Group), and other former R.A.F. bases, ate breakfast before briefing. Conditions at most bases were more primitive and pilots at many arose and covered a mile or more in the darkness to reach briefing. Only after both group and squadron briefings were they taken to improvised mess halls for breakfast.

Goodson and other pilots of the 4th, then, had their breakfast like "officers and gentlemen by act of Congress," in a style which evoked the envy and sarcasm of visitors from more spartan bases. Then trucks took them to group briefing, where Colonel Blakeslee outlined the mission.

The fighters would take off in pairs, Blakeslee said, climbing to an altitude of 24,000 feet, at which height they would cross into France in spread formation. The lowest squadron would be the 336th, which Blakeslee, or "Horseback Leader" would lead. "Horseback" was the code name of the 4th. Goodson, first lieutenant at the time, would lead the second flight in the 336th, just behind and to the left of lead flight.

The weather officer announced the forecast was good; only a few clouds and haze would be encountered. Intelligence didn't have to warn the men about the opposition. They knew what to expect. Group briefing finished, pilots departed for green Nissen huts that served as squadron headquarters, where they engaged in last-minute squadron briefings designed to clear up remaining questions and confirm order of flight and take-off. Pilots then checked out parachutes and flying gear. On a wall of each squadron headquarters was a blackboard, on which markers containing the names of the pilots were hung. Pilots glanced at the blackboard formation to recheck flying·position as they headed out for their planes.

Goodson greeted his ground crew, all standing by, and found everything in order. The armorer had checked and loaded guns, radio had been tested by a communications crewman, and the crew chief had checked engine and controls. He lowered his slim frame, and the clumsy equipment carried on it, into the compact Thunderbolt cockpit. He glanced at his watch. It was almost 8:02, start-engine time. The Pratt and Whitney radial fired away, after a few hesitations, and Goodson was ready to go. He taxied out as soon as he saw Blakeslee leave his revetment, for he was number five in take-off order and would lead the third pair of fighters off Debden's runway.

The dark green Thunderbolt (white-ringed cowling) kicked up a summer dust storm at it S-turned along the·taxiways. Now all over the field the sound of growling Thunderbolts could be heard. All three squadrons had started engines. Blakeslee pulled up at the end of the runway, glanced back. Goodson, with Lieutenant Bob Wehrman, as wing man behind, braked to a halt behind number four of 336th. Now Blakeslee was ready to go. P-47's were lining up in an ever-lengthening string at the end of the runway. He waved his hand and the first two 336th fighters, their code letters VF–B painted in large white letters on their fuselage, moved forward.

Horseback Leader lifted the seven-ton bird off the runway two-thirds the distance to the end. As soon as his wheels were off, numbers three and four, abreast, pushed throttles forward and began take-off runs. Goodson moved to take-off position as soon as they moved off, waited until he saw them airborne and signaled Wehrman to release brakes. Five and six were taking off.

When airspeed touched 100 m.p.h., Goodson began to ease stick back and the fighter began to fly. He turned in behind Horseback Leader when he had gained a few hundred feet altitude, and the group circled slowly around the field until the three squadrons joined up. Then Blakeslee set course for the English Channel and France, where certain action awaited pilots of the 4th.

The distance from Debden to the vicinity of Abbeville is well over one hundred miles. The English Channel lies eighty-five miles away, after which the 4th must pass over sixty miles of water. Abbeville is about ten miles inland on the Somme River, in the vicinity of famous battlefields of World War I, battlefields where the British held the line against the Kaiser's armies for four years. The 4th would cross into France forty miles southwest of Abbeville, near Dieppe.

The Thunderbolts climb at better than 150 m.p.h. on south by southeast heading. In thirty minutes they are west of Folkestone and passing out over the Strait of Calais, leaving the rolling green countryside behind. Below them, as they continue their climb, are Spitfires, also taking part in the mission. The Thunderbolts continue to gain altitude, though already above the Spits, and shortly after passing landfall out attain mission altitude of 24,000 feet. Now there are only minutes left before the coast of France will come into view. Pilots check gun and gunsight switches, gas gauges and instruments; there may be no time later.

They begin to look thoughtfully around the sky. The Luftwaffe's radar has surely spotted the oncoming armada (bombers and fighters) and it's taken for granted the yellow noses are already airborne. The 4th is in combat formation, each flight far out to the side of the other, staggered slightly. Individual fighters are also widely separated. Now at cruising speed, the P-47's are making between 250 and 300 m.p.h.

Over the earphones pilots hear the whine of German jamming. That and the roar of engines . . . and everything else is silent. The 4th flies on . . . a dim outline on the horizon appears ahead . . . France. Nerves tighten and heads rotate . . . no sign yet of German fighters. Down below the Spitfires, thin and graceful, ply on. They will probably get into the fight first. The Germans will have to climb up to meet the invading fighter force, will reach Spitfire level first.

Landfall gets nearer and nearer. The white shore and the green beyond are visible ahead . . . in a few minutes Dieppe comes into view. The 4th is now almost over landfall in . . . radio chatter begins to break the silence of the airwaves. Blakeslee's familiar voice rings out: "That'll be enough of that Goddamned radio chatter." Blakeslee is a stickler for radio silence. The Thunderbolts cross in. They are approaching the vicinity of Rouen. The bombers come into sight ahead! Someone suddenly yells over the radio—bogies below! Goodson searches the sky below, straining his eyes. Blakeslee calls: "There's a million of 'em . . .

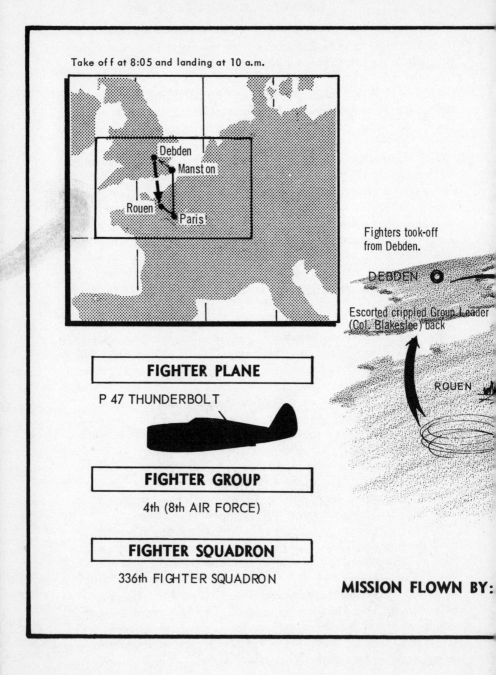

Take of f at 8:05 and landing at 10 a.m.

Debden
Manston
Rouen
Paris

Fighters took-off from Debden.

DEBDEN

Escorted crippled Group Leader (Col. Blakeslee) back

ROUEN

FIGHTER PLANE

P 47 THUNDERBOLT

FIGHTER GROUP

4th (8th AIR FORCE)

FIGHTER SQUADRON

336th FIGHTER SQUADRON

MISSION FLOWN BY:

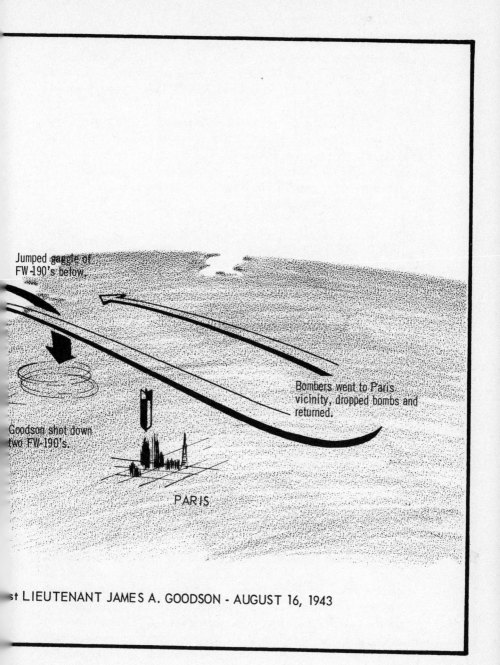

Jumped gaggle of
FW-190's below.

Bombers went to Paris
vicinity, dropped bombs and
returned.

Goodson shot down
two FW-190's.

PARIS

1st LIEUTENANT JAMES A. GOODSON - AUGUST 16, 1943

190's . . . down there!" Then, in rapid-fire order, Horseback Leader instructs the rest of the group to maintain altitude. To Goodson he blurts: "I'm going down, Goody . . . give me top cover." The 190's below are only a scattering of dots. Horseback Leader has a long way to go.

One of Blakeslee's wings goes up and he points his nose down. Goodson follows. Wehrman follows Goodson, who can now see the bandits more clearly. He estimates they are at 12,000 feet, and there are plenty of them. Spitfires are between the P–47's and the FW–190's. Blakeslee screams down . . . speed in the dive rapidly increases, 400 m.p.h., 450. The Thunderbolts are going almost straight down . . . Blakeslee is after the yellow noses.

The Germans are coming up in droves . . . several gaggles of them. But Blakeslee pays little attention to numbers. The diving U.S. fighters are now far below the rest of the 4th . . . the Spitfires are immediately below . . . and Blakeslee goes right through them. Now Horseback Leader slackens dive and alters direction . . . he has picked out two 190's . . . he's going after them. The P–47's curve behind their foe— there is much to watch—German fighters are all around, gray and black fighters, white-bordered crosses on wings, swastikas on rudders. The two 190's split-S and dive . . . for a moment they gain distance, but then the 47's—diving again—begin to close. The Germans continue their steady descent, reaching 500 m.p.h. But Blakeslee is right behind one of them. The other turns away.

Blakeslee banks left and closes the gap on his intended victim. Meanwhile 336th Squadron up above has headed into six FW–190's attacking the bombers head-on. Some of the P–47's become separated in the fast-breaking action, some pilots pull out of dives at great speed, feeling as though someone were pressing them down hard in their seats. At this moment, below, Goodson—trailing Blakeslee—spots three 190's ahead, maneuvering to get into position on Blakeslee's tail, and not far behind. They're cutting in on his rear in an effort to rescue the 190 now almost in Horseback Leader's sights. It's a tight situation . . . there isn't much time . . . Blakeslee is already in serious trouble.

Goodson rams the throttle forward and banks left to cut the three bandits off in the turn . . . the 190's are so close on Blakeslee he presses the mike button: "Break, Horseback Leader!" Blakeslee, hearing the warning, flashes into a vertical left turn, as tight as he can pull. The pursuing 190's follow . . . for a few seconds Goodson wonders . . . but Blakeslee doesn't shake the bandits. The enemy pilots are crafty. The three yellow-nosed fighters hang on to Blakeslee's tail . . . he's in a critical spot.

Goodson, standing on his left wing and hauling back on stick with all his strength, cuts in behind the three Germans. Blood drains from his head. He is closing . . . but is he closing fast enough? The last of the three enemy pilots is beginning to come into range . . . all of them are completely engrossed with Horseback Leader, oblivious to what's moving in on their rear. Goodson puts his finger on the trigger . . . about ready . . . the last bandit ahead grows larger and larger in his sight. He sees the lead 190 firing on Blakeslee, close enough to be registering.

Fire! He opens on the unsuspecting 190 ahead . . . the Thunderbolt's eight guns thunder, the recoil shakes every bolt in the fighter . . . ahead the armor-piercing and incendiary fifties are scoring. Good shooting! With light smoke streaming backward from his own guns, Goodson watches the gray bandit stagger as shells slam into him in rapid succession. Goodson is slightly above him and cutting in to his left. His fire is taking a heavy toll, especially at the wing roots. Pieces begin to fly back from the stricken 190. Suddenly a wing separates and hurtles back. Streaming smoke, the half-wing victim spins crazily and takes the plunge. The action is taking place at low altitude; Goodson realizes how far he has descended when he glances down for a split second at his victim. The trees are not far below.

Without a moment to spare, Goodson fixes his sight on the next bandit ahead, the second of the three which sneaked in on Blakeslee. He is still making speed enough to close. Blakeslee is taking every evasive maneuver in the books, but can't shake the 190's. Goodson executes turn for turn, cutting distance a bit in each, pulls in closer behind the second gray 190. Up front the leading Focke-Wulf is still shooting . . . Goodson must make it quick. His engine wide open, the dark, low-wing outline ahead draws slowly nearer.

The Germans are still unaware of Goodson, and, behind him, Wehrman—the only other P–47 support in the chase. Goodson puts his finger on the trigger again. The 190 is getting bigger and bigger . . . steadily the victim spreads out in the ring on the gunsight glass. Fire! Hundreds of shells converge on the dark shape ahead. This time fire is more concentrated . . . Goodson is closer to his victim. Strikes are visible all over the enemy . . . chunks and pieces of his aircraft tumble backward. The 190 begins to trail smoke . . . Goodson knows he's got him. A last short burst is too much for the German . . . he peels off and his nose goes down . . . straight down. The 190 dives down and down . . . then into the ground. Billowing smoke marks the spot of victim number two. No chute from this one either.

His rear secured by the faithful Wehrman (seeing quite a show on one of his first missions), Goodson locks his eyes on the remaining 190. If he can catch him, too, from behind, Blakeslee might be saved after all. He yells encouragement into the mike: "I've got 'em, Horseback Leader!" Blakeslee comes back: "The hell you've got 'em—he's got me!" Spurred by these words, Goodson coaxes every ounce of power from his engine, stares ahead at the remaining tormentor of 4th Group Leader. The enemy pilot hangs doggedly on to Blakeslee, just out of range. Goodson notices for the first time Blakeslee's Thunderbolt is streaming oil . . . he's been hit in the engine.

The chase continues. Goodson is coming on at six o'clock . . . seconds count. The Jerry tries to finish Horseback Leader off. This time Goodson is closing from dead astern. Flushed with excitement, eager to get rid of the last of the three 190's, the distance seems to narrow agonizingly slowly . . . but the Thunderbolt creeps up on the enemy's rear. The last few seconds are an eternity . . . finally the bandit is almost in range. Goodson lets the gray wingspan widen . . . presses the trigger. The eight guns roar and vibration rudely shakes the 47. Goodson sees no hits. Now certain he's in range . . . another burst . . . he makes out strikes . . . he is scoring! Abruptly, everything seems quiet. Goodson is baffled. He feels the trigger . . . he's still holding it down! But his guns aren't firing. Out of ammunition! The 190 ahead is hit, but hangs on to Blakeslee.

Goodson must think fast . . . he still has speed, he is easing right up on the 190. He decides to bank to one side and turn in on the enemy fighter. Maybe the sight of a Thunderbolt coming in for a gunnery pass from the side may scare him off . . . and maybe the German will see Wehrman, too, if he looks around. Something must be done to save Blakeslee. Using stick and rudder, Goodson slices gracefully to the side, reverses bank and points his nose at the enemy, now almost abreast of him. The 190 can't ignore the attack. And as Goodson approaches he breaks off.

The sight of the blunt-nosed P–47 approaching from his side, Wehrman behind, and the absence of comrades who were with him a minute earlier are too much for the enemy pilot. Goodson makes no attempt to follow the fleeing 190. He's out of ammo, concerned with the condition of Blakeslee's Thunderbolt. Pulling up close, he sees oil streaks

stretching the distance of Blakeslee's fuselage. He calls to inquire if
Horseback Leader can make it home. Blakeslee says he'll try, reports a
rough engine. Goodson assures him he and Wehrman will stand by
on the way home. Only Wehrman, of the three fighters in Goodson's
flight, has managed to maintain position throughout the battle. The
other two are not to be seen.

*An ME-109 pilot caught at the moment of bailing out of his
stricken plane somewhere over France.* (Air Force Photo)

Blakeslee sets course almost due north . . . the French coast is not
far ahead, but he sweats it out . . . his engine is steadily losing oil.
A cylinder, or more than one, has taken an enemy shell, and through
the hole oil is leaking out. The Thunderbolt might fly five minutes or
fifty. There is one way to tell—fly on and see. Goodson pulls up over
Blakeslee and he and Wehrman zigzag back and forth above . . . scour-
ing the sky to see if friend or foe is in the area. For a few moments all
goes well. Blakeslee is not losing altitude and has an escort. His chances
are improving.

Then, out the corner of his eye, Goodson spots a couple of suspicious
specks. The specks grow larger and larger . . . they approach Blakeslee

from five o'clock. They come on, making good speed. Goodson sweats it out . . . friend or enemy? The bogies' noses are blunt . . . not Spits, either 47's or 190's. The bogies grow more suspicious, are in perfect position for a firing pass on Blakeslee below. Goodson eases throttle forward and at the same moment recognizes the mysterious fighters as bandits . . . Focke-Wulfs!

Without ammunition, Goodson will nevertheless intercept. Though he'll be bluffing, Wehrman is able to fire. He carves out a sharp turn to the rear and Wehrman follows. The enemy, below, comes on. Goodson noses down, aims for firing position on the 190's. Blakeslee is approaching the Channel. Goodson keeps eyes on the approaching enemy fighters. He has altitude on them, a priceless advantage. He points his nose straight at the 190's. For a few seconds they close head on, then suddenly the 190's break. Goodson and Wehrman watch them streak away on a perpendicular course.

Goodson doesn't follow. Instead, he turns north again to overtake Blakeslee . . . who still holds altitude and heading, and steadily lessens the distance to the English coast. Goodson keeps throttle well forward to maintain high speed, and stays above Blakeslee as he approaches from behind, in case of further interference. He glances at gasoline gauges. In the swirling fight, so much of the time at high-throttle setting, he has consumed practically all his fuel.

He estimates remaining flying time sufficient to make England, but whether he can reach Debden is extremely doubtful. He wonders about Blakeslee. The group leader was flying wide open for a long time; his fuel must also be low. And Wehrman has had to follow the entire action in third position, a position which normally requires more fuel than lead, since turns must be a little wider and distance a little greater, following.

As he computes distance and fuel consumption, Goodson's attention is caught by something up front other than Blakeslee. Off to one side, low—at Blakeslee's approximate altitude—another fighter approaches Horseback Leader. A long look establishes his identity. Another FW–190! Goodson and Wehrman are near the coast and, luckily, have an altitude advantage. Blakeslee has just crossed out and the bandit obviously intends to curve into firing position behind the stricken P–47. He is some distance to the side. The escorts move to intercept. Once again Goodson bends on power. This time he will converge on the enemy fighter from the side, slightly ahead. Such a typical gunnery pass might impress the enemy pilot, who probably hasn't seen Blakeslee's escort.

Airspeed picks up as the two P–47's whistle down to defend their crippled comrade. The 190 below grows bigger and bigger, as the Thunderbolts lose altitude, and converge. Obviously the German doesn't see the two P–47's trailing Blakeslee above. Now they are sweeping down on him. But this pilot is more alert than his three comrades caught by Goodson earlier. He spots the two approaching P–47's and vertically banks away. Had he known, he could have paid attention only to Wehrman, and it would have been one against one.

The gray, low-wing enemy outline is swallowed up in the August sky to the west, and Goodson and Wehrman resume course behind Blakeslee. They would take up the chase in different circumstances, but there's no thought of abandoning Blakeslee. If Horseback Leader should go down, Goodson can circle the spot and give coastal radar stations enough transmission to get a fix on his position. Rescue craft would know exactly where to pick him up. This being summer, Blakeslee can last a long time in the water.

In winter Eighth Air Force fliers can survive the forty-degree water only twenty or thirty minutes. Pilots are sometimes pulled out of the North Sea in the dead of winter, down only fifteen minutes, having succumbed from exposure. August is about the best month to take a dip in the channel or North Sea, Goodson thinks, as he looks ahead at the black-stained P–47 Blakeslee anxiously nurses across the Channel.

His thoughts are interrupted. Out front, below, from somewhere, another fighter has suddenly appeared. Goodson watches him carefully for a few moments. FW–190! Is he one of the first two chased off, come back, or yet another enemy pilot who seeks to take advantage of Blakeslee's crippled condition? Slowly the bandit approaches Blakeslee from the rear. Goodson and Wehrman nose down to intercept.

As the 190 moves in on Blakeslee, the two Thunderbolts, slightly higher, slant downward toward the German. The game of bluff has worked so far. Goodson, of course, could leave interception to Wehrman, who has the guns to take on the enemy. But the sight of two fighters is more impressive than one. The two Thunderbolts turn into the 190—having pulled slightly ahead by now with greater speed—and point their noses, and wing guns, at the bandit. The German pilot sights the approaching escorts. He violently turns away to the south.

Goodson watches his foe hightail it home. For the third time he has saved Blakeslee from attack.

The coast of France steadily recedes. The three U.S. fighters, two milling above the other, continue the northerly course toward England. Goodson worries about finding a place to land, quickly. There's an emergency strip a few miles inland from the English coast . . . Manston. Blakeslee, obviously thinking along the same line, is heading straight for it.

The three fighters push on. In response to Goodson's call, Blakeslee replies he's okay, engine rough but running. He'll land the first chance he gets. Goodson and Wehrman look him over. They can't tell how much oil Blakeslee has lost, or how much longer he can fly. But his aircraft is covered. If he can last ten or fifteen minutes, the coast of England will be in sight. Meanwhile, they all sweat out their fuel supply.

Minutes pass slowly. Goodson feels tension loosening up. Now closer to England than France, he no longer worries about 190's. He's thankful a gaggle didn't descend on his two-plane escort.

Faintly, ahead . . . a thin coastline appears . . . England. For the first time, Goodson is sure Blakeslee will make it. The job is almost done. The three Thunderbolts fly on . . . the engines sound better now . . . stronger . . . they always do when land is sighted after crossing a long stretch of water.

Goodson scans the coastline, to make out a check point. Where is Manston? Where is the nearest field? He notices Blakeslee is beginning to let down slightly. He eases back on the throttle. He looks down at the fuel gauges . . . only a few gallons left. He must land at Manston with Blakeslee. He will fly on to Debden after refueling. Over Debden he'll have enough fuel to give them a victory salute. Two sure kills and one damaged!

The coast ahead grows higher and higher . . . nearer and nearer. Manston should be off to the right after cross-in if navigation has been accurate. The sight of England is cheering; the strange exhilaration of returning from aerial combat and possible death is something only airmen know. The green of the coast passes beneath. The three fighters are flying northward over Kent—the Strait of Dover off to the right. All three pilots keep eyes peeled for the emergency landing strip.

Ahead, and right, a huge emergency strip comes into view. Manston! The long runway is unmistakable. Many a crippled bomber and fighter has put down at this strip, located about as close to the coast of France as possible. And many a dead or dying bomber crewman has been removed from his riddled aircraft at this emergency field. Today Manston is green with summer growth, its long dark runway contrasting with the beauty of nature's summer.

Blakeslee leans into a slight turn and makes for the approach-end of the long strip ahead. He will land first, then Goodson and Wehrman. The altimeter needle spirals downward. Three thousand feet, 2,500, 2,000, 1,500 . . . Blakeslee has already called tower . . . his wing goes up in the approach turn . . . altimeter 1,000, 900, 800, 700, 600. He is on the approach. The green, oil-spattered fighter sits down nicely as Goodson and Wehrman look down from above.

Blakeslee rolls steadily along the runway . . . slowing. Then, halfway down the long strip, he turns off. Goodson, relieved, slices through the sky in a moderate turn to come over the runway. He peels off left in a climbing turn, throttle cut to lose speed. As airspeed moves below 200 he lowers gear; the thump tells him it is down. Goodson completes the circle and loses altitude rapidly, inclines downward toward the end of the runway.

He crosses the edge of the field at 130 m.p.h. and settles it in a few hundred feet from the end. His tires screech as they touch the hard surface, then tail wheel plops down. He lets the Thunderbolt lose its momentum and turns off. Behind him Wehrman is coming in over the end of the runway.

Suddenly Goodson is tired. The excitement and nervous tension loosen their grip. He pulls back the canopy and the fresh air mixes with the smell of gas. Helmet, goggles and mask come off. His sharp features, dark hair and dark eyes feel sunlight again. As he approaches Blakeslee's plane he can see where enemy cannon fire ripped holes through the engine—how close he came to losing a group leader. But Blakeslee is unhurt. Wehrman lands safely, which completes the short, fierce mission.

Blakeslee has praise for his "top cover." Few fighter pilots could have handled three bandits as quickly as Goodson had done. And Goodson was competing with the best. It has been a terrific day for Wehrman, new at the game; Goodson has high praise for his ability. A good wing man doesn't score the kills, is often picked off from the rear. But many an ace has been "made" by a conscientious wing man covering his tail at the right time and all the time. Goodson had never been alone in the battle over west of Abbeville. Congratulations in order all around!

As the three weary pilots talked, and morning waned that August day, neither Goodson nor Blakeslee had an inkling what the future held. The day's mission fully absorbed their thoughts. And for his great flying performance, and the destruction of two German fighters, damage to a third, Goodson was awarded the Distinguished Service Cross.

Ahead lay many missions for both pilots. Eleven months later, on a mission deep into Germany, Goodson was to be shot down by the enemy after hiking his score to twenty-eight, fifteen in the air and thirteen on the ground. Near Neubrandenburg, he was to end his flying in World War II, captured by the Germans. He was sent to a prisoner-of-war camp at Sagan (now Zagan). By this time Goodson was one of the most famous fighter pilots in the Eighth Air Force, and the Luftwaffe knew much more about him than in August, 1943.

Soon after capture, he was to come near death at the hands of the Germans once more. Taken to a Gestapo intelligence station near Stettin (now Szczecin) he was questioned and placed in solitary. He was called before the commanding officer and told he was to be shot. But Goodson, speaking fluent German, talked the officer out of the execution. Aboard a German train, which was taking him to a POW camp at Sagan, he glimpsed the heavy bombers and fighters of the Eighth Air Force once again.

It was in Berlin. His train had pulled into the station amid the wailing of air-raid sirens. Handcuffed to a German guard, he witnessed a devastating raid. People were caught by the suddenness and ferocity of the bombing. Friedrichstrasse Station was crowded with people trying to find shelter and escape the hail of bombs.

Goodson's guard asked if he would help—if handcuffs were removed —and he pitched in to help trapped civilians and care for the injured. Finally the train pulled out for Sagan. When it reached Frankfurt on the Oder, the Germans told him London no longer existed. They were convinced the city had been wiped out. And at Sagan officers at the prisoner-of-war camp told him they had been awaiting his arrival for a long time. One remarked it was too bad there was a party back at Debden that evening, and that Goodson must miss "Bubbles," the bartender at the pub in Saffron Walden, where 4th pilots hung out. The Germans knew the names of the batmen working in the officers' quarters. It was a strange experience.

Goodson was to remain at the POW camp until early in 1945, when the Russians approached from the east. Then the Americans were moved to Moosburg, near Dachau, to remain until American troops liberated them in April. They were to meet Goodson, who had set out alone with the help of a German friend, walking toward them.

None of this had happened as Goodson, Blakeslee, and Wehrman stood there talking, at Manston, the afternoon of the Paris support mission. But Blakeslee must have known, if the day's action proved anything, that here was one of the great figher pilots of the war. The Luftwaffe was to hear more from him in the future.

The Le Bourget raid was an outstanding Allied victory. Only four bombers were lost. The 4th lost but one pilot and shot down seventeen enemy fighters. Goodson himself dealt the Germans more damage than the Luftwaffe inflicted on the "Blakesleewaffe." It was a far cry from the days when the Luftwaffe ruled the roost over France.

And, for Goodson, the mission of August 16, 1943, was a memorable one. He had taken on the Luftwaffe's best, saved his commanding officer and scored two kills and a damaged—an important leg on his final score of twenty-eight victories. Had he not been shot down over Germany in 1944, his score would undoubtedly have been higher.

5 Lightning Over Huon Gulf

SEPTEMBER 4, 1943:

Captain JAY T. ROBBINS

Air Force Photo

"THREE Mile Drome" was the name unlovingly bequeathed by pilots and crewmen to the Army Air Forces' fighter base three miles east of strategic Port Moresby in New Guinea.

Three Mile Drome in 1943 consisted of a brown tent city, several small gray wooden buildings and a metal "prefab" runway. These modest military accommodations were surrounded by nature's luxury—lush foliage and beautiful and rare flowers, with the shining blue waters of the Coral Sea a backdrop offshore.

Temperatures in this latitude (ten degrees below the equator) were constant. Army-tan khaki was prescribed dress year round. This was the home of the 80th (Headhunter) Fighter Squadron of the 8th Fighter Group of the Fifth Air Force, which claimed the distinction of being the first U.S.A.A.F. squadron to destroy 200 enemy planes. It had been strengthened in the spring by the arrival of P–38 (Lockheed Lightning) replacements for its older single-engine planes, P–40 Warhawks. These new, twin-engined aircraft slightly softened the ordeal American pilots were being subjected to in this theater. Quarters were primitive and food below standard, and malaria was constantly exacting a heavy toll. Sometimes fifty per cent of the available pilots were incapacitated.

Moreover, the Japanese numerical advantage in aerial encounters was preponderant and U.S. fighter pilots seldom flew into battle in anything like even numbers.

But the new planes, the P–38's, and the fact that the Japanese forces had been pushed back from the vicinity of Port Moresby and were now on the defensive, were at least two big improvements since Lieutenant John D. Landers had been shot down over New Guinea nine months before.

Inside one of the four-cot pilots' tents, on the night of September 3, 1943, protected from formidable mosquito forces by mosquito netting, lay lanky, quiet First Lieutenant Jay Robbins.

A few hours earlier a mission had been laid on and Robbins, a native of Coolidge, Texas, was on the orders. At dusk that day, commanding officer Ed Cragg of the 80th had taken a call from Fifth Fighter Command headquarters.

Up on the northern coast of New Guinea, an American ground force was landing at Lae and Salamaua. The 80th's Lightnings could carry enough fuel to reach the area, patrol for an hour or two and return home. Next morning they had been ordered to do just that, so that U.S. ground forces would have fighter cover in case Japanese planes attempted to interfere with the joint operation.

Cragg had sent out messengers to round up his physically able pilots. They straggled in for a late briefing well after dark, Robbins among them. The tropical night outside was still, crickets chirped and southern stars shone down on the surf-edged fighter base. A small light in the 80th's briefing room cast its beams into New Guinea's darkness.

Cragg outlined a simple mission. The squadron had been on many similar ones recently; therefore, nothing unusual might occur. The 80th was to take off at first light, stage into Dobodura, near Buna, from which they would later take off and arrive at the assigned area over U.S. forces. From then until the end of the mission, the task of the Lightning squadron was to see that no enemy planes molested U.S. troops or ships below.

Everyone knew the Japanese Air Force had strong fighter forces at Rabaul—which could be brought to bear if the Japanese discovered the covering Americans in time.

But several uneventful missions had been flown by the 80th in recent days and an unjustified attitude of security had developed among the pilots. At the evening briefing course was set, take-off time agreed upon, and other preparations completed. The conduct of pilots reflected a belief that a routine mission was at hand, nothing more.

Japanese fighter squadrons at Rabaul were approximately three hundred miles from the scene of the ground operations, farther than the 80th Squadron at Port Moresby. Therefore, if the Japs didn't detect the coming of the Lightnings until they were patroling their assigned area, above the surface forces, the Lightnings would probably be forced to return to base before Japanese interceptors could reach the landing area. In these days, U.S. fighters usually had only an hour or two of flying time over assigned operational areas.

The last soft breezes of South Pacific night thinned into stillness preceding a September dawn. Pilots of the 80th Squadron not bedridden with malaria were getting last winks. It was 4:15 A.M. September 4.

A non-com pulled aside the mosquito net surrounding Robbins' cot. In his hand he held a paper on which was typed a list of pilots to be waked up. It was utterly dark, and Robbins didn't notice the intruder who had entered his sleeping sanctum. The non-com bent over and gave him a good shake.

"It's a clear day, sir," he said. With a start, Robbins sat up. Thoughts came to him now. It was the morning of a mission, a dawn take-off. In his tent Robbins pulled on his hearvy Army Air Force pants, slipped into a light khaki "issue" shirt. The heavy pants were a precaution, as were heavy shoes, to enable a pilot who came down in the jungle to walk out, if he had to, as had John Landers nine months earlier.

As Robbins buttoned his shirt he looked at his watch. It was 4:25 A.M. He stepped out of the tent and headed for the prefab mess hall, a drab olive-green building with a tin roof three hundred yards away in the darkness. Racing through his mind, in the excitement of pre-mission minutes, were thoughts of recent encounters with Japanese fighters.

For example, in an engagement southwest of Bogadjum, in July, he had run into a superior enemy force of Zekes while escorting bombers. In the ensuing dogfights, all over the sky, he had knocked down three enemy fighters—a feat not unnoticed in the command.

Only once before had he encountered enemy fighters. On that occasion he and another U.S. pilot managed to destroy a Zeke. They flipped a coin, after returning to base, to see who would get credit for the kill. Robbins lost. His record as of September 4 was thus three victories—all attained on one mission.

These memories skittered through his mind as he sat down for breakfast, a ritual every fighter pilot preparing to fly knew might be his last. The quality of the breakfast was depressing. Powdered eggs (again), toast with weevils, which the pilots picked out as they held their bread up to the light, coffee.

There were also salt pork, Australian jam, canned butter, and New Guinea water reeking with chlorine. Fifteen minutes passed as pilots of the 80th sat under the glary lights of mess hall tables. Conversation was at a minimum, quiet or spirited, depending on the reaction of the individual talking. The inevitable buildup of tension before a mission was in progress.

At 4:45 A.M., the sun still holding off an appearance in the eastern sky, Robbins and several other pilots left the mess hall and jumped into a battered weapons carrier. Others followed in a jeep. Only sixteen fighters were taking off.

Dawn was minutes away when the two vehicles unloaded pilots at the operations shack, on the strip, a mile from the safety of the mess hall, where non-flying personnel were now readying breakfast for those who always remained at the base, the permanent ground force complement. Theirs was a different war, more than one pilot thought to himself.

Before every mission pilots had to check in at the shack out at the strip, and then the parachute tent. The weather was reported good. The mission was to take off at dawn, fly northwestward, cross the Owen Stanley Mountains and land at the advanced strip at Dobodura. From there the pilots would take off and locate the amphibious operation and provide two hours' cover. The distance to the operations area was over a hundred miles.

After last-minute conversations in a faded white wooden building which had been confiscated at Port Moresby by a few over-enthusiastic G.I.'s, the pilots departed to pick up chutes and helmets at the parachute tent. Take-off was now minutes away, and a serious mood settled over pilots as they reached the chute tent, the last stop. Parachutes and helmets were carefully fitted and tested.

Each pilot, now heavily burdened, walked out to the dispersal area where his Lightning was parked. In the case of flight (four aircraft) and element (two aircraft) leaders, they flew permanently assigned aircraft. Others took what they were ordered to fly.

The pilot-to-crew-chief relationship of veteran pilots was naturally intimate. Robbins was flight leader of the third flight, leading four of the sixteen taking off, getting off ninth. As he reached his Lightning, crewmen greeted him with the traditional smile, not without admiration. There is never a lack of respect for fighter pilots in war. The often older, more experienced ground crew members know who is putting it on the line.

At a fighter base, one man flies the aircraft around which everything else is built. A fighter pilot can't blame sins of omission or commission in the handling of his plane while airborne on the navigator, bombardier or co-pilot. There are none.

Of all tasks assigned one man in World War II, none compared to the job of handling a fighter, in terms of co-ordination, mental alertness, split-second timing, mastery of technical detail, skill, courage, and judgment.

Robbins climbed into the cockpit, in the fuselage, between two Allison engines, each capable of over 1,100 horsepower. The chief helped strap him in, checked over instruments, controls, gauges, and switches, and a myriad of circuit breakers, indicators, dials, levers, handles, etc. It was still cool, and with the canopy back, and preparations complete, Robbins checked the time. It was 5:10 A.M.—time to start engines.

In seconds the port engine of the green-gray Lightning belched smoke. On its nose, in brightly-painted letters, was the name *Jandina*.

Robbins had named his fighter for the girl he was later to marry— an American nurse, then stationed in Australia. Taking the J from his name, and her name, Ina, and combining them with "and" in between, he came up with *Jandina*.

Robbins had met her while in Australia for a physical check-up some months earlier. He never lost sight of her afterward, used every leave to fly back to Melbourne, and finally capped the story by marrying her during the height of the war.

Ina was now asleep, however, as the sixteen Lightnings, their thirty-two three-bladed props spinning briskly, waited to taxi out to the end of the runway for take-off. The first white glimmers of daylight were visible, far ahead of sunrise, in the eastern sky.

The metal strip used for take-off ran east-west, and take-off was into the east.

The C.O. signaled his wing man, who in turn passed the sign on, and soon all the 38's were moving out toward the western end of the runway. Robbins rolled forward, following the number four man in the second flight.

The F–38, a P–38 Lightning fighter transformed into a fighter-bomber. (Air Force Photo)

The C.O., at the end of the runway, pointed his Lightning toward the eastern sky. An elderly sergeant, stationed at the starting end of the prefab, waved a reminder to him to get his flaps down. The runway was short, aircraft fully loaded.

Final engine check. First one engine, then the other was revved up, cleaned out. Instruments were checked for heat, pressure, and fuel. Then, still holding the 38 with brakes, he pushed throttles forward. Manifold pressure picked up quickly. Revolutions climbed.

As the big fighter shuddered from the pull of the roaring engines, Cragg released toe brakes and his lead plane rolled. It was 5:15. This process was repeated by each of the twin-engined fighters.

The ninth Lightning off was *Jandina.* Robbins could see the 80th's lead aircraft circling to his right. The eighth to take off was just off the ground, beginning a slow right turn, when he released brakes, jammed throttles forward to the stop.

The tenth, eleventh, and twelfth followed Robbins, after which came the last flight of four. Each pilot cut inside the one ahead, and the big wide right turn enabled the group to close up. The later a pilot took off the tighter his turn, and the shorter his distance. Finally, the sixteen planes were joined up. Major Cragg set course for the pass over the mountains as soon as the squadron was together, cruising speed set, wheels up, and in climbing formation. The Lightnings were pulling 33 inches of mercury with propellers turning 1,850 r.p.m.'s. They were making climbing speed of 160 m.p.h.

The pass ahead—only minutes distant—could be cleared at 10,000 feet but that was too close for comfort. An altitude of between 12,000 and 15,000 feet was the usual crossing altitude.

A tropical sunrise was now beginning to light up New Guinea, and the light revealed a September sky of broken cumulus clouds hanging over the mountains ahead.

Weather in this latitude was all important, though usually good. The pass over the Owen Stanley Mountains, however, was frequently socked in with solid cumulus, making it hazardous for fighters. Eager eyes, seeing more with each new ray of light, noted with relief that clouds were scattered to broken, with plenty of sky, now beginning to turn blue, between them.

Robbins' altimeter read 10,000 feet as the pass over New Guinea's backbone appeared straight ahead. Oxygen masks, so hot and sweaty at low altitudes in the humid New Guinea climate, became more comfortable, and at this altitude, 10,000 feet, full oxygen automatically came in through the oxygen mask.

The wheeze of breath became peculiarly noticeable through earphones amid a monotone developed by the continuous roar from the engines. It was like that experienced in an operating room, where the patient wheezes into a diaphragm. The somber sound was picked up by the throat mike in the oxygen mask.

In minutes the sixteen Lightnings were over the pass, heading for Dobodura. Soon they had descended to a lower altitude and had the advanced fighter strip in view. Cragg led the P–38's down, and they landed one by one. It was still very early in the morning.

Pilots climbed out of their aircraft and gathered in a small shack out on the field. Cragg would get final mission instructions from Fifth Fighter Command over the telephone in the shack.

Time dragged as the hours passed. The mission destined to make Robbins an ace would get off late. Finally, just after eleven o'clock, with last-minute instructions, final briefing was held and pilots started out to their aircraft.

In a few minutes the sixteen silver Lightnings were again taking off. As soon as they had gathered together, Major Cragg set course for the Salamaua and Lae area, where Allied ships were now discharging men and supplies in support of a major amphibious operation.

The sixteen fighters climbed steadily into the northwest. Altitude reached 8,000 feet. The waters of Huon Gulf were now in view to the right—Salamaua ahead. It was only minutes until dark outlines dotted the ocean ahead—the concentration of Allied ships.

It was a clear, bright day, and the waters of Huon Gulf, below, were blue green. Though it was September, in this latitude it was the eve of spring.

The sixteen Lightnings flashed in over the landing area near Salamaua shortly after noon, having leveled off in four flights at various altitudes. Each pilot had at his command two twenty-millimeter and four fifty-calibre guns, all located in the nose. These carried over fourteen hundred shells, which could be emptied in a few seconds.

The four flights had dropped back into a staggered formation as they approached the assigned area. They flew between 8,000 and 21,000 feet, separated by about 3,000 feet.

Coolant shutters closed, engines trimmed, 225 m.p.h. was registering on air-speed indicators as the Lightnings cruised above ships and men below. The fighters quickly flew to Lae, turned back and repeated their patrol run. For over an hour they whisked back and forth over the landing area, without incident. It was another routine mission.

The waters of Huon Gulf below shimmered in the sunlight, and the electric clock on instrument panel read 1:45 P.M. A pilot in the second (middle) flight blurted: "Bandits—ten o'clock high!"

The word "bandits" sent an electric wave up and down the spine of every pilot. This was it; this was what the years of training are all about. Robbins' flight of four was in the best position to greet the Japs first.

The American fighters were snaking slightly to the right when the

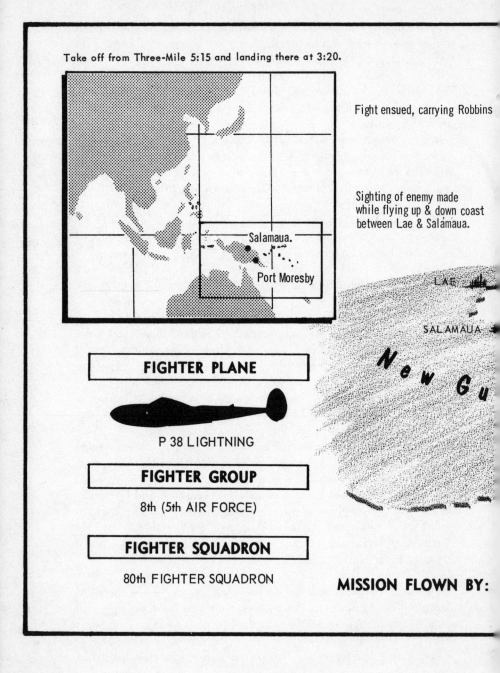

Take off from Three-Mile 5:15 and landing there at 3:20.

Fight ensued, carrying Robbins

Sighting of enemy made while flying up & down coast between Lae & Salamaua.

Salamaua.

Port Moresby

LAE

SALAMAUA

New Gu

FIGHTER PLANE

P 38 LIGHTNING

FIGHTER GROUP

8th (5th AIR FORCE)

FIGHTER SQUADRON

80th FIGHTER SQUADRON

MISSION FLOWN BY:

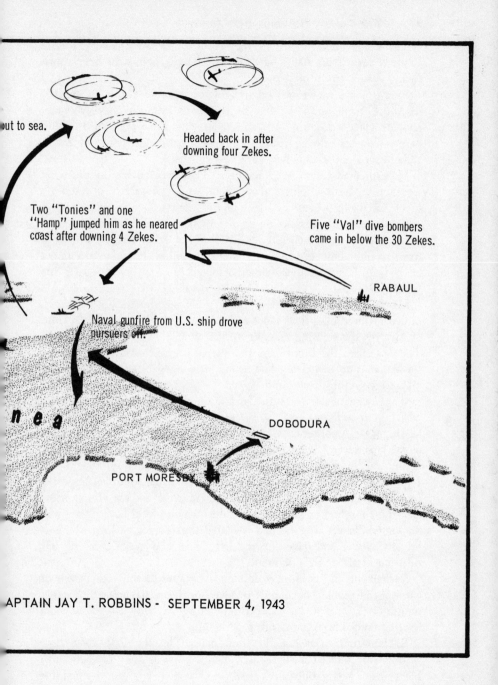

out to sea.

Headed back in after
downing four Zekes.

Two "Tonies" and one
"Hamp" jumped him as he neared
coast after downing 4 Zekes.

Five "Val" dive bombers
came in below the 30 Zekes.

RABAUL

Naval gunfire from U.S. ship drove
pursuers off.

n e a

DOBODURA

PORT MORESBY

CAPTAIN JAY T. ROBBINS - SEPTEMBER 4, 1943

enemy was sighted, and since they were at ten o'clock (left, ahead) Robbins turned his flight into the oncoming gaggle—which now was clearly Zekes—thirty of them!

By a quick turn, he headed straight for the enemy and became the leading U.S. flight in the race to intercept the Japs. At this moment another voice called in over the radio—that of a pilot in Robbins' flight—"Bandits below!" More bandits were below the gaggle of Zekes. Robbins now saw them—five Val dive bombers!

He estimated them at 12,000 feet. They were flying in the same direction as the Jap fighters above them, who obviously constituted top cover and were over 20,000 feet high.

But by now he was closing on the higher Zekes. He would violate every rule of aerial tactics if he dived on the easier targets, which, in turn, would allow the enemy fighters to follow him down and get on his tail. Much as these targets tempted him, he had to go for the Jap fighters first.

He gunned the engines, dropped wing tanks with a flick of his finger, pulled his nose up a little more and switched on his gunsight. In front of his eyes the sighting glass lit up, an orange ring with a dot inside. The Zekes saw the Lightnings and altered course to converge. Robbins turned on gun switches. The Zekes, still above the four oncoming 38's, were getting bigger and bigger.

It was a matter of seconds. On and on the Zekes came. They were weaving in and out, boiling around in general—all headed for the leading four Americans. As the Lightnings pulled up almost in front of the Japs, several of the enemy began to turn out in various directions.

One of the Zekes—now spreading out and almost on top of the Lightnings (which hadn't been able to gain equal altitude) appeared far out to the left, above. As the fighters came abreast, the stranger passed behind him and started a left turn which would have placed him on *Jandina's* tail, after he had executed the 180-degree turn. Robbins hit left rudder and gave *Jandina* left wheel and got a climbing left turn out of the roaring fighter.

Excitement and confusion developed because of the great speed of closure, the number of aircraft involved in the melee and the head-on nature of the initial clash, and threw all fighters into a wild scramble for that crucial advantage—firing position.

Robbins—not to be caught from behind by the lone Zeke now turning into him from above, left, held *Jandina* in the tight left turn, his course exactly opposite the Zeke. His two engines strained for every ounce of power—and he was now almost level with the enemy fighter.

He turned left again, seeking to get behind the Zeke. The Jap pilot also turned, but Robbins was gaining in the turn, pulling in behind him. At that moment he caught sight of several Zekes on his tail—far behind. Rubbernecking fast, he decided to go after the first Zeke, in an effort to knock him down before the enemy planes behind could close.

Now the lone Zeke nosed down, in an effort to outdive Robbins. *Jandina's* nose went down for the first time since the enemy had been sighted, began to pick up speed. By now Robbins had almost pulled in directly behind the enemy plane. The Japanese pilot had committed a fatal mistake when he failed to use his great turning capability and chose a dive.

The Lightning—which the Jap evidently wasn't familiar with—had a good initial diving speed, with two engines and great weight. This enabled Robbins to close the gap faster than the enemy had anticipated. *Jandina* was closing the Zeke at sensational speed.

The famous Japanese Zero. This one, captured at Buna, New Guinea, bears U.S.A.A.F. markings. (Air Force Photo)

Robbins twitched with excitement. He moved a finger to the wheel button and looked through the orange-yellow ring in his sight. The Zeke was filling it up. The enemy had only a second or two to turn, and realized his dilemma too late.

Fire! Two twenties and four fifties roared, drowning out the wide-open roar of two Allisons. Hits registered on the surprised Jap almost at once. It had to be fast; the enemy was also behind *Jandina*. At the root of the Jap's right wing, shells tore big holes. A light flame, and smoke, trailed out behind!

Robbins kept his gun button depressed. The smoke and flame increased. The diving Jap was mortally wounded. *Jandina's* shells were tearing chunks out of the Zeke, heavy black smoke billowed back, and then—the whole right wing tore off the trapped enemy plane and hurtled back through the air, off to Robbins' right.

He stopped firing, watched the wing go by. The rest of the burning enemy plane flipped over and started a vertical dive. No chute. Victory number one!

A second of relief, or satisfaction, flashed past. Then, his mind back on the churning battle, Robbins jerked wheel right to get out of the way of his pursuers behind. He pulled up out of his dive, still turning right, began to climb. They were no longer behind him. At that moment he spotted a cornered Lightning pilot. Several Japs had him boxed in; they were firing away and had a good chance to shoot him down.

The pilot in distress was at three o'clock, a little high. Robbins started the necessary right turn and continued to climb, heading straight for the dogfight. By now other Zekes were moving in for the kill and there were fifteen or twenty around the trapped American. *Jandina* aimed her nose for the pack.

The sight of the oncoming P–38 distracted some of the enemy. Several broke away and turned into Robbins, head on. He saw them clearly and put his finger back on the gun button—the distance closed. *Jandina*, wide open, was registering 300 m.p.h.

Robbins saw smoke and flashes from the nearest oncoming Zeke's wing guns. The enemy pilot had opened fire, but the range was too great. No thuds. He held his fire a few seconds, which seemed days, the enemy meanwhile firing away, closing. Finally, the Zeke flashing into range, Robbins pressed the button.

The Jap now turned slightly left and Robbins had to angle right to keep him in the gunsight ring. The two fighters flashed past each other. Robbins used only a short burst. No hits. Once before he had fired away most of his ammunition, on long, out-of-range targets. He had missed opportunities later in the day, when out of ammo.

He would not make the same mistake today. He had withheld his fire, spending only a short burst when the two planes, closing at a combined speed of about 600 m.p.h., were in range. He missed. But there were plenty of targets.

Another of the gaggle that had Robbins' comrade surrounded was now headed for *Jandina*. He was almost in range before Robbins saw him, and frantically maneuvered the Lightning into a firing position. He could see the twinkles of the enemy's guns. This time, though, the enemy didn't miss.

Jandina was being hit before Robbins could open fire. Robbins hit the firing button and both planes spouted flame and shell as they sped together. Now the Zeke began to take hits. Robbins winced as he heard the thump . . . thump . . . thump on *Jandina's* hull.

Jandina, however, could take more than the lighter Zeke. The twenty millimeters and fifties took a deadly toll. The Zeke suddenly pulled up. Robbins saw shells tear through the enemy's belly and into the wing. The enemy fighter was dragging a trail of heavy black smoke. He had absorbed a fatal dose. Robbins stopped firing; the stricken enemy had lost all fight. He went into a spin, falling fast. No chute. Victory number two!

The third encounter and second kill had consumed only a short burst. *Jandina* still had ammo left; Robbins didn't know how much. He looked down on the spiraling, yellow-burning, victim, headed for the blue water below. His engines were running smoothly; evidently hits he had taken were not serious.

The second victim burned fiercely, plunged down vertically. Robbins watched a second too long. A sudden cluster of holes in his right wing! The shock of being caught from behind was accompanied by painful shudders from *Jandina*. It took an instant for the danger to register. *Jandina* was being ripped by the shells of an avenging Zeke who had sneaked in on Robbins' tail.

Robbins lunged the wheel forward. He couldn't outturn the Zeke. Unless he could dive away, he was finished. *Jandina* was already damaged. Moreover, the initiative had now passed to the enemy.

The sudden dive threw Robbins against his seat belt. The Lightning dropped out fast, but the Zeke hung in, firing away. Now *Jandina's* nose pointed straight down. The weight of the Lightning and its initial diving speed came into play. Soon he was up over 400 m.p.h., picking up speed. That was too much for the Zeke—the enemy pilot dropped back out of firing range. Pulling away, still diving, Robbins spotted a Zeke down low . . . about 5,000 feet.

From above 15,000 feet, almost to 5,000, the Lightning had screamed straight down. Every rivet in the big fighter strained. Robbins knew he had to pull her out now, if he was to close on the Zeke below. He pulled back on the throttles. Then he stuck his head down, to hold as much blood in the head as possible, and eased back carefully on the wheel, hoping not to jerk the wings off, and completely black out. It was an awful test for a wing with shell holes through it. There was no certainty the wings could stand the strain.

Gravity drained the blood from the top of Robbins' body and his weight doubled and tripled as it pressed down on the seat. The Lightning was pulling out of the dive. Robbins' eyesight went gray, specks appeared, and his vision blurred—lack of blood! He was fighting to keep from blacking out completely. The gravity pull continued. But *Jandina* slowly and steadily pulled out.

Wings stayed on. Daylight returned in front of his eyes, and Robbins thanked God for the tough construction of the P–38. But now he was low—5,000 feet. The lone Zeke was still some distance away. He could see no other U.S. fighters in the sky.

Though they hadn't been able to stay in range, the enemy fighters above, behind, were following. The exasperating thing was that they were moving up on his sides, many of the Zekes between him and the New Guinea coast, since he had been heading out to sea, and they were behind, left. He would eventually have to turn toward land. He estimated he was now forty or fifty miles offshore. Slowly Robbins eased *Jandina* down, to close the bandit ahead, occasionally looking back to see if the Zekes were getting closer. He gave *Jandina* full power again.

Some of the Japs moved ahead out on each side. And now the lone enemy pilot ahead spotted him, tried to turn in behind the Lightning. Robbins also turned—left. His turn caught the Jap by surprise. He was suddenly aiming at his side, in the position of the stem of the letter T. Without waiting this time to get on his tail, which would have allowed some of the enemy to get behind him, Robbins lined up the gray Zeke in the sight ring for a deflection shot.

He was so close the Jap was at once in range. He pressed the gun button and *Jandina* roared. As the other Japs watched, the suddenly caught Zeke began to disintegrate along the left side from engine to tail. The deflection shot had been perfect. The Zeke went out of control, pieces flew off and light smoke trailed behind, as the victim headed for the waters of Huon Gulf, a few thousand feet below. Then the pilot straightened the Zeke up long enough to jump—went over the side. His parachute opened. Victory number three!

Robbins had no time to watch. Stung by the brazen victory, amidst their overwhelming numbers, the remaining enemy pilots closed in from every direction. Robbins, still at full throttle, turned toward land. Several enemy fighters were in his path—firing and coming in, head on.

The action was fast. Robbins had limited ammunition. He noticed a strange sound at the end of the burst which knocked down his third victim. One (or more) of his guns must be jammed. A Zeke loomed dead ahead, wings twinkling.

Robbins waited until he was in range. He pressed the button. Some of his guns fired, some didn't. *Jandina* shuddered. She was hit again. But the enemy also showed hits. The Zeke whizzed past. Robbins plight was getting desperate; he pressed his mike button and called for help. No answer. No sooner had this one disappeared than another bobbed up straight ahead. Once again Robbins put his finger on the gun button. The Zeke opened up first. Robbins fired only a short burst. This time he didn't feel any more hits.

Robbins dipped his nose, still pointed toward the coastline, down to 3,000 feet. Both throttles were full forward. The engines had done their best, but the strain was beginning to tell. As another Zeke turned in ahead, Robbins heard a dreaded sound. His starboard engine was missing, cutting in and out! Would it konk out?

There was no time to fuss about an engine. The Zeke was lining up for a pass. It was short, the Jap having barely turned in front in time to fire. Robbins gave him a short burst. He may have scored. But *Jandina* took more hits. The Zeke flashed past on the left. Robbins was down low, only a few guns firing—judging from the sound—and one engine missing!

The Jap that flashed by turned and lined up behind, to close in for a kill on *Jandina's* tail. Suddenly another Zeke appeared ahead, coming down on him. It was the fourth head-on pass in his effort to break through to the coast. By all odds, *Jandina* should have been in the water below before now.

Robbins pulled the wheel up slightly and lined up the gray Zeke perfectly. This time crippled *Jandina* was to impress the Japs again. Robbins waited until the enemy was without doubt in range. He pushed the wheel button down as the enemy filled the light ring. His remaining guns opened, and tracers flying at the Jap told him he was down to his last rounds.

But he was scoring heavily, so accurate was his aim. The concentration of hits centered in the belly. The Zeke turned away. Robbins banked after him, and with a deflection shot threw shells into the wing. It separated it from the fuselage! The Zeke plunged down to his right. Pieces were flying back and a brilliant orange fire enveloped the stricken enemy, whose gasoline tanks had ignited.

In seconds the burning wreck, in a death dive, hit the sea underneath. No chute. Victory number four! A cold sweat covered Robbins' forehead. It was hot on the deck. He had been in nine actions facing sudden death, was about out of ammunition, and one engine was missing. By any standard, it was recess time.

Robbins rubbernecked, to see what was behind him. No more Zekes appeared ahead. He had fought his way through the gaggle, fighting four separate engagements and destroying his fourth enemy fighter in the process of breaking through. Now his only chance was to get to shore before an engine quit, or before he was caught from behind. He gradually climbed toward the coast. But controls were damaged and he had to hold full left rudder with his foot continuously to maintain level flight.

To his dismay, he now spotted two Tonies and a Hamp behind him, closing. Where had they come from? He was at 6,000 feet. Suddenly one of them popped up in front of him. Robbins could only bluff. He lined him up for a head-on pass. The enemy's guns sparkled. One of *Jandina's* guns had a few rounds and threw them out. He scored hits! The Jap shot past. Robbins was happy to settle for that.

The others behind, however, were closing in, on the right and left. This was the time for the U.S. Cavalry to ride over the hill with bugle and flag, but no reinforcements appeared. He repeated his calls for help. No answer.

He was down to 1,000 feet when he noticed the enemy out on both sides. They were almost even with wounded *Jandina,* and preparing to make high-speed firing passes.

Robbins was faced with a split-second decision. He could jettison the canopy and jump out—and might be picked up. He could fly straight ahead toward shore—and would almost certainly be shot down. Or he could turn into every attacker, slip and skid his plane, try to throw the enemy's aim off, and simulate a counter-attack. He decided to try the last approach.

The Jap to his left began to peel off, and Robbins wheeled *Jandina* left, turning into the enemy, temporarily, for a head-on pass. The first dodge worked. The Jap fired, missed, and flashed by. The other peeled off, and once again Robbins turned into the enemy. This time the gun flashes in the Jap's wings registered. *Jandina* shuddered. Hit again!

Once more he straightened up, headed for land. A Tony was peeling off for a pass. The enemy now attempted to finish him off quickly. In rapid-fire passes, the Japs jumped him. Turning into each, skidding desperately with his rudder to throw their gunnery off, Robbins took each pass with a head-on approach of his own. Enemy shells ripped through *Jandina*, knocked out his radio immediately behind, and struck the armor plate on the back of his seat.

Robbins considered ditching *Jandina* in the water, getting out while still alive. Miraculously, he was uninjured. At this moment he noticed a number of ships in front, to his right. He turned in their direction, a last effort to survive. The enemy aircraft directly behind were almost within range, and Robbins went all the way down to the water to pick up speed.

He now closed the ships—which he made out as warships—cruisers and destroyers. As he strained to identify them, black puffs suddenly appeared nearby. Robbins thrust the wheel to his left, turning away sharply, displaying the belly silhouette of the P–38. The Japs behind turned also. The warships were opening fire on all the approaching aircraft.

But Robbins had to head for the warships despite the danger. It was a last chance. To Robbins' intense relief, the warships were American, participating in the amphibious operation he had been ordered to protect. Fortunately, ships' spotters identified him as an American fighter, and now his courtesy was to be returned, with compliments from the U.S. Navy.

Spotters aboard the American ships not only recognized the lone American, they realized the single-engined craft behind were Japs. They directed their anti-aircraft fire accordingly at the Japs dogging damaged *Jandina*.

Robbins swept over the warships, looking back. The anti-aircraft barrage proved too much for the enemy. The Japs at last turned back. *Jandina* had almost made it; land was just ahead. Robbins looked back, at a clear tail, with a great sense of relief.

To make it back to the base, he would have to climb to 10,000 feet on one sound engine, and it would have to carry him across New Guinea and over the mountains. He thought about landing on the beach. Once again he was game. He headed for the mountains and the haven of Three Mile Drome, pulling back on the wheel. The altimeter began to climb slowly. The port engine was running smoothly.

When he reached 8,000 feet, Robbins saw the sinister shadows of a group of fighters ahead. He made preparations to bail out. *Jandina* had no fight left. As he watched for oncoming fighters, his heart pounding, he made out the silhouettes. P-47's! Relieved, once again he set course for the familiar pass.

The altimeter slowly inched upward. *Jandina* climbed steadily. Soon the pass was in sight. He would clear the mountains. This was the last big hurdle. He crossed it at 11,000 feet. Robbins pointed his nose downward, aimed for Moresby, minutes away.

At the base, Robbins' crew chief waited and wondered. Ground crewmen knew the 80th had been in a fight. Some had straggled in already. Others had not. No one knew much about Robbins. He had been alone from start to finish in the wild aerial battles that day. Now the sound of his engines became audible to crewmen and fellow pilots at Three Mile.

Robbins had no radio. When he passed over the field, the crash truck and ambulance were summoned. They rushed to the runway. Robbins wondered whether his wheels would come down. He pulled the lever. They lowered slower than usual, but finally locked down. He cut back the throttles, glided in over the end of the prefab runway. The olive-drab crash truck and ambulance started engines. Jeeps with fellow pilots and ground crewmen cranked up and headed out for the runway. *Jandina* was on the approach. Speed 120 m.p.h.

Over the end of the strip, Robbins cut the throttle. *Jandina* hit and bounced. The landing gear held up. She rolled normally. He hit brakes. The big, crippled fighter slowed, and turned off the strip. Finally she was at a standstill. Robbins jerked back the canopy. He climbed out. It was 3:20 P.M.

He flopped on the ground nearby, as jeeps, trucks, and men on foot raced to the dear piece of ground he now guarded—crumpled, exhausted, at last defeated—but not by the Japs. Robbins was sitting, leaning over his knees, pale, shaky, and physically weak—his left leg, which he had kept jammed on left rudder to trim the damaged ship, almost numb. Ground personnel had comforting words. They tried to make him feel good.

One of them, looking at battered *Jandina*, offered a compliment:

"It must have been rough," he said. It had been quite rough, Robbins answered, which was the understatement of his career.

After being interrogated by Intelligence, still hot, tired, and shaky, Robbins had a request to make of Major Cragg—also safely back from the mission. He wanted ten days' leave. He would like to get away from it all—and see Ina. Robbins had earned it. Cragg granted it.

The repair crews went to work on *Jandina*. Two days later Robbins boarded a C–47 and headed for Australia. For ten days no one could put him on a mission. No one would wake him up before daylight, with a list of flying personnel in his hand. And he wouldn't be picking weevils out of bread, nor worrying about being shot at by enemy pilots fifty miles out over the water, alone.

In addition to Robbins' four kills, the 80th Squadron on September 4 destroyed seven other enemy aircraft. Major Cragg shot down two, as did Lieutenant D. C. Hanover, Jr. Captain J. R. Wilson, Lieutenant M. T. Kasper, and Lieutenant C. F. Homer were credited with single victories.

It was a major victory for Fifth Fighter Command and 80th (Headhunter) Squadron, eleven kills and no losses! Other U.S. fighter squadrons ran the score higher.

For Robbins—one of the great fighter pilots of the war—it was the war's most memorable mission, though the much-decorated Coolidge, Texas, ace wound up fourth highest of all U.S. fighter pilots in the Pacific, with twenty-two confirmed victories.

His awards included the Distinguished Service Cross, with Oak Leaf Cluster; the Silver Star, with Oak Leaf Cluster; the Distinguished Flying Cross, with three Oak Leaf Clusters; the Air Medal with six Oak Leaf Clusters, and many others.

6 *Cat and Mouse Near Emden*

DECEMBER 11, 1943:

Major FRANCIS S. GABRESKI

WHILE the aerial war in the Southwestern Pacific was taking a definite turn for the better during the latter half of 1943, important events were taking place over Europe.

The spectacular war between the Luftwaffe and British and American air forces took a dramatic turn when United States heavy bombers made their first daylight raid on the enemy homeland, January 27, 1943.

Although the A.A.F. had been bombing targets on the continent since July of 1942, and although the bombing of Wilhelmshaven (January 27, 1943) was not one of the great aerial attacks of the war, the mission was significant because it was the opening of the daylight bomber offensive against Germany itself.

Since 1942, the Eighth U.S. Air Force had been challenging the accepted theory in the R.A.F. and Luftwaffe, that defending fighters inevitably win a contest with bombers attacking in daylight. The Germans had learned a bitter lesson in 1940 when they attempted to smother England with daylight bomber attacks. Losses became so heavy the offensive was called off.

The British themselves had come to the same conclusion and were bombing Germany at night, and from the beginning urged the Americans to do likewise.

In anticipation of the inevitable American daylight attacks, Reichsmarschall Goering stationed two newly formed fighter wings in the two major approaches to Germany, Holland, and the German Bight. He was confident American daylight attacks would not succeed. The Americans faced the problem of providing adequate long-range fighter escort, and until the A.A.F. could protect its bombers all the way to and from German targets, the daylight bomber assault would experience its ups and downs.

Luftwaffe General Adolf Galland, chief of German fighter forces, rightly diagnosed the advent of daylight raids as a matter of utmost importance. Disagreeing with Goering's theory that German fighters could easily defeat the big U.S. bombers in daylight, he foresaw the larger and devastating raids which were to come later in the war. But Galland was in a minority. The American daylight offensive theory enjoyed support only from U.S. commanders and a few far-seeing allied and enemy airmen, who realized B–17 Flying Fortresses and B–24 Liberators, properly escorted, constituted a formidable force with tremendous fire-power—much more than the lighter, lesser-armed German bombers carried in the attack on England three years earlier.

Maximum success of the daylight bomber assault was not achieved, it is true, until American fighters could fly all the way to and from targets with the big friends, a condition which, of course, did not prevail in 1943. Even heavily armed Forts and Liberators, without strong escort, sometimes sustained shattering losses that year, in the period when U.S. theory was being proved the hard way.

At the time of the first U.S. daylight raid on Germany, January, 1943, the Allied strategic bombing offensive had been in progress only a relatively short time. While the R.A.F. had been bombing the enemy since 1939, the Germans regarded their night attack on the Renault works in Paris, on March 3, 1942, as the first attack strong enough to be classified as strategic bombing.

In the first phase of American daylight participation, A.A.F. forces were necessarily limited, results often meager. In these days U.S. bombers were often protected by Spitfires or Thunderbolts (P–47's) up to the borders of Germany, and by P–38 Lightnings over Germany, or part of the time over Germany. On the longer missions there was sometimes no fighter support at the point of deepest penetration, the

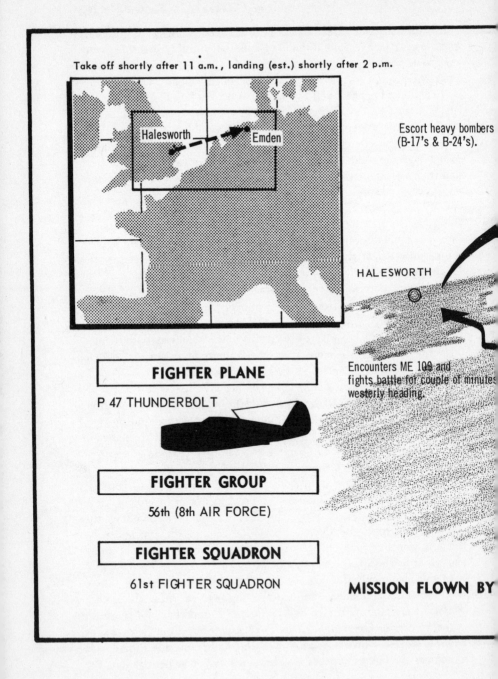

Take off shortly after 11 a.m., landing (est.) shortly after 2 p.m.

Halesworth — Emden

Escort heavy bombers (B-17's & B-24's).

HALESWORTH

Encounters ME 109 and fights battle for couple of minutes westerly heading.

FIGHTER PLANE

P 47 THUNDERBOLT

FIGHTER GROUP

56th (8th AIR FORCE)

FIGHTER SQUADRON

61st FIGHTER SQUADRON

MISSION FLOWN BY

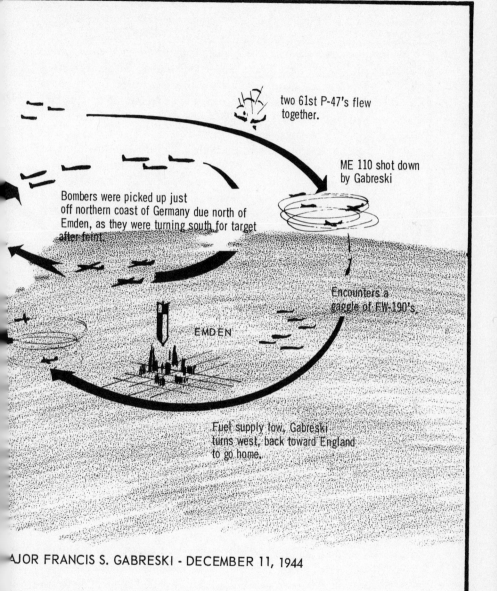

two 61st P-47's flew
together.

ME 110 shot down
by Gabreski

Bombers were picked up just
off northern coast of Germany due north of
Emden, as they were turning south for target
after feint.

Encounters a
gaggle of FW-190's

EMDEN

Fuel supply low, Gabreski
turns west, back toward England
to go home.

AJOR FRANCIS S. GABRESKI - DECEMBER 11, 1944

target vicinity itself. When Luftwaffe fighters caught the bombers without escort, maximum defensive results were most often achieved by ME–109's, FW–190's, and destroyer units armed with rockets.

On some occasions when this occurred, results seemed to vindicate Goering's judgment. And since, as General Omar Bradley notes in *A Soldier's Story*, the Germans finally waked up to the fact that the crucial task facing them, as of 1943, was the expansion of their fighter force, the prospect of reducing bomber losses was directly related to the strength and effectiveness of long-range U.S. fighter forces available to counter the attacks of increasing numbers of Luftwaffe interceptors.

In 1943 P–51 Mustangs were not yet operating from England, except for the first group to go into action, which went operational in the last month of the year. This long-range U.S. fighter was provided in numbers only in 1944 and 1945. In the interval, the Lightnings and Thunderbolts carried on, and the bombers were sometimes left for short periods (which seemed long enough to bomber crewmen) without fighter protection.

After the Wilhelmshaven attack, U.S. bombers steadily increased the strength and range of their operations. One of the bitterest battles fought by U.S. fighters and bombers of the Eighth Air Force that year, in which the bombers were threatened with heavy losses by German fighters, occurred December 11, on a mission to Emden. Flying escort on this mission was, among other groups, the famous 56th Fighter Group. The 56th, stationed at Halesworth, England, was to emerge from the war with more aerial victories than any other U.S. Fighter Group.

Leading a squadron of the 56th that day was Francis S. Gabreski, a blue-eyed, strong-jawed major from Oil City, Pennsylvania—the top surviving U.S. aerial combat ace of World War II. Gabreski finished the war credited with the destruction of 33½ enemy aircraft—31 in the air! It is the Emden attack of December 11, 1943, in which Gabreski participated, with which we are now concerned.

Aeolus had arranged a near-perfect, clear winter sky over the Continent as Gabreski pointed the red cowlings of sixteen Thunderbolts toward the eastern horizon that December morning. Pilots were, however, unaware of this good weather as they departed their Halesworth base, in East Anglia, England, shortly after 11 A.M. A layer of dark stratus hung over 'the English countryside at 5,000 feet as the 61st

Squadron (Gabreski's) of the 56th began a slow climb toward its bottom.

The weather officer had forecast clouds all the way to the target, though the day's action would be fought in generally clear skies near Emden. This Gabreski couldn't know as he searched the horizon of a cold, gray North Sea ahead, which joined the bottom of the cloud layer that seemed to stretch into infinity. To his comrades he was "Keyworth Blue Leader," the code word for the leader of the 61st Squadron.

The sixteen P–47's, heading east at a climbing speed of 150 m.p.h., reached the bottom of the clouds and gathered together in tight formation. Holding close, each pilot's eyes fixed on the plane ahead and not the instrument panel, the 61st cut into the soup and began the ordeal of climbing through the clouds.

The North Sea was visible minutes after take-off from Halesworth, as it was from most of the bases in the great East Anglia complex, from which the Eighth Air Force maintained its offensive against Germany. The 61st had taken off, joined up, and climbed into the murk at 5,000 feet, directly over the water, in a matter of minutes. For more than a hundred miles the Army Air Force fighters would be over forty-degree water, in which survival—if they were downed—would depend on a speedy rescue, within the hour.

Gabreski's altimeter registered a steady ascent, 6,000, 6,500, 7,000 feet . . . but gray murk still surrounded the sixteen fighters. Up above, ahead, the bombers plodded slowly on, also on an easterly heading. Field Order 198, outlining the mission, had ordered bombers and fighters to feint, flying east until northeast of Emden, then suddenly turning southwest and making straight for the target.

Only two hundred U.S. fighters, a modest force compared to fighter strength which would be used six or eight months later by the same Eighth Air Force, comprised the escort for the mission. Since Emden was not a distant target, fighters were to be with the bombers all the way.

Gabreski glanced at his altimeter . . . 8,000, 8,500, 9,000, 9,500 feet. Still in the stuff. Several of the sixteen Thunderbolts had slipped off into the gray unknown, unable to hold close enough to fly off their leader's wing. They had a compass heading to fly in such a situation and now climbed on instruments alone through the cloud layer.

Ten thousand feet, 10,500 . . . then instants of light. The sun above intermittently pierced the increasingly thin top. Now the altimeter registered 11,000 feet. The glass top of the canopy revealed flashes of hazy blue above. Then, suddenly, Gabreski's nose topped the cloud ceiling and all at once he was racing along over a fleecy cloud blanket, turned pink and orange by the sun. The nearness of the top of the clouds produced a sensation of great speed. Following Gabreski came the rest of the 61st, including those who had become separated, popping out of the clouds all around, quickly closing up. Gabreski ordered spread formation and gun and camera switches turned on, to prevent icing. The P–47's spread out into the combat formation and continued the long climb. They were reaching for 22,000 feet.

At briefing Gabreski had suggested this altitude, so the Thunderbolts would have a height advantage in case of trouble. The 56th wouldn't join the big friends it was to protect until the bombers were ready to turn southwest for Emden. There was ample time to complete the slow climb before picking up the heavies.

Above the clouds the sky was bright blue. Below, breaks in the cloud began to appear. The squadron silently continued its climb into the sun for fifteen minutes. By that time it was approaching the Dutch coast.

The blunt-nosed fighters crossed inland and droned on. Radio was silent, but the sound of German jamming became audible in earphones. Up ahead, the unexpected breaks in the cloud layer became larger and larger, revealing the northern coast of Germany. The North Sea had been crossed, Holland's northern coast skirted; the bombers could be expected to come into view soon. Eyes strained constantly to pick them out ahead. The B–17's and B–24's, however, were not leaving the familiar vapor trails, and would be less easily spotted, as a result.

Gabreski leveled out, increased the speed of his squadron to approximately 250 m.p.h. He had reached 22,000 feet. Pilots were on pure oxygen, temperature was forty degrees below zero, and engines were on superchargers. Down below the earth passed behind faster. It was almost time to rendezvous with the big friends. Alert eyes scanned the blue ahead.

Specks now became dimly visible up ahead—the bombers! The American force was already well inside German skies, and below practically all clouds had disappeared, contrary to the forecast. Any hope that bad weather would keep the enemy's fighters grounded disappeared. The distance behind the bombers rapidly closed. Now they could be distinguished in boxes—twenty to thirty bombers in each box—flying in a straight line. The 56th was almost in position.

The outlines of the bombers grew larger. Gabreski looked the closely packed heavies over. As he did, the lead box of the bomber stream caught his attention.

The near collision of a U.S.A.A.F. bomber's stick of bombs and an FW-190 which has just made a pass at the bomber. (Air Force Photo)

The lead bomber box is turning south, but there is something else—other aircraft in the sky! The specks ahead of the bombers now become larger. Fighters! They're not American. Pointed noses . . . ME-109's . . . attacking! Smaller, painted gray, the German fighters are flashing down head on into the big bombers, who open up with a gallant fire as they defend themselves and hold course, all now headed south.

Gabreski's heart jumps. His heavily gloved left hand rams the throttle forward. The 61st, above the bombers, races down into the battle. Even as he eyes the 109's ahead, he notices a more disturbing sight;

building up behind the bomber stream, some sixty large twin-engine rocket-firing destroyers are slipping in behind the Forts and Liberators, preparing to loose a barrage of rockets from behind. He will jump the twin-engined bandits first.

The rocket firers are at 20,000 feet, ahead and slightly below, right. Gabreski, now making 300 m.p.h., his nose down and turning right, races to break up the enemy formation before it discharges rockets. The red-nosed, black-and-white 47's bank to the right. A sudden yellow flash lights the sky above Gabreski's head.

Flaming pieces of burning aircraft shower through the sky, falling near the fighters! It takes a second to realize what has happened. Then a lump settles in Gabreski's throat. Two of his pilots have flown together in the turn! The crash was so solid, impact so great, both planes exploded. The pilots didn't get out. The 61st is down to fourteen planes.

The flash of that explosion caught the attention of the Germans lining up for an attack. Now they see the fast-moving American fighters sweeping in behind them. Instead of the cat, they become the mouse. Unlike the Forts and Liberators, the twin-engine enemy planes don't hold formation. Gabreski identifies ME–110's, ME–210's and JU–88's in the sixty-plane group. They break in every direction—right, left, up and down. The closing Thunderbolts split into elements or flights, and give chase.

Three ME–110's break down and away; Gabreski spots the twin-ruddered, twin-engine aircraft getting away. He shoves stick forward, roars down on the three fleeing rocket carriers. His speed cuts distance rapidly, and the wingspan of the German planes grows larger and larger in his K–14 sight.

The sky at this moment is a spectacular panorama of single combats merged into one great, confused aerial battle. German fighters spitting fire at the heavy bombers suddenly become aware of the predicament of their slower, rocket-firing comrades. Some disengage themselves from attacks on Forts and Liberators and plunge full-throttle into the fight between American fighters and German destroyers. By this time other U.S. fighters from other groups are hurling themselves into the developing melee at full speed, arriving on the scene from all directions.

The picture includes smoking American bombers, hit by the 109's, German destroyers desperately running from the eight-gunned Thunderbolts, duels between Thunderbolts and German 109's, and vertical columns of smoke above falling victims plunging to earth below. Parachutes begin to dot the sky.

Excitement and action come so fast pilots act from training and instinct alone in the game of survival, the Americans knowing even if they escape death when hit they will become prisoners if they crashland or bail out.

The last moments of a B-24 Liberator during an enemy fighter attack over Germany. (Air Force Photo)

Keyworth Blue Leader concentrates on the three enemy 110's ahead, disregarding the swirling battle around him, tense with the smell of combat and an impending kill. Through the sighting glass Gabreski watches the German planes get bigger and bigger. The Pratt and Whitney giant out front screams furiously, the roar of the wind stream adds to the howl. Gabreski methodically lets the sight ring fill with ME–110 . . . his finger anxiously touching the trigger button on the forward edge of the stick.

Seconds seem minutes as the enemy planes lose the race to get away, and the P–47 comes on, closer and closer. Gabreski has "tail-end Charlie" in his sight, the trailing ME–110 is in range! He pulls the trigger! The Thunderbolt shakes from eight recoils, the blast from four wing guns on each side. He sees tracers streak out at the victim ahead.

Looking through the orange light circle on the sighting glass, Gabreski sees his fire register heavily at the root of the enemy's left wing. Pieces fly back, concentrated fire pours into the enemy. Gabreski holds position and maintains fire. Caught from behind, the Germans are unable to react in time. Gabreski sees no return fire.

The German destroyer in Gabreski's sight is fatally damaged. The left wing is almost cut off. The ME–110 is smoking heavily and ready to take the plunge. Gabreski fires another burst. A wing lifts, exposing a straight white-bordered cross, and the 110 falls off into a death dive, stretching a smoke column earthward. Gabreski looks for the other 110's. He sees two taking heavy fire from his comrades. In seconds, both are trailing black smoke.

The flickers of light from the wings of his fellow pilots spell an end to the interception mission of these three German destroyers. Three fatal smoke streams mark their dives. Gabreski, flushed with triumph, scans the sky. He is separated from his comrades.

Below, he again watches his victim. The ME–110 continues its long plunge. Two chutes pop out behind. Gabreski again searches the sky. His brief chase has taken him from the center of battle. He looks in vain for the pilots of Blue Flight and the 61st Squadron. He has even lost sight of the P–47's which shot down the other two ME–110's. He is suddenly all alone. Pulling up again, he flies in the direction of the bomber stream, south. The Germans have not stopped the heavies . . . they are carrying on, nearing Emden. Gabreski will have a hard time catching up before they reach the target.

Flying south and searching the sky, he finally locates a group of fighters ahead. They are•surprisingly low . . . twelve o'clock. Sticking the blunt nose of his Thunderbolt down, Gabreski rings up greater speed to join. It will be good to have company again. Slowly he closes the gap. As he does, he has time to check fuel gauges. The indicators produce a weak feeling in his stomach. According to the gauges, he should be heading for England now. The full power used in his engagement with the enemy has eaten up his gasoline at an alarming rate. Gabreski worries lest he find himself without enough fuel to make it back across the North Sea. But he will join up with th.~ fighters ahead, at least, even if he has to depart shortly thereafter. The fighters ahead are almost within reach, anyhow.

Slowly he inclines downward toward the blunt-nosed fighters, which are continuing southward, toward Emden. They might not be from the 56th Group, but he will pull alongside nevertheless. A lone fighter is easy prey, especially when low on gas. Gabreski continues to look around, and behind.

He is almost on top of the fighters ahead. Somehow, they look different. He studies their silhouettes. For a moment he is baffled. Then . . . a chill runs down his backbone! He is closing an enemy gaggle!

The fighters ahead are FW–190's, radial-engined German fighters. Sweating, Gabreski turns carefully away, hoping desperately the Germans won't notice him. He avoids a violent turn, but quickly completes 180 degrees. Constantly looking back to see if the 190's will spot him, a sense of relief comes over him when he realizes that, miraculously, the enemy hasn't detected a lone American intruder. He pulls away rapidly, in the opposite direction.

As soon as he gains safe distance, Gabreski checks his fuel gauges. His supply is shockingly low. He should have headed home immediately after the fight with the 110's. Now there is no choice but to turn west without delay. With left stick and rudder, he brings his compass heading around to 260 degrees, but even now, finally headed home, calculations of flying time indicate a close finish. Normal fuel consumption will somehow have to be reduced if he is to reach Halesworth.

Having climbed rapidly since sneaking away from the FW–190's, he levels off at 27,000 feet and eases off the throttle. He pulls the red mixture control lever back to "lean," which reduces fuel intake in the cylinders, increases the air ratio correspondingly. It is a fuel economy trick. It causes the engine to run hotter, but saves precious gasoline.

Gabreski knows he jumped the 110's north of Emden. He flew south only shortly thereafter. He should be across or nearing the Dutch border. If so, he will have to fly the North Sea at its widest point between Holland and England—a distance of over one hundred miles. He glances at the countryside below, but can't recognize a single check point. A glance back at the fuel gauges shows seventy gallons remaining. (The Thunderbolt consumes a gallon a minute, or more, on an average combat mission.)

As he is reading the right tank fuel gauge, on the floor of the cockpit, his eye catches something moving out to the right. Looking up instinctively, he makes out, at three o'clock, a single bogy! Pulse quickens, eyes strain. Who is it?

The bogy moves in. He is on a crossing course, which will take him almost directly in front. The two planes are closing at an angle of seventy degrees, the bogy obviously making good time. Gabreski is cruising more slowly—on lean-mixture setting.

Closer and closer the unidentified aircraft comes. Gabreski considers changing course. But he can only turn east or south to avoid the stranger. And both these courses carry him deeper into Germany. Besides, the aircraft might be friendly. Yet, if this solitary fighter were friendly, why should he be heading 170 degrees? These unnerving thoughts race through his head as he watches the dark outline of the bogy grow larger and larger, both pilots holding their original courses, both surely looking the other over carefully.

His head right, eyes fixed on the single-engine aircraft, Gabreski grimly holds course. He can now see the bogy is a pointed-nose fighter —which means a liquid-cooled engine. That eliminates the Thunderbolt and the FW-190. Nor could it be a Lightning. The P-38 is easily distinguishable with its twin fuselages. Gabreski hopes desperately it will be a Spitfire. The bogy closes rapidly, now passes in front, and the shape of the fighter suddenly becomes familiar. ME-109!

With a start, Gabreski reaches for throttle and mixture control, then draws his hand back. He doesn't have fuel for a fight. No matter how well he fights, he loses, since he can't get back home after a fight. The Nazis are in control in Holland and Belgium, the two countries on the continent, other than Germany, he would be able to reach after an engagement.

Germany's best-known fighter, the ME-109. (Air Force Photo)

He watches the German cross ahead, from right to left, finally taking up a position at eleven o'clock. There he hesitates for a moment. Is it possible the German hasn't seen him? Gabreski sweats it out. He glances below to see if there is any cloud cover, but the clouds are further west, ahead in the distance. He keeps his eyes on the lone bandit, who sits out to the side like a cat tantalizing a mouse before the kill. The German is turning! He peels off to the right and starts in . . . on Gabreski!

Now the enemy is a silhouette, boring straight in toward Gabreski's rear. He will make a left turn when close, the usual gunnery pattern, and roar up from behind. As he comes in, Gabreski squirms. He can't fight, but must do something. He won't sit there and be shot down like a sitting duck.

The German comes in gracefully, but fast. It is a matter of seconds before Gabreski will see the twinkles from his guns. Now the 109 begins his left turn, from slightly behind; Gabreski's eyes are locked on the sleek gray enemy, now at his altitude and coming on fast. It is time for action. Gabreski turns sharp left, directly into the oncoming German. The quick maneuver throws the enemy's timing off, halves the time of closure, and brings the two planes flashing into each other at 600 m.p.h.

The German has only seconds to fire; his guns flash briefly at the onrushing American, and the two fighters whistle past each other. Gabreski turns back right, heading west immediately. The German knows the advantage of altitude; he pulls up, off to the right, gaining the advantage of height, and once again begins to cross over to the left. Gabreski flies on west, desperate, in despair, watching the trim 109 maneuvering for the kill. It is a nerve-tingling show.

The bandit completes his crossing, once again hesitates for a moment at eleven o'clock high. Then his left wing goes up and his nose once more points straight at the lone American. Gabreski watches the 109 dive in for another try. As the German pilot begins to roll out to the left, just getting in range, Gabreski once again cuts suddenly left and into him. This time twinkles from the enemy's guns appear as soon as Gabreski turns. But once more the sudden maneuver and rapid closure force the enemy pilot to overshoot.

He flashes past, as they meet head on, and pulls up. Gabreski once more turns right. He has felt no hits. Two passes and two escapes! The enemy is at two o'clock high, having retained his altitude advantage. Now he begins again to cross to the left, preparing for pass number three. Perspiration pours out of Gabreski's forehead. How long can this go on? His hands are clammy. For some reason he glances at the clock on the panel . . . it is 1 P.M.

Back in Pennsylvania this December Saturday it is 7 A.M. People are driving to work, thinking about Saturday night's parties, or the movies. Some are complaining about a scarcity of coffee or sugar. The sky above them is quiet, and nobody shoots at anyone else. Soft beds, safe from danger, are not appreciated. Good meals are plentiful. The war is a long way off. Gabreski is fighting for minutes—every minute an eternity!

And, on this very day, Prime Minister Winston Churchill is landing in North Africa for a visit to General Dwight D. Eisenhower's headquarters, near Tunis. Eisenhower, to become Supreme Commander of Operation Overlord, is still headquartered in Africa, where the invasion of Italy is the big news. D-Day, and occupation of Dutch soil, below, is as yet only a promise. Ike and Prime Minister Churchill are no doubt comfortably quartered. Keyworth Blue Leader is fighting for his life, cornered, the cards stacked against him, hoping to get back to base one more time.

The 109, left above, is back at eleven o'clock, to continue the grim contest. Right wing dips, left rises, and the German curves once again into Gabreski—who is carrying on in the tradition of the American fighter pilot, refusing to bail out, hanging on, trying for the near impossible . . . and scared stiff.

The German goes about his business carefully on this, the third pass. Gabreski knows the same dodge won't work. He grits his teeth as the German roars closer and closer, knowing he is almost within range. Then he yanks the stick back. As he pulls up, he sees sparkles on the leading edge of the enemy's wing. His nose hangs in the sky.

Thump! Thump! Crash! The cockpit is suddenly full of dust. More thumps! Gabreski is dazed. He feels a stinging sensation in his right foot. Something has exploded in the cockpit! He looks for the right rudder pedal. It isn't there. Nor is the heel of his boot. The German fighter flashes by. A twenty-millimeter shell had exploded just under Gabreski's right foot, knocking out the rudder pedal and tearing a hole in the fuselage. The engine has taken hits! Gabreski, realizing what has happened, recognizes a knocking, rough sound as that of a damaged engine. Only now does he realize he's in a left-turning spiral, having stalled at the top of his pull-up while being raked by enemy shells.

Crippled, falling in a spiral, low on gasoline and far from home, Gabreski's chances are practically nil, but some fight is still there. Down below he sees the cloud layer he sought in vain a few miles back. Glancing up, behind, he sees the enemy off to his right. The cloud layer is far below—11,000 feet. He is at 25,000. But Gabreski knows his chance when he sees it. Hoping the German will think him finished, for a moment at least, he continues the awkward-looking spiral downward.

The altimeter needle steadily falls. He keeps his eyes fixed on the 109. For a short interval the ruse works. The German hesitates and looks for a chute, or smoke. The P–47 spirals wildly down. The distance opens between the two planes. Gabreski needs just a few seconds more. . . . but then the enemy pilot recognizes his game—peels off. Gabreski rams the stick forward. He will have to make a run for it. The heavy Thunderbolt accelerates, but the damaged engine fails to give maximum power. The Thunderbolt hurtles straight down now—faked circles no longer necessary. Piling down behind him, full throttle, the enemy fighter takes up the chase.

Gabreski must win the race to the clouds. He has a head start. Initial diving velocity of the Thunderbolt is high, it being heavier than most fighters, so he is at once hurtling downward at tremendous speed. The enemy, however, has full power to augment his dive, and begins to close the gap. Gabreski anxiously watches the altimeter: 18,000, 17,000 16,000, 15,000! He fears he might pull the wings off his weakened fighter if he doesn't pull out, but the enemy is closing from above at terrific speed. He can't pull out right in front of him. The cloud layer is still a few thousand feet below. Gabreski must reach it. He continues his dive, will risk the G's of a pull-out at excessive speed. He keeps the stick forward. The screaming dive continues . . . Gabreski looks straight down. The white cloud tops rush up at him. He looks behind. The 109 is closing his rear . . . almost in firing range.

Now is the time to get into the clouds—the enemy fighter behind will be on him—in firing range—in seconds. Gabreski will have to dive into the clouds at a steep angle—and pull out inside. A high-speed pull-out in the soup is risky, but he must go in both steep and fast—to stay out of firing range of the bandit behind him. He hauls gently back and feels his weight thrown against the bottom of the seat. Blood drains from his head. Seconds drag. The nose of the big fighter pulls up slowly as the cloud top is reached. He can only dimly recognize the top of the cloud layer as he shoots into it, so little blood remains in his head. But he is at last in the stuff, and the German can't see him! He has won the race.

As he shot through the murky unknown, suddenly heaven, Gabreski kept a firm pull on the stick and concentrated all mental faculties on the instrument panel. The little round dials and flight indicators could save his life in this blind pull-out. He had to check descent and keep wings level to avoid a stall. The only way he could do this was to constantly read the instruments, acting accordingly.

Compounding the ordeal of entering the clouds in a high-speed dive was the fact that his engine had been damaged. He kept pulling back on the stick, forcing the altimeter to show a slower and slower descent, all the while enduring the pull of gravity which sometimes blacks out pilots, and which "grayed" him out. If he pulled back too hard on the stick he would lose vision, and the means to watch the instrument panel. Yet he had to check excessive speed and level off in the cloud—not mush out of the bottom, where the enemy pilot probably expected him to emerge . . . and probably lay waiting.

As he exerted tremendous effort to pull out, and maintain level flight on a westerly course, he noticed the oil-pressure needle was in the red. Low oil pressure was an ominous warning; Gabreski knew a shell had probably started an oil leak, and that his hot engine would get even hotter. There was nothing he could do about it. Meanwhile, he slowly straightened the rocketing fighter in the clouds. And as he brought her upright, straight and level according to needle and ball and flight simulator, a cold sweat drenched his body.

For several minutes, head forward and eyes hypnotized by instrument panel dials, Gabreski tensely flew on in the milky vastness at 6,000 feet. Engine rough, but running; fuselage holed, but flying; fuel low, but hoping, he carried on. Back home at Halesworth, crewmen were getting ready to receive their fighters after the mission. Gabreski, doing his best, wondered if he'd make it.

Gasoline gauges showed a steady drain of fuel. Fifty gallons left! Gabreski guessed he must at last be near the Dutch coast. He wanted to take a look. Inside the clouds he would never know. And flying for long periods in a shot-up plane, on instruments, builds up unbearable tension. He eased the throttle forward and pulled back lightly on the stick. The Thunderbolt's red cowl lifted and began to cut slowly upward in the murk; it was all the weak engine could do.

The P–47 climbed, Gabreski watching instruments every second of the way. He wondered where the 109 would be when he stuck his nose out of the top, and he knew that what he saw once out of the clouds, through holes in the almost-solid cloud layer, down below, would tell him whether he had a chance to make it back to England. Finally the altimeter reached 11,000 feet and the Thunderbolt, engine knocking, sliced through the top into the blue. Now he eased back on the throttle and leveled off. The first thing he noticed, below, through a break in the clouds, was the receding coast of Holland. He had a chance! Fifty gallons might get him across the North Sea, with luck and a prayer and tight fuel economy.

Instinctively, Gabreski switched his head from side to side and cleared his rear. He again looked back. Was that something at five o'clock? Keeping a westerly heading, enjoying the luxury of knowing up from down and being able to take his eyes off the instruments, Gabreski nevertheless kept his gaze fixed on the dot back there at five o'clock. Slowly the dot grew. And then he knew . . . the 109!

Surprised, and with a dread of re-entering the clouds, Gabreski waited just long enough to see the German getting too close, bade the sunshine good-by and dipped into the gray once more. This time he entered the clouds in a normal descent. Once inside, he turned again to the highly concentrated task of instrument flight. And now—for the first time—Gabreski turned to his radio in an urgent appeal for help.

He pushed one of the four push buttons on his radio, that reserved for emergencies only. "Mayday . . . Mayday . . . Mayday. Keyworth Blue Leader calling for a fix . . . Mayday . . . Mayday . . . Mayday. Keyworth Blue Leader calling for a . fix . . ." The emergency button was always monitored, and the reply came back almost instantly.

A radar operator back in England located him on his screen and offered encouragement. Gabreski told the operator he might not make it to land. The operator had his position fixed precisely, utilizing several radar receiving screens at various points along the English coast to get an accurate fix. If he went down, Air-Sea Rescue would at least know about it, and where he splashed. The radar operator gave him the course to Halesworth. During this dramatic exchange, Gabreski's eyes never left the instrument panel. He was still blind piloting a crippled fighter, in which a spin could be fatal. And he still didn't know how long his oil supply would last.

Back at Halesworth, operations is helpless; either the damaged engine will get him home, either gasoline will hold out . . . or else. Far to the east the Thunderbolt bangs louder and louder. Gabreski's nerves wear thin.

As the drama unfolds, minute by pulsing minute, German fighter pilots, no water to cross, touch down after interception missions. One of them, Hans Knoke, lands his Gustav 190 at Marx, south of the Luftwaffe's Jever station, but not until he has flashed across the field doing a victory roll, signifying his twentieth kill. Americans, landing at various fields in East Anglia, also display victory rolls. Gabreski has a victory, but for him there will be no roll.

Now he decides to drop down under the cloud layer . . . the German has surely turned back by now, else he will be caught in the same fuel squeeze. The stick goes forward. The altimeter needle turns counter-clockwise . . . 6,000, 5,500, 5,000 . . . the big sixteen-foot Hamilton Standard prop pulls the Thunderbolt out of the bottom of the clouds. Gabreski sees the choppy, cold water of the North Sea below. He glances at his fuel gauges; twenty gallons left! But at least he is out of the soup. He looks behind. The 109 is at last gone.

He may not reach Halesworth . . . the question is whether he will reach a field on the coast. Back at Halesworth Gabreski's crew strain their eyes. Sounds from the east arouse their attention. The 56th's planes are landing. They know Gabreski is either already down, or must come down soon. Nobody stays up. A hundred take-offs mean a hundred landings, good or bad, rough or smooth. And so each distant hum, each distant speck they heed, unaware of Gabreski's emergency call to radar stations along the coast.

Now down close to the water, leaning out mixture control until the engine runs rougher than ever, Gabreski looks ahead to the west . . . right and left and straight ahead . . . looking for land. He is flying a course to Halesworth furnished by the radar station. So low he can't see any distance, he scans the horizon ahead for a dark outline that means land, that magical four-letter word. And then . . . straight ahead, a dark shape sits on the sea's horizon. The coast of England! It grows bigger and bigger. Gabreski nervously looks on the floor of the cockpit, first on his right, then left. A few gallons in one wing tank . . . the other practically empty!

As the engine gets rougher and rougher, oil temperature moves higher and higher. Gabreski knows he can't fly much longer. Oil obviously dangerously low, he is nevertheless forced to fly on a mixture too lean for safety. Thus both a hot mixture and inadequate lubrication are burning up the engine's moving parts. Gabreski is literally spending the engine in a bid to get home; he knows this engine will never fly again; it will be removed and junked as soon as he lands—if he lands!

The coast is just ahead. Gabreski strains his eyes looking for a field —any field. He sees a city near the coast, by several large fingers of water. Ipswich! The Thunderbolt, laboring in its final minutes of agony, groans over the coastline. Halesworth is just a few miles further. If he sees another field first, he will go down. The seconds pass slowly. At last, ahead . . . HALESWORTH. The radar operator had vectored him straight in!

No time for elaborate before-landing check. The runway is clearly visible, and Gabreski lines up and pulls the landing gear lever, wondering if wheels will go down, whether some of the 109's shells ruptured the hydraulic system activating the gear. The wheels come down with a thump!

Gabreski eagerly pulls back on the throttle as he approaches the end of the black runway, looming up in front larger and larger. On the field below personnel in the control tower sense the situation, crash trucks and the "meat wagon" stand in position. The control tower clears the field and suspends traffic.

Airspeed drops to 130, then 120. The crippled fighter is twenty feet in the air as it sweeps in over the near end of the runway. Gabreski juggles rudder pedals and eases the stick back, all the way into his lap. The big fighter flops down with a crunch, landing gear stands up. He is rolling down the black pavement . . . safely on the ground! The smell of burning metal permeates the cockpit.

Body weary, tension suddenly ended, his shoulders fall, he suddenly goes limp. He's down, in England, after all. The big fighter rumbles down to the end of the black strip, slower and slower. All at once he's terribly tired. His strength seems to drain away. He turns off the end of the runway for a short roll, and lets the engine die.

From all sides vehicles and men converge on the still fighter, its silver underbelly holed by shells, its engine finished and smoking, the prop holed by a shell—this now visible as it stands strangely silent. Another hole, visible to those rushing up, is in the massive engine. All in all, the black-and-white checkered fuselage and red cowling, streaked with oil and shot full of holes, is a sorry sight. Gabreski shoves back the canopy and weakly looks out around him.

Mission 198 has been carried out. The enemy attack on the bombers near Emden was broken up. The 61st Squadron and the 56th Group have done well, and rung up an impressive number of kills. Gabreski has added another Luftwaffe victim to his total, his flight having destroyed three of the total.

Over five hundred bombers successfully bombed Emden. While seventeen were lost (170 men), they had not been decimated or riddled, as they might have been had not the fighters arrived at the very last minute. The range of the P-47's was such that, even arriving at the very last, they had only a few minutes in the target area. This was the constant problem of the Eighth Air Force, and the Germans knew it only too well.

Gabreski knew it was a near miracle he had survived the fight with the lone German fighter. His number had been up, as the law of averages goes, but there he was, at Halesworth, sitting quietly and still, while men, trucks, and an ambulance rushed to his side. It all seemed a little unreal now. Gabreski slid his helmet back. His black hair was soaking wet. A gentle breeze cooled his forehead as he stood up in the cockpit and looked around.

Non-coms jumped on the wing. Someone asked him if he was all right. The Hollywood line would have been to shrug it off, as just a breeze, a routine mission! Gabreski only said, in a tired voice, he was okay. One of the men said there were two holes in the engine. Another said the prop had been almost cut in two. And all looked at the hole under the cockpit where a shell had knocked out the right rudder pedal and entered the cockpit.

They crowded around and looked at Gabreski as if he might explode at any minute, do something unexpected. What was there to do? He slowly unhooked his chute and dinghy and dropped his helmet in the seat, then stepped over the side. The engine steamed, metal melted. A truck drove up to take him to squadron headquarters. Gabreski walked over and got in, still somewhat numb. The gathering around his plane continued to examine it in detail, wonder written on their faces.

The driver stepped on the gas and the truck took off. As they sped away, Gabreski turned back and took a last look at his plane, now sitting still on the ground, lonely in the middle of the field by itself, the big prop strangely motionless, it seemed, after hours of turning—such necessary turning! He kept his head back and took a long look. It grew smaller and smaller as they left it out there on the field.

7 ME-109 at Six O'Clock

DECEMBER 22, 1943:

First Lieutenant JOHN T. GODFREY

National Archives

ONLY eleven days were to separate the most harrowing experiences of two of the war's top aces. First Lieutenant John T. Godfrey of the famous 4th Fighter Group, bitter rival of 56th, had only a single kill to his credit on the morning of December 22, 1943. By that afternoon he was to be on his way to becoming the second-highest-scoring U.S. ace in the European Theater of Operations.

Godfrey's position in the 4th Group's flying list for December 22 was Purple Two, 336th Squadron. That meant he would be flying in the fourth flight of the 336th Squadron, one of three squadrons in the 4th. There were four fighters in a flight, and each flight had a color. The fourth flight in the 336th Squadron was Purple and position two meant Godfrey would be flying the wing of Purple Flight Leader (Purple One). Their orders were to rendezvous with a formation of heavy bombers over the latter's target, Münster, Germany.

The code name for the 336th Squadron was Horseback. Therefore, Godfrey's code name was Horseback Purple Two. The other two squadrons in the 4th had different code names, but the same color designations for flights within their squadrons.

Godfrey's lone victory to date had been sweet revenge for his brother, Reggie, who had been lost at sea when a German U-boat sank his ship. The brothers, from Providence, Rhode Island, had been close and Godfrey had named his fighter *Reggie's Reply*.

On December 1, three weeks earlier, he had been on a mission over the Continent when he spotted a single enemy ME-109 below. Leaving his comrades, he dived after the unsuspecting German and closed in from behind. It was a short engagement. The eight fifty-calibre wing guns from Godfrey's P-47 shattered the 109 before the German could take evasive action. The 109 spun out, into the deck, on fire. That was kill number one, but more important it was *Reggie's Reply*. The Luftwaffe was to hear more from Reggie's brother before the war was over.

Only two months earlier, Godfrey had flown his first combat mission. He flew the wing of Captain Don Gentile, another of the war's great aces—killed in a crash several years after the war. On this mission the fighters escorted heavy bombers to Emden. The weather turned sour on the return flight and Gentile succumbed to vertigo. He spun out.

Godfrey stayed with his element leader to the end. Fortunately, Gentile managed to recover in time to save two lives. A lasting friendship had begun and Gentile ever afterward marveled at the feat Godfrey performed that day, September 7, 1943, when on his first mission he was called upon to fly formation with an element leader tumbling earthward, out of control—and did it! The friendship lasted throughout the war and Gentile and Godfrey went on to destroy over fifty Luftwaffe planes, to become the greatest one-two punch in the Eighth's Fighter Command. The fine-featured, dark-haired Godfrey had perhaps the sharpest eyes in the Eighth Air Force.

Before daylight on the first day of winter, December 22, 1943, Technical Sergeant Lawrence Krantz of Madisonville, Ohio, climbed out of bed, paid a breakfast call at the enlisted men's mess, and headed out to a revetment where Godfrey's red and silver Thunderbolt stood exposed to the English winter.

Krantz and his assistants had work to do. He was crew chief, responsible for keeping *Reggie's Reply* flying and in perfect working order. Before a mission ice and snow had to be scraped off wings, engine warmed up, a number of checks performed, and the fighter made ready for flight.

An armorer loaded the eight wing guns. Each took 300 shells, and that meant loading 2,400 shells. Film had to be loaded into the wing camera, which automatically operated when the guns were fired.

A radio man checked vital and intricate radio equipment. Each fighter had a four-way radio, push-button type. The pilot could listen to his squadron leader on one channel. On another he might tune to either his fighter group or bombers being escorted. One was for Air-Sea Rescue in the English Channel or North Sea, guarded night and day, and the other brought in radar vectoring assistance, often needed to get home.

Krantz checked such things, installed oxygen, drained tanks and tried to keep warm. He had completed most of his job when the December sky whitened in the east, revealing low-hanging scud in every direction.

Meanwhile, on the second floor of the brick building which was pilots' living quarters, a batman walked down the hall. When he came to the room occupied by Godfrey and Robert Richards, Godfrey's roommate, he opened the door. It was 7:45 A.M. "Good morning, sir," he said. "Briefing is at nine o'clock."

That—to every fighter pilot in the ETO in World War II—was the beginning of a mission. Godfrey sat up, threw aside heavy cover compensating for lack of heating fuel in England, reached for heavy socks and clothing and purple R.A.F. flying boots.

Washed and dressed, he was soon descending the stairway to the officers' mess on the first floor. The smell of coffee, fried Spam and fresh eggs greeted him. Only pilots on flying duty got fresh eggs. Around the long breakfast tables pilots of all three squadrons ate and fought tension. It was 8:45 A.M. when Godfrey finished.

The jeeps and trucks that carried pilots to group briefing were already lined up outside. Pilots poured out and climbed into them.

When they pulled up at the briefing room, pilots streamed inside and sat on folding wooden seats in orderly rows, facing a small raised platform. At the back of the platform was a huge wall map of Europe. In front of it was a curtain which was now pulled aside.

The mission was marked by bright-colored string over the exact course fighters were to follow, denoting where they would pick up the bombers, etc. As soon as all pilots were seated, Colonel Chesley A. Peterson, Group Commander, took over. The tall, wiry, blue-eyed com-

Take off 12:45 p.m., landing at Downham Market 4:05 p.m.

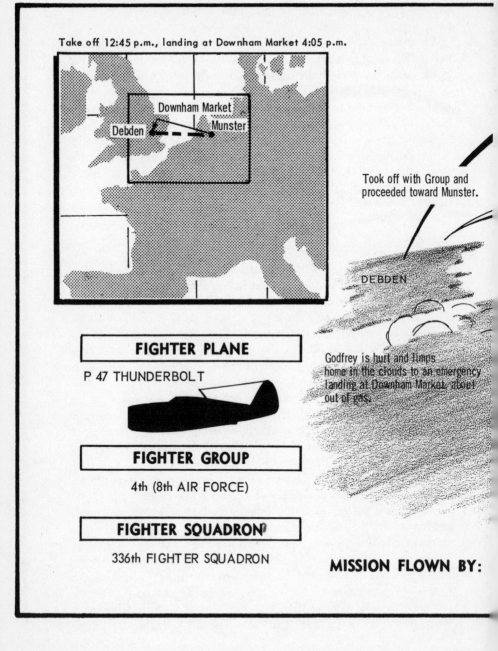

Downham Market
Debden
Munster

Took off with Group and proceeded toward Munster.

DEBDEN

Godfrey is hurt and limps home in the clouds to an emergency landing at Downham Market, about out of gas.

FIGHTER PLANE

P 47 THUNDERBOLT

FIGHTER GROUP

4th (8th AIR FORCE)

FIGHTER SQUADRON

336th FIGHTER SQUADRON

MISSION FLOWN BY:

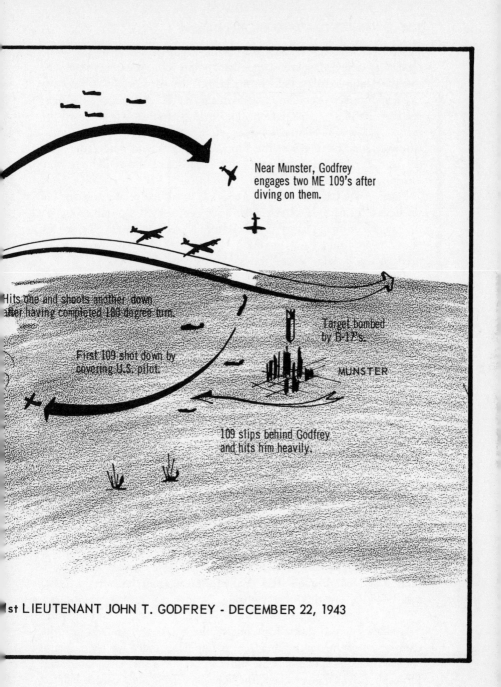

Near Munster, Godfrey engages two ME 109's after diving on them.

Hits one and shoots another down after having completed 180 degree turn.

First 109 shot down by covering U.S. pilot.

Target bombed by B-17's.

MUNSTER

109 slips behind Godfrey and hits him heavily.

1st LIEUTENANT JOHN T. GODFREY - DECEMBER 22, 1943

mander was nearing the end of his tour. Eight days later he was to be rotated to a less dangerous and demanding job. At twenty-three, he was the youngest full colonel in the U.S. Army Air Corps. He had been the first American squadron leader in the R.A.F. and his was the most celebrated name to emerge from the Eagle Squadrons. He outlined the mission. It would be the longest yet flown by the 4th. The target, Münster, was just north of the Ruhr. The 4th was to rendezvous with the heavies near the target, and bring them home. Other fighters were escorting them in.

Peterson set take-off time for 12:45. It would be a late mission. He read out a list of code letters. Each letter represented a certain point on the map of Europe. (Every pilot carefully copied the letters on the back of his non-writing hand, in ink.) He repeated the code words to be used on the mission several times.

Times were read out . . . the time the group would reach landfall out, landfall in. Course settings were announced. Radio call words, the distress signal, the order of flight, the point where the bombers would be picked up, and the bomber markings were all explained by the C.O.

On his signal, each pilot synchronized his watch. "Good luck," were Peterson's last words.

Outside the skies were damp and cloudy. Fog added to the bleakness of the December setting. When the weather officer stepped on the briefing platform, most of the pilots knew what was coming. Clouds were expected to extend for a considerable distance upward. Clouds were also expected to cover much of the Continent, especially around the target, Münster, three hundred miles to the east.

Weather would be heavy over the North Sea and Holland, the shores of which would be reached at the halfway mark on the trip in. Next, the intelligence briefing: the Luftwaffe had steadily been strengthened during 1943, now had more day fighters defending Germany than at any time since the A.A.F. began operations. Large numbers of enemy fighters could be expected. And flak—it would be heavy. The minutes had ticked by. Briefing was over. Squadrons were ordered to report to their individual headquarters. Vehicles once again hauled the pilots away, for the last time that morning.

Godfrey jumped down from one of the trucks and walked into the ready room of the 336th Squadron. A few pilots called for cheese sandwiches from the squadron grill and some went to the parachute room. Unlocking their flight lockers, they checked flying suit, G-suit, helmet, oxygen mask, boots and gloves . . . several pairs. They ate, talked, and lounged around. For more than an hour they waited. Then they began to don flying gear.

After strapping, zipping, and pulling flying gear on, each man slipped into a Mae West life preserver, then wriggled into his parachute. Heavily-loaded pilots waddled into the squadron briefing room for a last short briefing. It was 11:45 A.M. Outside the winter sky was depressingly dark.

Squadron planning was brief; time was short. The squadron commander checked flight dispositions, order of take-off, take-off time. He wished pilots good hunting. It was time to get to the aircraft.

Godfrey, clumsily weighted down, made for *Reggie's Reply*. Krantz had everything ready.

He strapped Godfrey in and connected the oxygen hose from Godfrey's helmet. Both tested the oxygen supply. (Over 10,000 feet oxygen was necessary, and was arranged to flow through the hose automatically, as needed.)

Krantz hurriedly checked Godfrey's G-suit connection. The G-suit was new. It was designed to prevent blacking out. Through a small black hose, from an air pump connected to a gravity device, air would rush into flat rubber bags strapped to Godfrey's arms, legs and abdomen when there was danger too much blood would drain out of the upper parts of his body—because of aerial maneuvers—and cause a blackout. That was the purpose of a G-suit—to enable U.S. pilots to retain sight longer than an enemy in periods of severe pull-outs or turns, when the pull of gravity drew the blood from the upper parts of the body, especially the head, and caused a loss of vision.

Seconds remained before start-engine time. Godfrey looked toward his squadron leader. At 12:37 Krantz saw the squadron leader's propeller turn. He waved to Godfrey, who pressed the energizer button, then the starter button. The 2,000 horsepower radial engine coughed thunder. Smoke kicked out of the stacks intermittently. Soon the cylinders fired evenly.

Godfrey checked instruments, now lighting up. Purple One—nearby —began to roll. Godfrey, Purple One's wing man, pushed the black knob of the throttle forward with his left hand and released brakes. The heavily-loaded fighter rolled sluggishly ahead, and Godfrey turned in behind Purple One on the taxi strip, a few hundred feet away.

Purple Flight—four planes in all—was now taxiing toward the end of the runway, four aircraft in line. It was 12:43 when they pulled in

behind the other flights at the end of the runway. Several hundred feet
down the runway Colonel Peterson waited, looking back. When he
saw that Purple Flight and the spares had arrived, he prepared to take
off. He eased throttle forward. The Pratt and Whitney roared louder
and it became harder for Peterson and his wing man—off to his right
—to hold the fighters.

When the mercury reached halfway to the red line Peterson spiraled
his right hand and brought it down in a forward motion. The two lead
fighters began to roll. The next two would follow as soon as they lifted
off the runway. Peterson and wing man left the runway at 12:45. The
mission outlined in Field Order 207 was on.

Thunderbolts in pairs rapidly hurtled into the air. Two, four, six,
eight, ten, twelve . . . now it was Purple One and Two in front,
watching to see the wheels of the two fighters ahead lift off the concrete
runway.

They dragged off, and Godfrey watched Purple One for the sign.
With engines roaring and brakes hard pressed to hold *Reggie's Reply*
back, he saw Purple One throw his right hand down. Off came the feet
from brake pedals.

Speed picked up slowly. With extra gasoline tanks underneath and
a full complement of ammunition, convincing a Thunderbolt to fly was
not to be taken lightly. If the engine cut out three-fourths the distance
down the icy runway, a pilot might not be able to stop on the re-
mainder.

Godfrey's air speed indicator registered sixty, picked up faster . . .
seventy, eighty, ninety. The runway was running out. The Thunderbolt was beginning to bounce. Airspeed passed one hundred; Godfrey
hauled back on the stick and forced the big bird to fly. When she stayed
airborne, he reached down and retracted landing gear and milked up
flaps, to cut wind resistance and increase speed.

A string of pairs of 4th Group fighters circled upward to the left,
each pair behind, cutting something off the turning circle of the pair
ahead—closing the gap. The 336th Squadron leader was making an ex-
ceptionally wide turn to allow the squadron to join up. In a matter of
minutes, the squadron was together—the lead flight ahead, second
flight behind left, third flight behind right, and Purple Flight (the
fourth) behind and right of the third.

Behind flew a couple of "spares" which followed in case anyone had
to abort. A spare was also often sent home as escort for a pilot who

turned back because of engine trouble. As enemy territory was approached, spares usually turned back if they hadn't been needed.

Debden was forty miles from the North Sea. The four flights of 336th's red-nosed P–47's climbed into the dreaded low-hanging soup after assembling in squadron formation and setting course. As each pilot went into the stuff everything outside became gray. The major task suddenly became staying close on the wing of the fighter ahead.

Pilots are trained to keep eyes off the instrument panel when flying in thick stuff, and strict orders are to fly off the wing in front. That means jockeying the throttle constantly with the left hand, never taking eyes off the pilot ahead. Jockeying the throttle is necessary because no two engines perform exactly the same and because rudder and aileron corrections are always different, and made at different times. Therefore, the flight path of every plane is a little different, requiring its specific power setting, changing from time to time, to keep in close formation off the wing of the pilot ahead.

The Thunderbolts bored steadily upward—silent except for the steady roar of engines. Complete radio silence was observed. The altimeter hand circled slowly, clockwise . . . 3,000, 3,100, 3,200, 3,300. The airspeed indicator registered 160 m.p.h., regulation climbing speed for fully-loaded P–47's.

The cloud bank was solid. Minutes passed. Half an hour had elapsed since take-off. It was 1:15 and the 336th was still climbing in the soup. Pilots felt the strain. In all this time, only seconds (in stolen glances away from the aircraft ahead) were available for checking instruments, switching gas tanks, and watching engine temperatures and pressures.

By this time 336th's fighters were above the choppy windswept waters of the North Sea. But only the amount of time in flight told pilots they were over water. They were still on instruments. Altitude reached 13,000, 14,000, 15,000. Oxygen masks were now bringing in pure oxygen.

As the long ordeal of blind flying dragged on, one pilot lost contact, then another. Three or four were now on their own, maintaining the course setting but separated from the rest of the squadron. On and on the 336th's Thunderbolts flew, fighting weather, fighting ice, fighting for altitude.

Suddenly a light spot appeared . . . then it was gone. In a minute another lighter area could be seen. Then it was dark again. But that was a long-awaited sign. The top was being reached. Just a little longer, and the squadron would pull out through the top—into the sun.

The lighter spots appeared more frequently. Then a very light gap passed overhead. And another. A sight of blue, for an instant! Then another. Then the top at once, and the squadron shot out of the cloud into gleaming sunshine—long awaited.

The climb continued. The blue sky made it easier. The stragglers who had lost their lead planes in the soup all broke out at relatively close distances, and were able to join up again. The squadron leader signaled all aircraft to spread into semi-combat formation. Visibility was now excellent. Pilots had no trouble maintaining contact.

The coast of Holland lay ahead below the clouds, minutes away. Except for the roar of the engines only one sound was heard, the wheeze from breathing through the oxygen mask. This necessity of life flowed with each breath. Twenty thousand feet! The 336th's fighters leveled off.

Now the radio picked up a faint sound, a distant, high-pitched whine. It was German jamming. Always it was there . . . the Luftwaffe invariably knew when a high formation was coming in.

Already pilots were searching the sky in all directions. The search ahead was for small streaks of wispy, white specks (contrails left by the four-engined big friends were more readily visible than the B-17's themselves).

The coast of Holland was crossed. Though the Continent was still nine-tenths covered, through cloud breaks pilots could see they had crossed in over the shoreline of enemy-occupied Europe—Fortress Europe, Hitler called it.

The aerial armada plowed on through Holland's December skies without incident. No enemy aircraft was sighted. The German border lay below—the Belgian border to the south. Godfrey switched gas tanks, checked his instruments and looked around. Nothing happened.

Outside it was forty below. The extra gloves felt good. Godfrey checked his gun-warming switches. Guns could freeze up in such weather. His flight was at the rear of the squadron and he was to the left of his flight leader. He kept looking around. Training had stressed the importance of seeing the enemy first, before he saw you. Clouds and Germany passed below. For some time the squadron flew on, all eyes now probing the sky ahead for telltale contrails. Then they came into view ahead—the bombers! They were very close to Münster.

Flying at a speed between 250 and 300, the Thunderbolts closed the gap fast. Soon the fighters were approaching their big friends. Pulling up behind, they had to throttle back to keep from leaving them behind. They could slow down only so much, so S-turns and zigzagging were required.

The squadron spread out a little more, climbed another two thousand feet to 22,000 and zigzagged continuously above the B-17's. Black puffs began to dot the sky near the bombers. Eyes scanned the air above,

The curving vapor trails were made by U.S.A.A.F. fighters escorting B-17's on a raid. (Air Force Photo)

behind, and ahead, seeking to detect the approach of enemy fighters trying to sneak through to the bombers.

Godfrey spots something moving below. Darting along above the clouds, in the opposite direction—two dots . . . aircraft! They wouldn't be friendly, at that altitude, going in that direction. Still, they are too far away to be sure. Godfrey presses his mike button: "Two bandits, one o'clock low!"

The call charges the atmosphere. Back comes the reply: "Can't see 'em." Godfrey replies, "Follow me down. I'll show 'em to you!"

With that, charged with excitement, Godfrey pulls the lever to release belly tank, shoves the stick forward and right, and steps on right rudder. The airspeed indicator comes alive and the extra tank tumbles wildly away.

But no one follows Godfrey down. There are no orders to leave the bombers. And, also, Godfrey has no wing man. He is—or was—Purple One's wing man. Purple One sticks with the bombers.

A diving right turn brings Godfrey screaming down; the altimeter shows a loss of 4,000 feet. When he spotted the planes below, Godfrey estimated they were 6,000 feet beneath him—at 16,000 feet. They grow bigger and bigger as Godfrey dives. The silhouettes are not American . . . single engines, inline engines . . . ME–109's!

He presses the mike button again, "They are bandits. Come on down, cover me!" But the 336th roars on overhead, with the bombers, in the opposite direction. Godfrey has now completely reversed course. He is behind and below the bombers and roaring down on the Germans from above.

He flips on gun switches. An orange sight ring appears on the optical gunsight glass, directly in front of his eyes. He has descended 6,000 feet, is indicating better than 400 m.p.h.

The two Germans are flying just above the cloud layer. They weave in and out of several cloud tops that extend up as high as 16,000 feet. The 109 on the left is higher than his wing man to the right, who is slightly behind.

Godfrey decides to pull in behind the lower ME–109, on the right. He is ringing up great speed, closing the Germans fast, too fast for careful, well-timed firing. Accordingly, he cuts throttle, all the while keeping his eye on the lower 109. In drama-packed seconds, Godfrey looks around him. He is a loner, attacking two of the enemy, and there are probably others around.

The 109 ahead, right, grows larger in the sight. Godfrey puts his finger on the gun button. He is still closing his intended victims at an excessive rate. Now the crosses on the wings of the dark gray German fighters are visible.

Not far away, unknown to Godfrey, Lieutenant Vasseure H. "Georgia" Wynn, of Dalton, Georgia, is screaming down to his assistance. Wynn is not from the 336th. He is in the 334th, one of the other two Debden squadrons, an R.A.F. veteran who won't turn down a call for cover from a daring pilot.

Wynn and the 334th had been near the 336th. He had seen the bandits Godfrey called out, and when he heard Godfrey's call for cover decided he'd provide it, no one else seemingly in the mood. He dispatched belly tank, rolled off to his right in a diving turn, and followed Godfrey down.

Godfrey is on the unsuspecting enemy's tail. His long dive has built up such speed he frantically pulls throttle back further, but the dark fighter outline ahead looms bigger and bigger—as if rushing toward him.

The Thunderbolt won't slow down. He is going to shoot past him despite everything he can do. The enemy's wing span fills the sight ring. Instantly Godfrey's right forefinger pulls back on the stick trigger. Eight fifties spurt fire and shell. *Reggie's Reply* shudders.

The German fighter pilot has been negligent . . . his opponent slipped in on his tail. He is to pay the price. Shells rip into the low-winged enemy fighter. Godfrey's shooting is good.

The German fighter staggers. Dusty puffs mark the spot . . . American fifties tearing holes in the 109. Pieces of metal fly back from the puffs into the slipstream. The Luftwaffe pilot desperately banks into a sharp right turn, so tight Godfrey can't follow, with greater speed.

The German is trying to circle behind Godfrey. As he curves to the right, slightly up, outturning his foe, his chances appear good.

Godfrey is in a tight spot. Wynn comes to the rescue. Approaching from behind, he pulls in behind the 109 pilot as he circles. Once again the German has an unseen follower. Godfrey sees flashes from Wynn's guns. Then he glances ahead at the other 109, now just barely forward and above to his left.

He will go for the second one. Throttle forward, stick back. Left rudder. Up surges the P–47. The German ahead apparently hasn't seen what happened to his wing man. Is it possible? *Reggie's Reply* lifts nicely and rapidly closes from right to left.

The gray 109 grows larger and larger. It is suddenly filling the sight ring! This time Godfrey has plenty of time. He is overtaking the enemy at the right speed. Fire! Instant hits! The low-winged 109 begins to shed fragments, which fly off behind, passing below *Reggie's Reply*.

Godfrey keeps the firing button down . . . by now hundreds of shells have streaked for the German. Godfrey sees the wings of his enemy wobble back and forth. He is taking heavy, concentrated fire at point-blank range. The yellow nose spinner of the 109 spins slower . . . pieces continue to fly back through the air. The 109 begins to trail smoke. Godfrey has him!

Reggie's Reply is down to 150 miles an hour. Godfrey literally tears the German plane to pieces. The enemy's controls are shot away. His engine smokes heavily. Godfrey's shells still find their mark. The German throws back his canopy and goes over the side! He passes twenty-five yards below *Reggie's Reply* headed home, below.

Three pictures from the gun camera of an Eighth Air Force fighter record the death of an ME-109. (Air Force Photo)

Godfrey looks down at the falling pilot. Pieces of his burning plane are flying back, hitting *Reggie's Reply*. Thump! Thump! Thump! He yanks back on the stick to get above the flying debris. Thump! Thump! Thump! Out of the corner of his eye he sees twinkles. Enemy fighter! On his tail. Firing and hitting! A flash of terror, and a wild yank at the controls! The 109 sitting back there is squarely on his tail, pouring 20-millimeter fire into him at a fatal rate. Godfrey twists and turns, but he can't shake him . . . he has no speed . . . the 109 can easily follow his every maneuver. Ominous bangs begin to register in the cockpit. Time is short. He is trapped like a sitting duck.

No comrade is behind to pry the enemy loose this time. A last chance flashes through his mind. In the R.A.F. he had been taught to yank back on the stick, hit full right rudder, in an emergency. This produced a flick roll. It's worth a try. There's nothing to lose! Godfrey pulls the stick into his stomach and jams his right foot down hard. Instead of a flick roll, *Reggie's Reply* gives a violent lurch and the tail comes whipping over the nose. Something is wrong. The P–47 is tumbling! Tail over nose and nose over tail, and the fighter heads down toward the cloud bank below, tumbling out of control. Godfrey, desperate, is unable to bring the plane out of this wild descent.

The German is unable to follow the tumbling Thunderbolt. He assumes his foe is finished. No one tumbles purposely. Such violence can easily break an aircraft in two. Godfrey is hit, smoking, and heading for the clouds, tumbling out of control. The German pilot is satisfied. (He must have received credit for a kill.)

Cold sweat covered Godfrey's forehead. His fighter was almost surely finished. Nothing he tried would right the aircraft. He was thrown violently around in the cockpit. Tumbling down and down, *Reggie's Reply* disappeared into the cloud layer below.

Now everything was revolving gray. The violence of the fall continued unabated. Godfrey prepared to bail out. There is a limit to the tumbling a pilot can stand. He reached for the canopy. But the viloence of the tumble and the terrific force of gravity constantly threw him back against his seat, then against seat belt, forward and backward, rendering him almost helpless.

Seconds seemed years. As a last chance, Godfrey managed to grab the throttle and stick and push them both forward. The engine roared and something seemed better. The violence lessened. Speed increased.

Godfrey was going straight down, but he had powered his way out of the tumble.

Down through the cloudy gray December above Germany the crippled red and silver Thunderbolt roared, full throttle. Godfrey looked at his instruments. Shot up! No airspeed indicator. He tried to pull the aircraft up—straight and level, but the ominous dive continued, Godfrey now unaware of the angle of flight. Speed continued to build up.

Mentally and physically exhausted, hands shaking, Godfrey suddenly shot out the bottom of the clouds at 2,000 feet! The shock brought him into action. He hauled back hard on the stick and prayed he could pull out in time. At his great speed, more than 500 m.p.h., it would be close.

Reggie's Reply might break up under the great strain, too. Slowly the fighter's nose lifted. Blood drained from Godfrey's head, his G-suit pumped. But the aircraft held together, despite the pull of gravity. Had some of the enemy's cannon shells weakened the wing structure wings would have separated in the pull-out. Nevertheless, it would be close.

A few feet over the trees *Reggie's Reply* straightened out at the bottom of a great arc. Godfrey leveled off and began to climb. He had missed "going in" by a scant hundred feet!

The engine ran smoothly, but instruments were badly shot up. With a sense of relief, he noticed the compass worked. With that he hoped to get home. He swung into a western heading, gradually climbing. He was dangerously close to the ground and enemy anti-aircraft fire might open up at any moment. The thought became frightening. Godfrey headed for the bottom of the clouds. He would go home in obscurity.

At that moment black puffs filled the sky around him! Desperate again, Godfrey yanked back on the stick, climbed into the bottom of the clouds. He tried to fly on compass and altimeter. Needle and ball (showing the aircraft's altitude) didn't function.

Godfrey glanced back and forth from altimeter to compass. They weren't enough. He was attempting what would have been dangerous in a fully functioning fighter—flying two hundred miles on instruments, at low altitude, where a mistake was often fatal.

Godfrey sensed something was wrong. His speed increased. He hauled back on the stick—to bring the nose up. The speed increased nevertheless. He pulled back again. Nothing would stop it. Speed continued to increase. All at once the red-nosed fighter flashed out of the bottom of the clouds, spiraling toward the ground on its side. Godfrey had been a victim of vertigo!

Flipping the low wing up just in time, Godfrey escaped the trees a second time. Flashing over fields and houses, he realized he was approaching a town. Just as he saw the city, gunners below saw him. Once again smoke puff, dangerously close! He was on the deck, only a couple of hundred feet over the trees. This time the flak was small stuff, white smoke and orange golf balls.

Fire was so intense Godfrey turned back. One hit in the right spot would bring him down. And he had a hundred miles of water to cross, after reaching the shore of Fortress Europe—if he reached it.

Godfrey turned back eastward, to dodge the flak. Physically and mentally he was becoming frayed.

He now turned north. After a few minutes, he turned west again. This time he managed to escape anti-aircraft fire. For ten minutes he flew along smoothly, hopefully.

Godfrey knew he was over Holland. He strained to see the coast. Instead, he suddenly saw an airfield. He had flown straight over it! The Luftwaffe would surely send someone up after him now. To hide from pursuers, he decided to try the heavy clouds again.

It was a hard decision to make. Once again he pointed the nose up, fearful the enemy would soon be on his tail, and headed for the dark stuff. Pulling up into the bottom of cloud bank, he kept his eye glued to the altimeter and compass. He went in at 2,000 feet.

The shot-up Thunderbolt climbed steadily. The altimeter read 3,000, 3,500, 4,000, 4,500. Godfrey sweated. He was well up in the stuff now, and he knew it extended above him to approximately 15,000 feet. The altimeter gained feet, but more slowly. Then the altimeter stopped registering gains.

Godfrey worried about airspeed, which began to increase. The compass varied back and forth. He looked at the altimeter again. The hand was moving down . . . he was losing altitude. Once again desperate and shaky, Godfrey pulled back on the stick to gain altitude. Nothing happened . . . he pulled back harder.

The altimeter recorded faster descent. He was the victim of vertigo again. Trying wildly to figure out the angle of his aircraft, Godfrey kept losing altitude . . . 3,000, 2,500, 2,000. Out of the cloud—and there it was! The ground was coming straight up for him!

He pulled the stick back as hard as he could, pulling up the low wing at the same time. It was like dive-bombing practice . . . but the question was whether he could pull out in time. The G-suit pumped and things turned gray. He pulled back harder. Still the ground passed behind slowly. He was having trouble coming out. But the trees were moving to the rear. The nose was coming up.

Godfrey whistled over a forest at 400 m.p.h., so close he couldn't have jumped. It was less than a hundred feet this time. It was a third nerve-cracking pull-out, with death standing by. Cockpit shot up, shaking, physically slipping now, Godfrey stayed on top of the trees. He would make a run for it hedge-hopping. He corrected his course. Then there was a burst of flak, off to one side! This time Godfrey didn't let it turn him back. If they hit him, they hit him. He pushed the throttle forward, flew through the fire. The small flak resembled roman-candle balls, or golf balls, leaving tracers.

Godfrey was through it. For fifteen or twenty minutes he flew due west. Small stuff came up at him again. Through it again. He was surely near the coast of the North Sea. But where was it? Every minute seemed an hour. Still the coastline didn't appear. The red-nosed, well-holed Thunderbolt continued on, on the deck, due west.

After what Godfrey estimated as twenty minutes, a dark horizon ahead revealed the North Sea. It was only minutes away. Godfrey was so low he hadn't seen it earlier. The clouds were still just above, at 2,000 feet, now sometimes 1,500, lowering slightly ahead, over the water.

Reggie's Reply flashed over Holland's western shores. Godfrey lowered the nose. From approximately a hundred feet he went to five. He was hugging the water below, in which he could last only minutes if he splashed.

Water spouts appeared just ahead! Coastal flak towers were lining him up. If they hit too close ahead, they would knock him down. The spouts were big ones, made by 88's. Godfrey had to get off the deck.

A sharp tug at the stick sent the red-nosed fighter skyward as splashes registered all around. If he could get away from these long-range guns, he would be out of the last danger from the Germans.

There was one way . . . into the cloud bank again! Three times Godfrey had spun out of the clouds. Three times he had barely pulled out. It was not easy to fly up into the lurking danger overhead another time. But it had to be.

Into the bottom, at about 1,500 feet, *Reggie's Reply* disappeared for the last time. The coastal guns could shoot only five or six miles. In a few moments he would drop down and get on top of the water again —out of range. He tried to fly by compass and altimeter. He was in trouble again. The altimeter hand began to fall. He didn't know which wing was down. He knew he was spiraling; yet he pulled back on the stick. He was helpless, frightened, reacting by instinct.

There it was! The water came up at him. He had shot out of the cloud bottom in another spiral spin. Hands shaking, confidence gone, Godfrey pulled back on the stick with all his remaining strength. The big nose of the P–47 slowly began to move ahead of the water below, then toward the sky. At a bare minimum—for the fourth time that day —Godfrey straightened out the big fighter on the deck, a few feet from the water. He corrected course to due west, and flew on. At last he had outrun the German guns.

Godfrey reasoned he could make it across the North Sea, but couldn't be sure. There was no radio to call Air-Sea Rescue should he go down. The thought of running out of gas began to prey on his mind. He checked gauges again and again. He leaned out the mixture, chopped the throttle.

Minutes ticked by, five, ten, twenty, twenty-five. Gasoline was good for fifteen or twenty minutes more, only. The coast of England must soon appear on the horizon ahead. Godfrey strained his neck, looking for land. He began to wonder if he had missed his course. Would he run out of gas over The Wash—north of the projecting land bulge where so many Allied airfields were located?

Then, a thin strip of color change appeared ahead. England! The Pratt and Whitney droned on. Godfrey eased off some of his tight-fitting gear, earphones, etc. No need for earphones when the radio didn't work. But he still faced the task of finding out where he was, where Debden was.

In a few minutes *Reggie's Reply* streaked over landfall at scarcely a hundred feet. Godfrey didn't recognize any landmarks. He was lost. He scanned the countryside—friendly countryside at least—searching for an airfield . . . any airfield. He had only minutes of fuel left.

Something black lay ahead. He headed for it, thought it might be a hangar. He made out a runway. It was grass, but even that looked good. Several black hangars and a grass runway . . . it was Downham Market, west of Norwich, in East Anglia, and close to The Wash.

He flipped over on a side and turned into a downwind leg, then an approach. No radio, no landing instructions . . . he was just coming down. He flipped the flap lever. Flaps whined down. He lowered landing gear. Without an airspeed indicator, he made a power approach and came in hot.

The grass came closer and closer. It roared past under his wings. Thump! The landing gear held firm. He was rolling fast. He chopped the throttle, stood on the brakes. Ahead, as he lost momentum, he saw a little brown and gray R.A.F. tower; it was the operations tower, on the right of the runway.

He continued down to it, drew abreast, turned off the runway and cut the engine. He pulled the canopy back, jerked off his mask and helmet. Then he unstrapped, pulled up and over the side, and stepped on the wing. He slumped to the ground, leaned on the spattered fighter.

The R.A.F. operations officer ran out to see what he could do. As he approached, Godfrey, holding on to his plane, emptied his stomach, and pleaded: "Have you got anything to quiet me down?"

"Some Irish whiskey. . . ."

Godfrey had a tumblerful. He sat down . . . for half an hour. The R.A.F. officer asked few questions. He was a veteran. Slowly Godfrey collected his wits. The drink killed some of the tension. Another thirty minutes passed, Godfrey sitting still, resting, thinking.

Now his thoughts returned to Debden. Maybe he'd fly back. He looked over *Reggie's Reply*. Holes in the wing, in the cockpit, but none in the engine. And the controls worked. The R.A.F. had filled his tanks. He decided he would fly home—it was a twenty-minute flight. He didn't want *Reggie's Reply* to be left at an R.A.F. field—from which it might never return.

He told the R.A.F. lads he was going home, thanked them for the drink. They cleared him for take-off. With no belly tank, and little ammunition, he would be light. Take-off would be easy. So, after more than an hour, *Reggie's Reply* lifted off the runway. His gear retracted without a hitch.

Twenty minutes later, never having flown over 1,000 or 1,500 feet, Godfrey eyed Debden. He passed over the field and wiggled his wings. Below they got the signal. Business stopped and Horseback Purple Two was cleared to land. With no airspeed indicator, Godfrey came in hot again. If flying speed is lost in a landing attempt, the aircraft flips over in the first stage of a spin and goes straight in.

He thumped down, applied brakes, turned off on the taxiway. He pulled back the canopy and headed for the revetment he had left at

12:38. Crew Chief Krantz had given up hope . . . but somehow he was staying at the revetment . . . waiting.

Godfrey taxied closer and closer. Krantz was standing up, trying to see if the Thunderbolt that landed was his. He recognized *Reggie's Reply* and ran toward the injured machine. He waved to Godfrey, grinning. Godfrey taxied in, cut the engine and climbed out. Non-coms rushed over from other revetments, from all directions. A truck sped out to pick him up. There were questions and wild shouts. Godfrey heard little. He said a few words to Krantz, shook hands, and climbed into the truck. They watched him drive away.

At squadron headquarters the truck stopped. Godfrey crawled out. He walked into the ready room. Eyes popped. The intelligence officer wanted to question him . . . obviously surprised. Godfrey answered his questions. The I.O. gave him another drink. He took it.

Wearily he climbed aboard another truck and headed for the mess hall. He thought he should eat. As he walked into the mess hall, Colonel Peterson caught sight of him and came over at once. He congratulated him on his aggressiveness, but told him sternly that leaving the squadron and the bombers was not the thing to do.

He was there to fight, Godfrey replied. If he saw something and didn't take advantage of it, the advantage might be lost. Peterson heard him out. He knew the bombers had gotten through. Losses had been light, Münster successfully bombed, and Godfrey had shot down one ME–109 and damaged another. Peterson decided not to finish his reprimand. Instead, he offered to buy Godfrey a drink.

December 22, 1943 had been a long day. It had been the most memorable of all combat days for John T. Godfrey, even though he would score thirty-six kills before the war was over.

And though he wound up his fighting career as one of the A.A.F.'s highest-scoring aces, wearing the Distinguished Flying Cross with eight clusters; the Silver Star, one cluster; the Air Medal, four clusters; and many other awards and medals, never again did death ride beside him in the cockpit so long on a single mission.

PART *3*

SUPERIORITY AND VICTORY

8 *First Strike at Berlin*

MARCH 6, 1944:

First Lieutenant ROBERT S. JOHNSON

WHEN Adolf Hitler or-
dered Reichsmarschall Hermann Goering to send the
previously unbeaten Luft-
waffe into an all-out assault
against England in the summer of 1940, little did he
realize this was the first
round in an aerial struggle
which would eventually
leave Berlin, and the rest of
Germany's cities, in heaps
of rubble.

The Luftwaffe seemed in-
vincible. It had been tempered in the Spanish Civil War, had destroyed
the Polish Air Force in a couple of weeks, and had paved the way for
the stunning Nazi victory over France and the low countries in May
and June the following year.

Flushed with victory, only the Royal Air Force remaining between
a German invasion of England and complete triumph over his foes,
Hitler was confident the Luftwaffe would rise to the occasion and
establish for Germany aerial supremacy over the skies of England and
the English Channel—a prerequisite for Operation Sea Lion, the
Wehrmacht's invasion of England.

In the first days of the all-out Luftwaffe offensive the Germans em-

147

ployed the strategy of attacking R.A.F. airfields and the aircraft industry and enemy planes wherever they could be found. Although the R.A.F. put up a stiffer defense than Goering had expected, the Luftwaffe inflicted considerable damage and the R.A.F. was strained to the breaking point.

The Germans then made a momentous decision. They switched the strategic objective of their aerial assault to terrorization of the British people, and began heavy bombing attacks on London and the larger cities. It was a fatal error, and whatever chance the Luftwaffe had of winning supremacy in the skies over England disappeared. The experts differ as to what the outcome would have been had the Germans continued their attack on the aircraft industry and the R.A.F., but most agree the margin would have been a close one indeed had the R.A.F. emerged victorious.

The first great aerial climax of the war, then, came in the late summer and early fall of 1940, when fighters of the Royal Air Force, their backs to the wall, began to exact a toll of German bombers even the Luftwaffe could not endure. The Luftwaffe reduced the scope of its attack, turned largely to night bombing, where spectacular successes were achieved on some occasions—as in the great incendiary raid on London late in the year. But these attacks did not crush the R.A.F.—the principal objective of the Luftwaffe's assault when it began in earnest, August 13.

The great German raids of 1940 on London and other British cities spread a wave of horror throughout the civilized world, but they were but an omen of the terror that was to come to Germany late in the war —from the air. This ominous clue to the future was recognized by few in 1940. Germany then faced no war on two fronts. German airfields were located less than an hour's flight from London—on the coast of France. Berlin seemed relatively safe from major attack. The distance from British fields to the Nazi capital was great and no fighter in the world had the range to escort bombers that far.

But by the latter half of 1943 Allied bombers were heavily assaulting Germany. The Luftwaffe's fighters then aimed for a victory similar to that of the R.A.F. in 1940, and in the summer of 1943 German fighter strength stiffened considerably. When a large, four-engined force of U.S. bombers attacked the Messerschmitt works at Regensburg and Schweinfurt, the Luftwaffe threw approximately 300 interceptors against the bombers, shot down 60 and damaged 138, with a loss of only 25 fighters.

The Eighth Air Force attacked Schweinfurt again on October 14.

Although fewer bombers were dispatched, and a tighter defense formation attempted, German fighter strength had increased and 60 bombers were shot down and 140 damaged—out of a raiding force of 229! (291 bombers took off for Schweinfurt and 229 actually attacked.) Thirty-five German fighters were destroyed.

Such losses created a problem in the U.S. command. The effect on bomber crew morale was not unnoticeable. The Luftwaffe was rapidly increasing the strength of its day fighter force to counter the American threat, and this was responsible for increasing U.S. losses. In the six months from April, 1943, to October, for example, day fighter strength in Germany rose from approximately 152 to 765, and in France from approximately 307 to 505.

The Luftwaffe challenge had to be answered. It was countered in several ways. The Eighth Air Force had already requested long-range fighters, so the bombers could be escorted all the way to distant targets. The need now became obviously urgent.

An immediate relief for the bomber crews was a switch from precision bombing to area bombing, as practiced by the British. The weather actually made area bombing a logical step as it worsened in the autumn of 1943. In November, flying conditions were the worst in years.

The R.A.F. can be said to have opened the extermination campaign against Hitler's capital on the night of November 18–19, 1943. On that historic night the British sent 444 heavy bombers over Berlin. The Eighth U.S. Army Air Force had already joined in the Strategic offensive against the enemy. On July 4, 1942, the first American raid on the Continent was made by six Boston light bombers, which attacked Luftwaffe fields in Holland. The next month, on August 17, eighteen B–17 heavy bombers staged their first daylight attack on the Continent, bombing targets at Rouen-St. Otterville.

The A.A.F. made its debut over Germany itself on January 27, 1943, when a force of B–17's bombed Wilhelmshaven. As its bomber strength and fighter escort forces grew, the Eighth Air Force extended its daylight bombings deeper into Germany. Fifteen months after the first A.A.F. bombing of Germany and four months after the first large-scale R.A.F. raid on Berlin (November, 1943) a small force of thirty B–17's bombed Berlin. Two days later, on March 6, 1944, the first large-scale American attack on the Nazi capital was carried out. On this day 660 heavy bombers dropped 1,600 tons of bombs on Berlin in broad daylight, protected by long-range U.S. fighters, which now made the bombing of Berlin feasible.

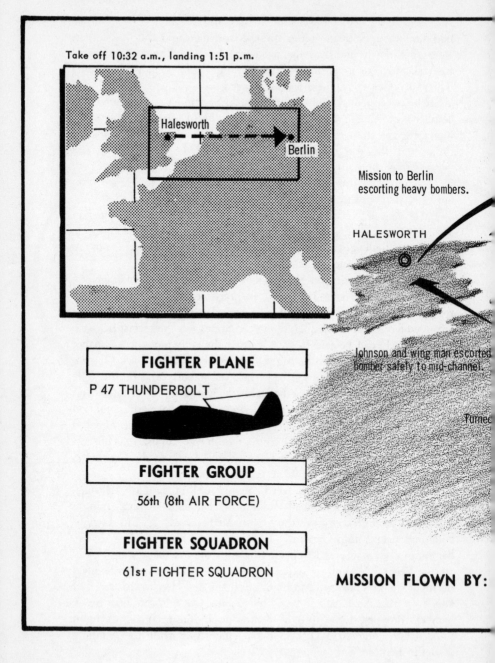

Take off 10:32 a.m., landing 1:51 p.m.

Halesworth

Berlin

Mission to Berlin
escorting heavy bombers.

HALESWORTH

Johnson and wing man escorted
bomber safely to mid-channel.

Turned

FIGHTER PLANE

P 47 THUNDERBOLT

FIGHTER GROUP

56th (8th AIR FORCE)

FIGHTER SQUADRON

61st FIGHTER SQUADRON

MISSION FLOWN BY:

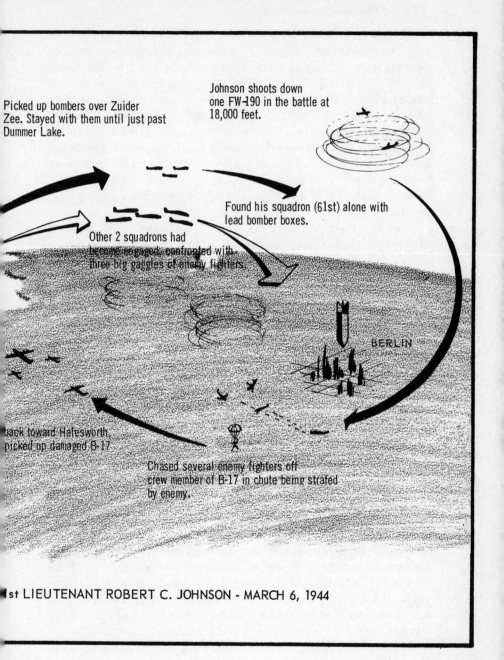

Picked up bombers over Zuider
Zee. Stayed with them until just past
Dummer Lake.

Johnson shoots down
one FW-190 in the battle at
18,000 feet.

Found his squadron (61st) alone with
lead bomber boxes.

Other 2 squadrons had
become engaged, confronted with
three big gaggles of enemy fighters.

BERLIN

back toward Halesworth,
picked up damaged B-17

Chased several enemy fighters off
crew member of B-17 in chute being strafed
by enemy.

1st LIEUTENANT ROBERT C. JOHNSON - MARCH 6, 1944

The Luftwaffe's reaction to the assault on Berlin was naturally vigorous. The threat of extermination soon became a grim reality to Germans in 1944 as the R.A.F. struck at night, to be followed by the A.A.F. next day, even as Berlin attempted to dig out and put out the fires caused by the raid the night before. A year after the first American raid on Berlin, in March of 1945, notwithstanding record German fighter production in 1944, the "round-the-clock" offensive against the German capital reached its peak. In this fiery climax the Eighth Air Force dispatched more than 1,200 heavy bombers on its Berlin missions —and, worst of all for the Germans, this great bomber assemblage was escorted all the way to the target and back by more than 800 long-range fighters.

From the night of November 18–19, 1943, then, until April 10, 1945—when the last American daylight raid on Berlin was carried out—the Battle of Berlin was waged with ferocity and persistence. On some of the raids the A.A.F. lost hundreds of airmen in the space of a few hours to determined German fighters. The most costly year, in over-all losses, was, of course, 1944, and the worst part of 1944 the early months, when Allied fighter strength available for these long Berlin missions was not what it came to be in the last six months of the war.

Losses on the first large-scale American attack on Berlin were very heavy, about which more will be learned in this chapter. But the A.A.F. was only beginning. The German capital was bombed five times in the opening week of the American offensive. Two days after the first heavy attack, on March 8, 1944, another massive raid was carried out by Eighth. On this raid the A.A.F. lost 54 aircraft and 396 airmen, an indication of the bitterness of the Battle of Berlin in its early days. But losses would have been higher had not long-range U.S. fighters provided escort all the way.

As the campaign wore on, the Fifteenth Air Force in Italy participated in the bombing of Berlin and relative losses decreased as American fighter forces became stronger and more and more fighters became long-range types. The R.A.F. also increased the tempo of its assault, and losses in its early large-scale attacks are a grim indication of the savage fight which raged in German skies on the route to Berlin at night. For example, on the night of March 24, 1944, the R.A.F. admitted the loss of 73 aircraft on a Berlin raid—a loss comparable to the destruction of a battalion of troops in a few hours!

The Battle of Berlin, then, was one of the greatest aerial battles of the war, extending over a period of eighteen months, at a cost of thousands of American, German, and British airmen, and scores of thousands of German civilians on the ground below. Pilots and crews who went on missions to "Big B," as the German capital was called by Allied airmen, flew death-laden skies, withstood the ordeal of heavy flak, cannon, rocket, and machine-gun fire from Luftwaffe fighters, which streaked in from all sides, and the sometimes grim task of limping home over long stretches of hostile territory and the vast, dark wastes of the North Sea.

In 1928, at one of the early air shows at Post Field, Oklahoma, eight-year-old Robert S. Johnson watched spellbound as three Army pilots —the Three Musketeers of World War I—did their stuff. Right there and then Bob Johnson set his heart on becoming an Army pilot. Sixteen years later, on March 6, 1944, Johnson was leading a Group of U.S.A.A.F. fighters on the first heavy American bombing of Berlin. In the meantime he had grown up, joined the Army as a cadet, won his wings, reported to a combat area and become a leading fighter ace. The Three Musketeers had done a good job.

Bob Johnson was the first American pilot in Europe to equal the aerial combat record of Captain Eddie Rickenbacker of World War I, who ended the war with twenty-five confirmed victories. (Rickenbacker undoubtedly scored additional kills not credited to him. His total also includes four balloons.) In the Pacific, Major Richard I. Bong beat Johnson by a nose to the distinction of being the first U.S. pilot in World War II to surpass Captain Eddie's record. The ace of aces for his country in World War II, Bong was credited with forty kills at the end of the war. But he was not to live long afterward. In the year following Japan's surrender he met death in a jet fighter in California. Johnson, however, finished his combat before the Allies invaded France, returned to the United States, and is still in aviation—with Republic, at Farmingdale, New York.

Bob Johnson scored twenty-eight kills, all in the air, from June 13, 1943, to May 8, 1944—less than a year. He was the fourth-ranking of all American aces in aerial combat, and the second-highest scorer in the air in the European theater. His feat in downing twenty-eight German aircraft in less than eleven months stands alone in the history of operations of the A.A.F. in Europe.

Curiously, Johnson's aggressiveness in combat involved him in deep trouble on the day of his first kill, and probably prevented his victory total from being higher than it was. The incident which was to affect his career occurred during a mission on June 13, 1943. Flying with the 61st Squadron of the famous 56th Fighter Group, Johnson spotted twelve Focke-Wulf 190's below his squadron. When the squadron didn't go after the enemy fighters, Johnson bade the others a hasty farewell and dived on the unsuspecting bandits, shooting one down in an audacious surprise attack. The legendary leader of the Wolfpack (56th Group), Colonel Hubert Zemke, adopted the same tactics and shot down two of the enemy fighters.

Johnson was reprimanded for leaving his squadron when he returned to base after the mission. He was so sternly chastised he dared not venture out of formation for a long time thereafter, although he disagreed violently with the strategy being followed at that time by most A.A.F. squadrons—in general, waiting to be attacked. Some time after his initial kill, having missed several golden opportunities to attack, Johnson was caught from behind maintaining formation and almost shot down.

Finally, tactics were changed, though over objections from high-ranking air officers in the theater. Major General O. A. Anderson at last won approval for his proposal of more aggressive escort tactics for the Eighth. Thereafter, Johnson would never again sit still waiting to be attacked. And, realizing Johnson's philosophy of battle had been a good one, his comrades who had dubbed him, tentatively, as an over-enthusiastic and unpredictable pilot began to extend their apologies. Henceforth the squadron went after the Jerries with gusto, and more victories.

Ironically, Johnson could never qualify for fighters in gunnery—in which he so obviously excelled in combat. Beginning Texas A. & M. in the fall of 1941, Johnson thought better of it and joined the Army as an aviation cadet November 11 of that year—twenty-three years to the day after Captain Eddie Rickenbacker and other American pilots in France celebrated the end of the war in Europe by shooting off rockets and burning gasoline on their field behind the front lines in France.

He completed flying training successfully, except gunnery, which necessitated his designation as a bomber pilot, and final training in twin-engine aircraft.

Six months after Pearl Harbor, however, he managed to be assigned to 56th Fighter Group—no one was worrying about his gunnery then—and in less than a year's time found himself in England preparing for combat with the formidable Luftwaffe.

He arrived in England with the 56th Group on January 13, 1943. Technically, the group began operations that winter, but because the 56th had to await the arrival of a full complement of aircraft, most 56th pilots had to wait until spring to begin operations.

In April, having requested assignment to the forty-eighth position in the group (tail-end Charlie of the last of the three squadrons), Johnson flew his first combat mission. Six months later he was an ace. By March 6, 1944—the date of the first heavy U.S. daylight bombing of Berlin—Johnson was one of the war's leading aces, leading the 61st Squadron of Colonel Zemke's famed Wolfpack, which was protecting the first three boxes of heavy bombers on that historic attack.

Every American pilot in the Eighth Air Force knew that sooner or later the Eighth would join in the attack on Germany's capital. Therefore, after fourteen months of raids on other targets inside Germany, when U.S. bombers and fighters were ordered to fly to Berlin on March 3, 1944, pilots had been anticipating the event. On that day, however, the bombers were forced to turn back because of the weather.

A small force of bombers blazed the way the very next day, March 4, without encountering unusual difficulties. Late on March 5 orders were prepared directing 800 heavy bombers to attack Berlin next day. Naturally, receipt of the orders at bomber and fighter bases around England caused a ripple of excitement and anticipation. The United States had been at war with Hitler's Germany for two years and three months. The Eighth had been operating from England for more than a year and a half. It was time Hitler's capital felt the weight of the Eighth's bombs, and looked up at the awesome sight of four-engined American bombers unloading lethal cargoes over Germany's greatest city in broad daylight—the city Luftwaffe Chief Hermann Goering had said would never suffer such an ordeal.

But in March, 1944, the task of providing fighter escort for heavy bombers on such a long mission was formidable. Not many of the new long-range fighters, which made the Berlin attacks possible, were yet available. There were P–38's and P–47's, for the most part, which were not able to fly in and out, all the way, and do battle with the enemy also. Thus a schedule had to be worked out for some of the fighters to escort the bombers a certain distance, then be relieved by other fighters, a partial relay process.

The 56th Group, which emerged from the war the second highest-scoring outfit in the Eighth Air Force, flew P–47's throughout the war;

therefore was equipped with Thunderbolts in March, 1944. The 4th Group—56th's greatest rival, which finally came out with top honors by a hair (in the victories race), had just been equipped with P–51's. Both 56th and 4th were among the many fighter groups assigned escort duties for the Berlin attack. The Thunderbolts of 56th would split into two groups for the mission, thirty-five fighters making up each group. The understrength groups would rendezvous with the bombers as they approached Germany, and provide penetration support.

At this time the Nazis occupied the Low Countries and France. Every pilot knew, when he took off on an escort mission and crossed into enemy-occupied territory, that an hour or two later he would have to fly back across the North Sea to England. If he was forced down in France, Holland, or Belgium, short on fuel, it meant capture by the Germans. The enemy, then, was not the only worry of fighter pilots. Each sweated out his fuel supply on the longer missions, especially pilots in P–38's and P–47's.

On the night of March 5 pilots of the 56th were alerted and told a major mission would be flown next morning. Since the number of pilots in the group was not what it was later in the war, 56th fliers knew most of them would participate. With that knowledge, and the forecast that tomorrow's weather would be good, the group's fighter pilots hit their sacks at Halesworth early. Unlike bomber pilots, and crewmen, many did not learn they were going to Berlin until next day.

At 4:30 A.M. next morning, the drone of heavy bombers in the winter darkness above roused Lieutenant Bob Johnson from his slumber. Dressing in O.D. pants and shirt, silk scarf and leather jacket, and carefully checking the knife he carried in his right boot, Johnson made off into the blackness for a Nissen hut mess hall. There he grabbed a few slices of bread, toasted them against the side of the iron stove in the center of the hut, and drank his coffee. In a few minutes he departed for the operations room of 61st Squadron, where pilots checked the position they would fly, and also their flying equipment. They still did not know their destination for the day.

A jeep carried 61st Squadron to group briefing—where the answers to a lot of questions awaited pilots. A curtain hid the big wall map from view. After pilots from all three squadrons had taken their seats, the group intelligence officer stepped up on the platform at the front of the room and pulled the curtain string.

Pilots let out a howl. The ribbon marking the route stretched from

England to . . . Berlin. Amid whispers and excitement, the I.O. briefed the group on flak, expected enemy resistance, and escape procedures. The weather officer followed—explaining conditions pilots would encounter on the way into Germany and back.

The three squadrons of the 56th were 61st, 62nd, and 63rd. Commanding officer of the 61st, Johnson's squadron, was one of the war's great aces, Francis S. Gabreski, whose most memorable mission appeared in Chapter 6. Johnson was one of 61st's flight leaders, destined to emerge from the war in Europe second to Gabreski in the number of confirmed aerial victories. The 61st, then, was an outstanding squadron.

The group commander, Colonel Hubert Zemke—one of the greatest of the war—completed the briefing. He announced that 56th would divide into two groups. He would lead A Group and Johnson would lead B. The group's executive officer, Lieutenant Colonel Dave Schilling —who was to become the fourth-ranking American ace in the E.T.O.— was not scheduled to fly, nor was Gabreski.

Johnson, then, was to have charge of thirty-five P–47's, half the group's total effort. Take-off was set for 10:32 A.M. If the group encountered no opposition from the Luftwaffe during escort duty, it was to descend to low altitude on the way home and strafe targets of opportunity. After a few last words from Zemke, gripes that the mission was either too short or too long, and exclamations—as pilots eyed the long route-marker ribbon stretching to Berlin and back—group briefing ended.

Pilots and officers of the 61st climbed on their jeep and headed back to the squadron building. After a short ride the jeep arrived and the daily race for the six-holer was on. Pilots leaped from the still-rolling jeep. The driver won last honors in this morning ritual, since he had to park the jeep. Fighter pilots on combat duty were never bothered by irregularity.

At squadron briefing Johnson made his talk brief. He merely confirmed the order of flight, outlined a few general rules for close-in and combat formation, and warned his men to be on the alert. Pilots then went to their lockers and pulled out parachutes, Mae Wests, helmets, etc. Johnson took with him one glove—for his left hand, which would rest on the metal throttle handle much of the time in flight. In March over England and Germany temperatures above 20,000 feet were below zero, and while the cockpit was partially heated, it nevertheless became quite cold at higher altitudes. Pilots lounged around and the morning grew late.

It was a few minutes after ten. Johnson wished his men luck and they walked out to their aircraft. In a couple of minutes he stepped up on the wing of a blunt, red-nosed Thunderbolt, the words *All Hell* painted on its side. Before the day was over Keyworth Red Leader— that was Johnson's code identification—and *All Hell* would weather an experience approximating the aircraft's name.

The fat fighter kicked over a few minutes before 10:32, and after Johnson listened to a few words of encouragement from his crew chief, the radial-engined Thunderbolt, a 150-gallon extra tank slung beneath its belly, rolled away toward the end of a black-surfaced runway on which 61st would take off. Without a hitch, the other fighters of B Group fell in behind Keyworth Red Leader and followed him toward the runway.

Half the fighters lined up on the end of one of Halesworth's two runways and the other half on the other. At 10:32 A.M. Keyworth Red Leader and his wing man roared off toward the far end of one runway. As soon as they passed the intersection where the runways crossed, two fighters on the other runway began to roll. In a few minutes the thirty-five P–47's were all safely off, turning in a wide left turn, and rolling out on course, almost due east. Colonel Zemke's thirty-five fighters—the rest of 56th—were only a short distance away.

The few clouds which covered England were easily topped in a shallow climb. To conserve fuel, power was set at 1,800 r.p.m. and 29 inches of mercury. Johnson looked behind and around; his P–47's were in perfect formation, closed in properly behind. He was leading three understrength squadrons, totaling thirty-five fighters in all. Normally, a squadron sent out sixteen planes on a mission.

Making better than 150 m.p.h. in the gradual climb, the group rapidly left the English countryside behind. The Thunderbolts roared on upward . . . out over the North Sea and toward the coast of Holland. Altimeters registered steady gains . . . 6,000, 7,000, 8,000 feet. Now superchargers were cut in and pilots switched to belly tanks, to use up that gasoline first, since the extra tanks would have to be jettisoned quickly in case of imminent action.

Altitude registers 10,000, 11,000, 12,000 feet. Below nothing can be seen but a vast expanse of water. The width of the North Sea at this latitude is over a hundred miles. It is a cold dip for the pilot who is forced down, either going or coming. The blunt-nosed fighters slice upward into the sky . . . pilots check their gun switches . . . begin

For as far as the camera can see, sixty-eight B-17's and B-24's over Germany on the way to their target. (Air Force Photo)

to look for the outline ahead which will reveal landfall in—the Dutch coast. The altimeter needle reads 15,000, 16,000, 17,000 feet. The coast of Holland can't be far away. Johnson orders the three squadrons to spread out into combat formation.

The Thunderbolts wing out wide, come into almost line-abreast formation, continue slanting upward. Altitude reaches 23,000, 24,000, 25,000 feet. Now the coast of Holland is visible ahead. Each pilot flips on his gunsight switch. The yellow circle on the sighting glass appears. Altitude 27,000 feet.

The group crosses landfall in. The landscape below is blurred by a general haze, but the sky is cloudless. The group passes over Walcheren Island . . . and then in above the Zuider Zee. Up ahead the lead boxes of bombers come into view, clusters of small outlines, more than thirty bombers to a box—B-17 Flying Fortresses. Johnson points the group toward the big friends. Of the three squadrons, the 63rd leads the way, Johnson's 61st is slightly back, and Lieutenant Mike Quirk's P-47's are next—the 62nd.

The dots ahead grow larger. As the fighters approach the bomber boxes, the squadrons split and curve into position around the heavies. One squadron leader takes his eight P-47's directly above the bombers, Johnson banks left and eases up on that side, and Quirk guards the right flank. They stay several thousand feet out from their big friends —begin to S-turn, to keep from running away from the slower bombers.

The spearhead of the aerial armada streaks on through the Dutch sky at 24,000-25,000 feet—one squadron of fighters above. For a short time the silent procession drones on inland. Then it reaches the vicinity of Zwolle. Heavy flak bursts dot the sky. The fighters maneuver radically to be on the safe side—but the guns below are aiming at the bombers, where the bomb load, on its way to Berlin, is carried.

A group of unidentified specks ahead . . . pilots tense. The bogies are small—fighters. The 56th readies for a fight. On come the bogies . . . at the 56th's altitude. As they approach nearer, Johnson leans into a slight left turn to meet them head on. They come closer and closer . . . now their blunt noses are identifiable . . . they are coming right through the 56th's formation! At the last moment, with pilots' fingers itching near trigger buttons, someone calls in identification— the bogies are P-47's! They fly right through the 56th. It is a new group. It is a dangerous situation . . . but the inexperienced pilots get away with it . . . they flash on by and back . . . no one slips and fires at his comrades.

For a few minutes the flight continues uneventfully . . . then bogies
are spotted off the side. Once again escorting fighter pilots tighten up
. . . the bogies come on, closer . . . blunt noses! FW–190's or P–47's?
On and on come the fighters . . . now they are almost on 56th. "Those
same boys," someone yells over the radio . . . and once again the
Wolfpack holds its fire, and curses. The orderly flight continues. The
sky is clear. The bombers leave no vapor trails.

Then, ahead, lies the German border. At this moment Lieutenant
Quirk's eight P–47's break hard right. They go into a dive . . . Johnson looks hard but can see nothing. Johnson maintains position. Quirk's
fighters rapidly disappear below. Then, on the radio, Johnson hears
shouts from Quirk's men . . . they are in a fight! They spotted a
gaggle of ME–109's climbing up for an attack. They jumped the enemy
fighters and are having quite a battle. Quirk estimates the gaggle at
about thirty fighters.

Johnson calls and asks the location of the dogfight. No answer. He
calls again, hoping to get into the fight. Quirk is too busy . . . and
maybe the 62nd wants the bandits for themselves. Pilots in the two
squadrons with the bombers envy 62nd. Johnson pulls wide, to the
left, to search a little wider. The other squadron curves right—to the
south—for the same purpose. But neither finds the enemy fighters.
Johnson curves back in toward the bombers as the stream is approaching Dümmer Lake—an unmistakable landmark on the route to Berlin.
The other squadron is still to the south, so Johnson comes in close to
the bombers and flies over the boxes. As he reaches the front box, he
leans into a left turn. The three boxes of bombers 56th is protecting
fly silently and majestically on—dozens of Forts in each closely packed
box.

The blunt nose of *All Hell* heels around toward the north . . . and up
ahead Johnson spots suspicious specks. It's 11:40 A.M. They're closing
on a southerly course. Johnson watches as they come closer. They
must be the same P–47's that have already flown through the 56th twice.
He speaks over the radio to seven 47's behind him: "Watch these
monkeys ahead." At the same time he realizes the oncoming gaggle
isn't P–47's. Bandits! Into the mike he yells: "Hell, they're Focke-
Wulfs!" Thunderbolts drop tanks, spread out further and wheel out
into position to turn in on the enemy fighters as they come through.
The Germans are heading for the leading box of bombers. Johnson
is so close to the bombers there's no chance to stop the enemy fighters
before they reach their objective.

The gaggle now is fast approaching—FW–190's and ME–109's clearly identifiable. Johnson times his maneuver to the second. As the Germans reach his vicinity he swings into a sharp right turn to pull in behind . . . throttle wide open. The fighters flash together at 600 m.p.h. In a second they are past the Thunderbolts and boring in on the lead box of bombers. Johnson pulls a tight right turn and is on the tail of the bandits almost immediately. The bandits ignore the U.S. fighters and go for the bombers. Now the big friends get set for the shock of attack . . . guns of each Fortress train on the German fighters as the March air is filled with cries of warning and the excitement of combat.

Distance is so close between the German and American fighters it's impossible for Fortress gunners to distinguish between friend and foe. Johnson watches the enemy ahead draw into range . . . he's overtaking them. To his left he catches sight of another gaggle, slightly east. In a split second, his eyes pick out a third gaggle above. Each enemy formation contains thirty to forty fighters!

Johnson's eight Thunderbolts, all that are available at the moment to protect the bombers, close the range behind the gaggle in front. But the Germans are already on the bombers. The sky lights up. Enemy twenty-millimeter shells throw white bursts into the bomber formation. Rockets leave a zigzag smoke trail as they streak into the heavies. The B–17's, ten fifty-calibres to a bomber, open up with all guns. The Germans fly right in. The Thunderbolts follow . . . too late to turn off now. The bombers shoot at friend and foe. The P–47's open up on the Germans ahead and German thirty-calibre machine guns and cannon and rockets clutter up the air. The fighters flash through the formation, under and over and by the sides of the bombers.

Parachutes begin to dot the sky. The action is so fast, so deadly, it's hard to comprehend. The other two gaggles of German fighters have picked the second and third boxes of bombers and bore in . . . splashing fire and shell through the formations, unhindered by defending fighters. The 61st Squadron, right behind the enemy gaggle, passes through and by the lead bomber box and down and out, hanging on and firing away. Johnson sees scores of parachutes. One B–17 is cut in half . . . the tail assembly glides off in one direction . . . the rest of the fuselage and wing in another. Ten men were safe and sound in the Fortress seconds ago. Other B–17's drop back out of the lead box, trailing smoke, crippled. Several plunge earthward, trailing a black column of smoke. Now a hundred parachutes fill the sky!

Several enemy fighters smash into the big bombers. A huge flash of fire follows and both planes go down. It is a savage encounter. A number of enemy fighters are burning. The Americans are taking a heavy toll. Johnson closes four FW–190's at about 18,000 feet. He slams throttle the rest of the way forward, approaching from five o'clock. So far he hasn't scored a kill and planes are falling all around him.

The German Focke-Wulf 190. (Air Force Photo)

The FW–190's draw closer into range, Johnson at full throttle. He watches the four 190's closely—they're making good speed, in two elements—ahead, slightly left. He looks through his sight ring—one of the bandits is now almost filling it.

Just as *All Hell* flashes into range behind the Germans see the danger to their rear. The four FW–190's break sharply up, in pairs. But Johnson is opening fire. The Thunderbolt roars and shakes . . . and the 190 directly ahead takes hits.

Johnson pulls stick back and hangs on behind the climbing enemy. *All Hell* spits tracers and shells, which converge on the gray-black, radial-engined fighter. Johnson's fire is accurate and inflicts fatal damage.

The enemy's engine is hit . . . his propeller seems to spin slower. Pieces of the FW–190 fly backward. Something moves on top . . .

suddenly the enemy pilot leaves the cockpit. He jumps at good speed
and falls rapidly. Then, a chute opens below. The FW–190 plunges
earthward.

Enemy fighters are scattered all over the area, in singles, in pairs
and larger groups. Johnson, flushed with victory, spots a lone bandit
and banks sharply to come in on his tail. He looks back to check
his wing man—a new pilot—is shocked to see a German squarely on
his tail. He racks around and turns into the enemy as fast as he can,
breaking up the attack. Now some thirty falling planes fill the sky.

Again he sees a target ahead. He maneuvers for position, but remembers to check his wing man. Right behind him is another German
fighter. For the second time Johnson breaks off his attack and turns
sharply to make a pass at the enemy fighter. In all his combat he has
never lost a wing man. The bandit breaks away as Johnson threatens
to close his tail.

The scene up above is bedlam. Burning aircraft and hundreds of
parachutes dot every corner of the sky. Johnson has never seen so many
burning aircraft and chutes. He notices another fighter curving in behind his wing man, and, almost by habit now, stands on a wing and
turns into the enemy. He succeeds, for the third time, in driving him
off. It's a strange battle. By now he could have scored several victories
had he not bothered about protecting his wing man.

Up above Johnson sees two FW–190's firing away. Four men in
parachutes dangle in front of the enemy fighters' guns. He yanks
the stick back and *All Hell* climbs at a sharp angle. He can see the
burning B–17 now, from which the Americans jumped. It's above him.
All Hell climbs toward the enemy fighters. As they prepare to make
another pass at the parachutists, Johnson—still out of range—opens
distracting fire. The tracers catch the attention of the enemy planes
. . . they drop their noses down toward the climbing P–47's to converge. Only Johnson and his wing man are left together. The other
six P–47's of 61st Squadron are scattered in every direction.

The two enemy fighters grow larger and larger as they approach at
great speed. Johnson sees the light flashes from their wing guns. He,
too, opens fire, but observes no hits. As they close, the Germans break to
Johnson's right and continue to dive. Johnson shoves stick forward and
hits right rudder and plunges after them, burning inside at the thought
of enemy fighters machine-gunning airmen in parachutes. For a moment
the Germans, with their greater diving speed, pull away, but then the

two heavier P–47's come on strong and Johnson can see the FW–190's are no longer gaining.

By now all four fighters are just a few thousand feet above the ground. They continue their steep dive . . . in the direction of Hanover, not far away. The distance begins to close. Airspeed climbs at a rapid clip . . . 325, 350, 375, 400, 425, 450. The two Thunderbolts are gaining. The German pilots realize they're being caught from behind. Without warning, they suddenly part . . . the enemy element leader's wing man turns sharply to the right. Two targets. Johnson must choose. He and his wing man stay with the enemy leader, the other German fighter gets away.

The distance is closing . . . and Johnson is almost in range. The FW–190, now leveling out, tries an old trick. Suddenly the thin dark exhaust smoke from his stacks disappears. Johnson's left hand races for the throttle, jerks it back. The enemy is cutting his engine to make the Thunderbolts overshoot, and zoom out in front of his guns. *All Hell* slows up . . . but still eases up on the German fighter . . . just about right. Now the 190 pilot stands on his left wing in a vertical turn. Johnson cuts tight behind him, cutting him off in the turn, not going too fast to stay in there on the enemy's tail, as the German pilot had planned. The cut-off turn brings Johnson into range. He presses the firing button. Eight fifties roar and shake *All Hell*. Tracers mark an aerial path to the German fighter. Johnson pulls the stick into his stomach and sees the silhouette of the low-winged enemy fighter pass through his gunsight ring from tail to nose . . . proof he's outturning his foe. His shells rake over the top of the enemy fighter, from tail to engine nacelle. For a second or two *All Hell* spits shells at the German at close range. Johnson is on top of his victim now and banks to the right, pulls up to come around for another pass. As soon as he gets another glance at his foe, turning to come in from behind again, Johnson notices the enemy fighter is diving. Already close to the ground after the first long dive, Johnson pushes stick forward and *All Hell* streaks after the fleeing German. This time the chase is short. The crippled enemy fighter can't make top speed. The Thunderbolt walks right up on him in the dive, easing up through the smoke stream and into point-blank range. The enemy fighter's wingspan fills the orange sight circle and Johnson fires again. Shells reach out to the German fighter. The 190 noses down, hit again. Now the earth is racing up, straight below. The enemy fighter doesn't pull out.

Suddenly Johnson sees an FW–190 on his wing man's tail. He hauls stick back and breaks off the chase, turns into the enemy fighter, drives him off.

Johnson is too low for comfort, and begins the long climb back to high altitude. His wing man is in position. He wonders if the 190 went straight in. In protecting his comrade, again, he lost sight of his foe at the critical moment. He can claim only a probable!

The two Thunderbolts slice upward through the clear sky and Johnson looks up in search of the bombers, and whatever action might be in progress. He sees nothing. Altimeter registers steady gains and the fighters soon find themselves back at altitude . . . 15,000, 16,000, 17,000 feet. Still climbing, he makes out bandits at two o'clock high. About six of them, FW–190's and ME–109's, are firing on a lone B–17. Johnson gives *All Hell* right stick and rudder and continues his climb . . . straight into the German fighters. His wing man sticks in position. Full throttle.

The distance closes rapidly and Johnson gets ready to open fire, coming up on their rear. The approaching fighters are now almost at the same altitude and Johnson puts his finger on the trigger. He lines up one of the bandits in his sight. Fire! His guns spit and *All Hell* shudders from the vibration. The Germans now break sharply left and go into a dive. Johnson rolls over to his right and starts down again, in another vertical chase following two 109's.

The enemy fighters have speed on the two P–47's and pull away. Johnson's two Thunderbolts keep them in sight and at full throttle rapidly increase speed. But Johnson knows he can't stay over Germany much longer at full throttle, with gasoline burning at a terrific rate. He has been taking on German fighters for a long time now, and his fuel supply is running low.

Still, he begins to gain gradually on the 109 directly ahead and decides to hang on a while longer. Slowly the enemy plane grows larger in his sight . . . speed building up in the roaring dive. Down and down they go, close to the deck again . . . and Johnson begins to approach firing range. Now, almost ready to close the enemy, he spots two other bandits approaching, just as he begins to slacken the angle of dive, following the nearest bandit ahead.

The distance to the target is great, but Johnson is in a hurry. He opens with *All Hell's* eight wing guns. Shells streak out, marked by the flight of tracers. The Thunderbolt shudders. But he must break off the encounter. The enemy fighters coming to the rescue are almost on him, and Johnson turns in their direction. They flash by, as the great speed of each pair of fighters brings them together in seconds. Johnson doesn't turn to take after them. Never can he remember having started so many attacks in one day, only to have to break off before attaining victory. Today the sky is full of Germans. He must start home without delay.

A glance at the enemy fighters shows they are pulling away to the east . . . they choose to fight again another day. Johnson is relieved. His ammunition is low, but fuel supply is his main problem. The North Sea ahead is quite wide when crossing it with limited fuel. Climbing once again, Johnson spots a flight of four P–47's not far away, heading west. He calls on the radio and identifies their marking; they're Keyworth Red Leader's second flight. They, too, have seen plenty of action. All six of the P–47's join up and head for England. Johnson orders each pilot to throttle back and use as little gas as possible.

One of the P–47's of the squadron is badly damaged. As they head west the pilot of the damaged Thunderbolt radios he can't make it. His engine has been hit and is through. Johnson tells him to bail out at 18,000 feet. But the pilot, Lieutenant Andrew B. Strauss, replies it's too cold at that altitude. He will go down to 5,000. The other pilots watch in sympathy, escort him down. He points his P–47's nose toward the deck for the last time, loses altitude rapidly. Then they hear him call —at 6,000 feet: "So long, you guys. I'm cutting off my radio, rolling over and dropping out." And he does.

Strauss's chute billows open and the stricken fighter spirals crazily down. His body swings back and forth, like a pendulum. Strauss can't arrest the motion. He drops closer and closer to the ground, still swinging back and forth, strikes the earth on the back of his neck and head. His comrades above circle and watch, hoping he will get up. He stands up, rubs his head and looks up. He sees his friends up where he was minutes before, who will soon be back at Halesworth. Then he puts his hands in his pockets and slowly walks away from the spot where he landed.

The rest of the 61st has to resume the flight home at once. Johnson points his growling fighter toward England. The others follow. The sky is now largely clear of German fighters. Johnson's Thunderbolts climb back to safe altitude and cross into Holland. Ahead they see a lone crippled Fortress, and provide an appreciated escort. Johnson won-

ders how many others won't come back this far. Soon they are out over
the North Sea.

Watching gasoline gauges constantly during the last part of the
flight, the 61st makes it across the North Sea, flashes in over England. In
another fifteen minutes the big fighters are landing at Halesworth. As
they lose altitude and come down for a landing, Johnson notices the
clock on his instrument panel. It is 1:51 P.M., still early in the day—and
the Wolfpack has been deep inside Germany, run into four big gaggles
of enemy aircraft, and returned home. Big B has been an exciting
mission.

Shortly after touching down, and taxiing *All Hell* to the parking area,
Johnson and other pilots are answering questions for the intelligence
officer. Pilots agree the Luftwaffe threw the works at the first three
boxes of bombers—more German fighters than most of them had seen in
a long time, more than many had ever seen! U.S. losses, as a result, had
been heavy.

Though Berlin was bombed successfully, the Eighth lost 69 bombers
(690 men), not counting fighter losses, which were light (11 aircraft),
in its first major daylight bombing of Berlin. The 56th happened to
be escorting the boxes singled out by the enemy as targets for their
attacks. Some of the other boxes were almost untouched and some
of the other fighter groups missed most of the fighter action. Johnson had had little to be worried about, or envious over, when Mike
Quirk spotted a gaggle of ME–109's and dived on them, though
at the time he feared Quirk would get in all the fighting for the day.
That had been only minutes before Johnson's squadron spotted the
three large enemy gaggles queuing up for a strike at the three lead
B–17 boxes. The battle that followed had far eclipsed Quirk's dogfight.

Johnson and the Eighth Air Force profited from the experience of
the grim battle, in which so many Americans in the lead boxes were
killed—in just a few minutes. The inevitable conclusion was reached
—American fighters must get further out and away from the bombers,
to be in position to head off enemy gaggles preparing to attack. Johnson
suggested 56th try such defensive tactics in the future. (Eventually the
higher-ups ordered such tactics for all fighter groups.)

On March 15, on another major bombing mission, the new tactics
were put to the test. Escorting fighters stayed well out ahead and to the
side of the bombers. Success crowned the effort. Although every attack
was not broken up, losses were relatively light, and pilots agreed the

system paid dividends. The German fighters were intercepted by the Americans on several occasions before they could get their mass attacks organized, and many of their fighters were scattered before they were able to make the first pass on the bombers.

So the first great daylight raid on the enemy capital, which was one of the bitterest battles ever fought in the skies over Germany, was significant in several ways. For Johnson, it was one of his last missions. On May 8 he completed a second extension of his combat tour and was sent back to the United States shortly after, leaving for the States the very day the Allies landed in Normandy. Back in the U.S.A. he went on tour and helped sell government bonds—traveling over the country in a P-47. He had another great fighter pilot with him on the tour, a P-38 pilot from the Pacific, credited with twenty-seven victories at the time, Richard I. Bong.

After touring the States with Johnson, Bong managed to get back into combat, and destroyed another thirteen enemy planes before the end of the war. That gave him forty aerial kills, the all-time unofficial record for an American fighter pilot. At the time of his bond-selling tour with Bong, Johnson was the highest-ranking aerial combat ace from the European Theater of Operations, with his twenty-eight confirmed aerial kills. That was, at the time, one more than Bong had to his credit.

For his gallant attempt to break up the enemy's fighter attack on the bombers, while heavily outnumbered, on March 6, 1944, and for the destruction of an enemy fighter (possibly another), and aggressive leadership and daring in combat, Johnson was awarded the Distinguished Service Cross. His P-47 group had destroyed seven German fighters on the mission while losing only one. When he had completed combat, he wore, in addition to British and French decorations, the D.S.C., the Distinguished Flying Cross with eight clusters, the Silver Star, the Purple Heart, the Air Medal with four clusters and other medals. His unit, of course, had been awarded the Presidential unit citation.

These honors for the youngster they had said was deficient in gunnery, for the cadet who was sent to twin-engine school because he couldn't pass a gunnery course! This for the boy who, at age eight, thrilled to the bravado and daring of World War I's Three Musketeers and who decided then to be an Army pilot—and did it.

9 *A Game of Bluff at Sorau*

APRIL 11, 1944:

Captain HENRY W. BROWN

Air Force Photo

No ONE would ever refer to a fighter mission as pleasant, amusing or entertaining, but a few of them can be viewed—at least in retrospect —as containing grim elements of humor. One of these experiences occurred to one of the war's top-scoring American aces on a dangerous and successful strike over Germany as the aerial war approached a crescendo two months before the Allied invasion across the Channel. The mission took U.S. aircraft to the vicinity of Berlin—and took place just a month after the costly Berlin raid described in the preceding chapter.

Second Lieutenant Henry W. Brown, of Dallas, Texas (later in the war shot down and captured), played the pulsating and leading role in the affairs of April 11, 1944. Brown flew with four P-51 Mustangs of Blue Flight, 354th Squadron (355th Group), that memorable day.

The mission began normally enough. Field Order 295 from Eighth Air Force Fighter Command directed a number of fighter groups in England to escort bombers on a mission to Sorau, just outside Berlin. It directed various fighter groups to pick up the bombers at different points along the route, providing the bombers a continuous escort, in shifts.

The 355th was directed to rendezvous with big friends near Dümmer Lake and escort them to the target. After the heavies had bombed the target, the group was to scatter its three squadrons for descent and strafing of German ground targets, conditions permitting.

With these orders awaiting him and more than forty combat missions under his belt, Lieutenant Brown climbed out of bed at 4 A.M. on Tuesday the 11th, at Steeple Morden Airbase (home of the 355th), dressed and set off for briefing.

Not long afterward pilots of all three squadrons sat silently in the big Nissen hut which served as group operations and listened to instructions from Group Leader Everett W. Stewart, weather and intelligence officers. Group briefing took forty-five minutes. At the conclusion pilots had carefully copied code words, course settings, bomber markings, emergency radio call signs and all the other data which would give each pilot the maximum chance to return to base alive that afternoon. The flight to Sorau was to be made low, at 13,000 feet. Stewart would fly with the 354th Squadron.

Pedaling bicycles back to squadron headquarters, a smaller Nissen hut about a mile away in the darkness, pilots of the 354th looked up into the early spring sky for a sign of the day's weather. The first faint light of approaching dawn revealed familiar scud. It was damp, cold, and muddy at Steeple Morden.

After a short squadron briefing, where strafing tactics and the order and position of flight were outlined for each member of the squadron, pilots pedaled to the mess hall—another wet mile by bike—to down a hasty breakfast of hopped-up orange juice (vitamin-stocked), powdered eggs, toast, marmalade and coffee. Then it was back to the ready room at squadron headquarters. The roar of bombers already airborne at nearby bomber bases, which had begun at 4 A.M. and which could be heard for miles over the English countryside, was now dying down. Most of them were now on their way.

Flying clothes on, pilots of the 354th started out to parked fighters, warmed up and carefully checked before daylight by ground crews. Brown rolled up to the *Hun Hunter from Texas* shortly after eight. His fighter already proudly exhibited a row of swastikas painted on the fuselage below the canopy—indicating enemy kills. He had long ago become an ace.

The 354th Squadron took off first among three squadrons at Steeple

Morden, since the group commander was flying with 354th. Its code name was Haywood. Each of the four Haywood flights was designated by a color, the lead flight being Red Flight. Brown was Haywood Blue Four.

Stewart taxied his fifteen fighters (the squadron was one fighter short of normal strength) to the end of Steeple Morden's north-south tarmac runway minutes before 9 A.M. After checking mags and going through the laborious cockpit check that was S.O.P., he gave his wing man a signal and 354th began to take off. The roar of straining, wide-open engines echoing through the countryside, the 354th lifted into a great joining circle around the field, pair by pair, and once the squadron joined up, Stewart pointed the white noses of his fighters toward Berlin.

The fifteen white-nosed, green-winged P-51's slanted upward toward low-hanging scud covering England, one of three squadrons. The 356th and 357th squadrons flew just behind. Visibility was excellent and squadrons climbed in string formation—one flight behind the other. One by one, at 3,000 feet, flights swept into gray scud, and were lost

One of the latest wartime versions of the P-51 with added firepower and a "teardrop" cockpit for greater visibility. (Air Force Photo)

from sight momentarily as they continued climbing, breaking out in a matter of minutes as clouds proved quite thin. Above, as the flights broke out of the clouds, brilliant sunshine filled the sky.

Landfall out was reached at altitude 7,000 feet, the coastline identifiable through breaks in the cloud layer. Squadrons, maintaining a steady rate of climb on an eastward heading, now above the sea, were ordered into widened combat formation. As the Mustangs maneuvered into the wide, slightly staggered positions, pilots flicked on gun switches and checked engine gauges, jockeying the throttle to keep a constant 160 m.p.h. rate of climb and proper flying position of combat formation.

The crossing of the North Sea, which would take more than twenty minutes, continued. Ahead lay the shores of the Dutch coast, a hundred miles from English beaches. The group maintained radio silence as mile after mile of water passed below. The climb lifted the Mustangs higher and higher as they neared landfall in. The only disturbance to mar the grim silence of the beginning of the mission was the ominous sound of German jamming, which became audible over earphones as the group approached the coast of the Continent.

The group attained mission altitude of 13,000 feet, and leveled off, on course and on time. Pilots changed from fuselage tank, an added tank built into the space behind the cockpit, to drop tanks. The idea was to burn fuel from the fuselage tank, which adversely affected flying characteristics of the Mustang, and from the drop tanks, which might suddenly have to be released, as soon as possible. Added to allow U.S. fighters to perform extra-long fighter missions, the two drop tanks (over 100 gallons of fuel in each), the 92 gallons in each of the wing tanks, and slightly less in fuselage tank, gave the Mustang a 500-gallon fuel capacity, made it the longest-range fighter in the war.

With this fuel load, about 2,000 rounds of fifty-calibre armor-piercing and incendiary ammunition, and the weight of a big Rolls-Merlin liquid-cooled engine all added to the normal weight of airframe, radio equipment, etc., the aircraft barely produced a flying margin. A malfunctioning engine, if turning out slightly reduced power, would not lift it off the runway. It took all the engine's 2,000 horsepower to make an overloaded P–51 a flying machine, and until pilots consumed fuel in the fuselage, and dropped extra tanks, they were too cumbersome to engage an ME–109 or FW–190. This was the price paid for greatly extended range.

Brown had burned fuel only in the fuselage tank and ten gallons from left wing tank, to make space for drainage, when the coast of

Holland was sighted. Vapor trails left behind by bombers headed for Sorau became visible in the clear sky ahead. The cloud layer far below became thinner and thinner. Visibility was unlimited.

The Dutch landscape was crossed quickly since the Mustangs were making better than 200 m.p.h. in level flight. The group unceremoniously crossed into Germany; eyes now constantly raked every corner of the sky, but the Luftwaffe was not yet putting in an appearance. Up ahead dots that were heavy bombers hove into view. The 355th Group was making its rendezvous according to plan. In a few minutes, with the blue waters of Dümmer Lake below, the three white-nosed squadrons of the group had pulled into position around the four-engined bombers they had been ordered to protect. The big friends were no doubt relieved as their little friends put in their prompt and timely appearance.

For Lieutenant Brown, and other pilots in the group, the mission had been "a piece of cake," as an English pilot might say. The target was within reach and with good visibility Sorau was certain to get an accurate American prescription. The bothersome task of S-turning and circling—so as not to run away from the bombers—and the constant watch in every direction occupied escorting fighters. The air armada droned on in the direction of the German capital. Still the Luftwaffe, which reacted so sharply to attacks in the Berlin area, failed to molest the bombers.

The stream of heavies was nearing Sorau. Berlin came into view. Fighters gracefully rolled out further to the side in expectation of flak. The long string of Flying Fortresses and Liberators had to hold course and level flight, while bombardiers checked computations, preparing to unload lethal cargoes. Meanwhile black puffs soon began to burst below, ahead and behind the bombers—88-millimeter flak. Through this fire toward the designated target, Sorau and its Focke-Wulf assembly plant, the heavy bombers plowed relentlessly on. Bomb-bay doors folded down and the bombing climax approached. American fighter pilots watched, unengaged in clear skies, as a rain of bombs showered down on the target below, producing sharp flashes and billowing black smoke as they shook Hitler's Germany in a death grip. So far it had been easy.

Box after box passed over the target and through the flak bursts and completed the bomb run. How many bombers the Germans had hit Brown couldn't say. But casualties among those protected by 355th—which he had been watching—had been light and enemy fighter resistance nil.

Before it was destroyed by P–47 strafing attacks, this had been part of a German panzer division retreating in France. (Air Force Photo)

Black smoke columns stood high in the April sky as the American bomber force, each plane lightened by the dispatch of its bombs, turned and hurried on its way home. For fighters of the 355th Group the time had come to leave further escort of the bombers to other fighters. Accordingly, with the relieving fighters in view, the three squadrons of the group signaled good-by to the big friends and hungry eyes began to look over the sunshine-lit German countryside east of Berlin. The 355th's squadrons prepared for strafing attacks and relieving fighters moved in to protect the bombers.

Over the radio orders come from Group Leader Stewart. The 354th, 357th, and 358th squadrons are to separate and find targets of opportunity. The squadron leaders of 357th and 358th acknowledge. Stewart lowers the white nose of his P–51 and turns away from the other two squadrons. White, Blue and Green Flights follow in that order. The full squadron is descending at an accelerated rate. Drop tanks have gone tumbling. The fighters are at last free to maneuver and dive.

Down below the enemy homeland becomes a target, and pilots search the clear landscape of Berlin's suburbs and nearby fields, roads and rivers. Speed increases as the fifteen Mustangs slowly turn and descend, like hawks searching out prey. All eyes fix intermittently on Stewart, now Haywood Leader, who will call the signals.

A voice breaks radio silence: "There's an airdrome down there," Haywood Leader acknowledges the call. It is Strausberg Airdrome, one of the airfields surrounding Berlin, a few miles to the east of the capital. Blue Flight is to go down and strafe it. The other flights will look for other targets. "All right, we'll go down," Captain Curtis G. Johnston, Blue Flight Leader, announces. "I've got the field in sight. We'll get in a string and go down to attack."

At these words, nerves tighten; every pilot in the flight studies the German airfield below. Haywood Blue Leader sharpens the angle of dive and points his fighters toward an area west of the field. Airspeed passes the 300 mark and continues to climb. The four fighters gradually spread out as they whistle lower and lower. The landscape comes up faster and faster. Trees, woods, and roads all grow steadily larger. The enemy airdrome is now clearly in view—its round concrete flak towers visible on the edges. Buildings, a single long runway, and parked aircraft are plainly visible as altitude disappears. The Mustangs of Blue Flight are but several thousand feet high, still diving.

Brown watches with excitement as Johnston, now almost on the deck, begins to lessen dive angle and banks left, straight for the western edge of the enemy airdrome. *Hun Hunter* is making 400 m.p.h. Brown trails the other three fighters in his flight, and occasionally glances back to clear his rear. Up ahead he sees the outline of Blue Leader's Mustang down on top of the trees, the streams of smoke trailing back over the wing . . . he's opened fire.

Second, third, and fourth fighters prepare to hit targets. Brown sees the low-wing silhouettes of Blue Two and Three lowering over the trees to attack. He moves stick slightly left and bores in . . . now the fighters ahead are having it out with parked aircraft. Tracers mark the path of fire from the onrushing fighters and dirt and buildings splatter as fifty-calibre shells rip criss-cross paths across the airfield.

Blue Flight is streaking over the edge of the field, headed almost due east, on a course that will carry the four Mustangs across the southern tip of the field's north-south runway. On this side of the southern end of the runway Brown makes out a number of buildings and a prominent flak tower. As he flashes over the edge of trees surrounding the field he dips his nose and gets the tower and buildings in his sight ring. Suddenly two JU–52 transports, parked side by side off the south end of the runway, appear dead ahead. Blue Three is firing at, and hitting, the JU–52 on the left. Suddenly it explodes. Brown hits right stick and rudder and brings the one on the right into his yellow sight ring, firing away immediately. The Luftwaffe transport gets the brunt of heavy fire at once and shudders under the impact of armor-piercing metal. Incendiaries slap into torn gas tanks and ignite its fuel.

He lifts his nose slightly, to stay airborne, roars over his victim and starts a slow left turn. The flight comes around for another pass. As he approaches for the second strafing run, Brown spots a JU–88 bomber on the field ahead. Lining it up, he flashes in over the airdrome again and opens fire. His shells walk up to the enemy aircraft and register all over wing and fuselage.

Something moving catches his eye. His head snaps left. An FW–190 is racing down the runway . . . taking off to intercept. He jerks stick back and left and shoots up into a chandelle, banking left. The enemy pilot is daring—attempting a take-off in the middle of a strafing attack! Brown, several hundred feet high, now parallels his course, on a north heading, watches the Focke-Wulf lift off the runway and retract wheels. He turns sharply left again, to pull in behind the enemy, who also turns left.

The FW–190 is making surprising speed, but Brown has momentum left from his long dive and closes in behind the radial-engined German fighter rapidly. The gray silhouette of the low-winged enemy grows larger and larger. Brown moves his finger on top of the firing button and the wingspan of the German begins to fill his sight ring. The enemy pilot is staying low, desperately attemping to outrun the American. His outline gets bigger and bigger on the sighting glass twelve inches in front of Brown's eyes. Matching every twist and turn, the Mustang hangs in on his tail and closes the gap. The enemy pilot senses his danger. His FW–190 is wide open, still in a left turn and still just off the deck, but now Brown has him in range—250 yards. Fire! At the same time he pulls back the throttle to reduce speed.

Even so, aim must be good, for *Hun Hunter* will overrun the enemy fighter. The Mustang shudders from gun recoil; the 190 takes hits immediately. As he races up on the trapped enemy Brown holds the gun button down and a concentrated barrage pours into the fuselage and wings of the gray fighter. The Mustang's guns, spitting ammo at a rate of better than eighty shells a second, smashes the enemy craft to pieces. Wing parts, chunks of the fuselage and all sorts of debris fly back off the German aircraft. Brown is at point-blank range At that moment the 190 emits flashes of white fire, streams smoke, loses huge chunks of cowling.

Then . . . it noses down and dives into the ground below! The 190 bounces up over a fence, bounces again and again. Brown thunders over the wreckage as the enemy pilot jumps out and dashes away from his smashed aircraft. It was fast and accurate gunnery at its devastating best, leaving the American fighter's guns red hot, and Brown breathless. Now Brown banks sharply around and makes several passes at the downed 190—trying to set it afire. But the 190 won't burn and *Hun Hunter* runs out of ammunition.

He pushes the throttle handle forward again and leans into a right turn, checking his tail. The sleek Mustang has no pursuers; Brown looks for the rest of the flight. It seems only seconds since he took on the 190, but the other Mustangs are not in sight. They had time to make several additional passes on the field while he was shooting down the enemy fighter, and have pulled up and probably headed home.

Brown hauls back stick and checks his fuel gauges. He will go home alone. The Mustang cuts upward gracefully through a blue sky arching up in every direction, heading west. But nowhere are friendly fighters to be seen. He has fuel enough to make Steeple Morden and his aircraft is undamaged. Still, it would be good to have company. The other three fighters of Blue Flight no doubt lost him when he unexpectedly chandelled left, to take after the 190. He presses the mike button of his radio: "This is Haywood Blue Four calling Blue Leader . . . what is your position?"

Back over the airwaves came a voice in reply: "We're joined up and heading home on a westerly heading." Brown, climbing into the west, searches the sky ahead. His flight is nowhere in view. He will try to overtake them on the way home. He adds power and watches the altimeter needle spiral . . . 8,000, 9,000, 10,000 feet. He is crossing the outskirts of Berlin. Suddenly dark puffs dot the sky around him. The 51 lurches and tosses about. Brown peels off into a steep dive—down to the deck. He pulls out just above the trees—full throttle to the west. Now small-arms fire streaks up at him from below. Banking radically, he leaves Berlin behind. Once again he begins to climb. Slowly he gains altitude. At last he reaches 10,000 feet, then 12,000, 13,000, 15,000.

Up ahead he makes out four dots—fighters! They look like P–51's. Brown feels a sense of relief. The four fighters fly a westerly heading at approximately 15,000 feet. He adds throttle to close. The flight ahead couldn't be Blue Flight. There would be only three fighters left in it. Could it be Haywood Leader, or White or Green? The distance closes, the low-winged twelve-o'clock outlines grow larger. In the blue sky the thin wing line is only a gray silhouette. Brown studies the four fighters to make an identification. The Mustang is gaining and the last of the four gray fighters is now almost within range. These Mustangs are hard to identify . . . no distinguishing marks, yet they are close.

Too close not to be identified. A pang of fear grabs his stomach! His heart jumps. The fighters ahead are ME–109's, their low, rounded rudder unmistakable! Now almost on top of the fourth fighter in formation, he must cut throttle and try to sneak away undetected.

The fourth ME–109 is at this very moment filling his sight ring, dead ahead, a perfect sitting duck. It's a great opportunity to pass up. But he is out of ammunition. Disgusted, fearing for his life, his left hand leaps for the throttle, cuts power to zero. Why doesn't the enemy see him? Slowly the momentum dies. The Mustang slips back from the fighters ahead. Brown dips his nose slightly, hoping to escape in the blind spot at six o'clock low. He can't understand why the German pilots aren't clearing behind them. If they had, in the last minute, he

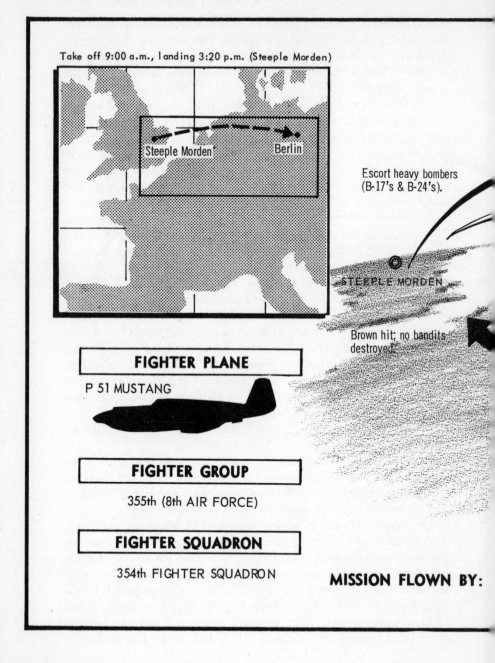

Take off 9:00 a.m., landing 3:20 p.m. (Steeple Morden)

Steeple Morden   Berlin

Escort heavy bombers
(B-17's & B-24's).

STEEPLE MORDEN

Brown hit; no bandits
destroyed.

FIGHTER PLANE

P 51 MUSTANG

FIGHTER GROUP

355th (8th AIR FORCE)

FIGHTER SQUADRON

354th FIGHTER SQUADRON

MISSION FLOWN BY:

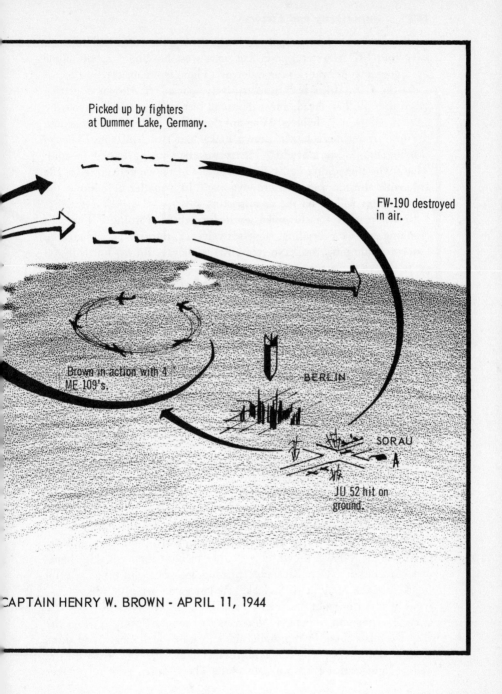

Picked up by fighters
at Dummer Lake, Germany.

FW-190 destroyed
in air.

Brown in action with 4
ME 109's.

BERLIN

SORAU

JU 52 hit on
ground.

CAPTAIN HENRY W. BROWN - APRIL 11, 1944

would surely have been spotted. He picks up the mike and calls: "I have four ME–109's at 15,000 feet on a west heading . . . no ammo . . . does anyone want to come down?" There is no answer.

As the P–51 drifts back unobtrusively, power off, Brown is getting away after all. Far ahead, a few thousand feet below, something moving . . . two dots . . . fighters! Who are they? Still falling back, watching the four 109's like a hawk, Brown makes out two Mustangs. They're climbing on a western heading. He realizes the 109's have them in sight. That's why they didn't notice him behind! They're maneuvering for the kill, with altitude and position advantage. In a matter of minutes the enemy pilots will be on the unsuspecting 51's.

Brown reaches for the mike, excitedly yells a warning: "Two 51's climbing on west heading, angels twelve or thirteen . . . there are four 109's jumping you!" No reply. Radio silence. Brown hurriedly repeats the vital warning: "The two Mustangs climbing out on a west heading . . . four ME–109's are jumping you from six o'clock high. Break left! Break left!"

The Mustangs suddenly turn sharply left, still at a disadvantage, but at least they seem to have heard. Brown can't be sure. The 109's turn left also, and close the gap. Did the Mustangs really hear? Brown rams the throttle all the way forward. With a roar, the Mustang lunges out at the enemy fighters. The Americans are in a bad way. Even if they heard the last warning, they may be unable to shake their pursuers, who have both speed and height advantages, the two trump cards in fighter combat.

Still undetected by the enemy, Brown might surprise the 109's from the rear and break up their attack. The three Americans might then have the best of it, even if only two are armed, or at least a good chance to get away in the resulting surprise and confusion. And the Germans might think more than one Mustang has sneaked in from behind. Brown decides to take the gamble, in an effort to save two lives.

The two Americans out front below are in a sharp left turn and the enemy flight follows. Brown cuts sharper to head them off. He shouts over the radio: "Two Mustangs turning left—keep turning . . . I'll break into the 109's at six o'clock!" At last came a reply: "Okay . . . we've got 'em in sight and we see you!"

At that moment the enemy discovers the danger closing in from the rear. Number three in the flight suddenly rolls on his back and dives straight down. Brown is closer to number four, who begins to fill the yellow light circle of his gunsight glass. The German pilot in number four is on the spot. He has no way of knowing Brown's ammunition is spent, obviously is following instructions to stay with the flight. Meanwhile the two leading 109's open fire on the two Mustangs, all six aircraft now standing on their left wings in a tight turn.

"Break right!" Brown yells to the Mustangs, closing fast on the enemy. One Mustang flips right wing down and left wing up, and breaks down and to the right. The sudden maneuver, plus the presence of the Mustang on their tail, checkmates the enemy pilots. Then the other Mustang rolls out of the left turn and dives away. The 109's decide to continue the sharp left turn, hoping to shake Brown, who hangs on, now well within range of the last foe. Meanwhile the two rescued Mustangs grow smaller and smaller to the west. Brown glances back in dismay, even while turning sharper and sharper in a tightening Lufberry with the 109's. The Mustangs are disappearing rapidly in the direction of England!

Alone with enemy fighters, without ammunition, Brown is in a grim spot. The enemy planes bank tighter and tighter. He responds, gives the Mustang full trim for turning, puts down ten degrees of flaps, continues to turn inside the enemy, already within range of the last enemy fighter. He now inches up dead astern, closer and closer. Standing on his left wing tip, blood draining from his head because of the pull of gravity in the tight turn, Brown can only bluff. He thinks about staying in the Lufberry until out of gas . . . thoughts reach out in all directions for a solution. There is none. Tracers from the leading enemy's guns spray the sky behind him. Almost chewing up the tail of the last 109, with the other two leading, he sees the answer unfold.

Unable to stand the expectation of imminent destruction, the trailing 109 suddenly flips over right and straight down! Brown pulls the stick in a little harder and raises his head to get the number two 109 in the sight, still on his side, still mashed into his seat by the terrific weight of gravity exerted by the tight left turn. The round-and-round Lufberry continues. Outturning the 109's, he creeps up on number two. But seconds are hours in the roaring, desperate circle. The enemy pilot in number two position tries every trick to shake the lone Mustang, slanting up and down in the turn, pulling tighter and tighter. Brown almost blacks out from loss of blood but inches up on the second of the two remaining German fighters. He is closing the range. The tension becomes too great for the enemy. Following the example of his comrade, number two suddenly rolls out of the tight turn, on his back, and goes straight down.

For a second Brown watches him disappear, then fixes his sight on the lone enemy fighter. Three down and one to go! The flight leader continues his effort to outturn the Mustang. The two fighters are a half circle apart. Brown can see the 109 directly across the turning circle. This time he finds it harder to close the gap. The enemy is cunning; if he should close the Mustang, his guns can do something about it. Only if Brown outturns the remaining enemy can he make his break for home. Once more he pulls back on the stick as tightly as body and eyes can stand. For several seconds it's hard to tell whether he is gaining or losing in the turn. Then, gradually, the Mustang shortens the distance!

Black crosses, edged in white, are clearly visible on the wings of the remaining German fighter as the white-nosed P–51 outturns the last bandit and unmistakably moves into firing position, slowly but emphatically. Brown grimly holds stick back, sees the enemy's tail grow larger and larger. In seconds the last of the four 109's will come into range.

The German Flight Leader, finally convinced the Mustang can outturn him, doesn't wait for shells that would have never come. Like his Luftwaffe comrades, he suddenly levels his wings, then turns over on his back and points his nose toward the fatherland below. A feeling of relief comes over Brown. He has outfought four enemy planes without firing a shot and without having been able to. He relaxes his right hand, the stick eases forward and *Hun Hunter* rolls out of the Lufberry to the right. The great tension diminishes. He can straighten up head and shoulders without having to use all his strength. He pulls back the throttle handle.

A rattling noise! The Mustang shudders and vibrates. It sounds as if someone were beating on the outside of the plane. The Mustang bucks. Then he knows. The vibration is not the engine . . . *Hun Hunter* is taking hits!

Brown glances left. Holes through the left wing! A swoosh over the right wing—an ME–109 flashes past, out front! The enemy overshot . . . luckily . . . his speed and timing thrown off when Brown reduced throttle. The enemy pulls up—almost straight up. The German pilot, fearing the wrath of Brown's guns as he slides helplessly out into range, continues up in a vertical climb.

Not knowing whether other 109's are around, Brown quickly rolls over on his back and split-S's. The enemy fighter who caught him from behind was probably the first enemy pilot to split-S at the beginning of the Lufberry action. He would have had the time to climb back up and slip in on the lone Mustang from outside the turning circle. Brown's damaged Mustang screams down, all the way to the treetops again. The enemy doesn't follow—a stroke of unexpected luck. Brown glances at the compass to set a westerly course, rubbernecking to protect his rear, fully expecting another 109. The compass needle is erratic, then immobile. He pounds the instrument . . . no response. Shot out! He begins a slow climb, scans the sky for friendly aircraft heading home. None in sight. Looking back and down anxiously, for the enemy he has so far bluffed, Brown guesses the way home and sets course—maintaining high throttle setting to clear the area quickly. He eases back a little more on the stick.

The altimeter registers 8,000, 9,000, 10,000 feet. Down below the clouds are thickening; ground navigation is soon to be impossible. He must have navigational help. Like an answer to his prayer he hears voices in his earphones . . . The radio is working. He presses the transmitter button: "This is Haywood Blue Four . . . just shot up by an ME–109. Compass knocked out. Am trying to fly home without it. Wish someone who is flying home would tell me what the position of the sun is on the canopy." He waits for a reply. In a few seconds there comes a strange voice, unknown to this day: "Put the sun on the second screw from the front on the top left railing." Brown replies: "Roger. Thanks a lot."

He looks at the sun. He is heading too far north. Had he followed this course it would have taken him far astray over the North Sea. He eases the stick to the left and toes left rudder. The sun swings into position over the second screw from the front. He straightens out on course. He will go home by sun navigation, until he can pick up a radar station in England. Though still over Germany, Brown appraises chances of getting home as better than during the desperate encounter with enemy fighters. His engine is running smoothly and his fuel supply ample to complete the flight to Steeple Morden. For the first moment in a lifetime, confidence wells up inside—that he will make it home.

Up to 20,000 feet and keeping a silent vigil in all directions, the lone Mustang continues its path through the skies over Germany. Dümmer Lake appears below . . . and then passes behind. What must be Holland comes into view through holes in thickening clouds below. Next comes the Zuider Zee . . . and then the thin strip of Holland that separates it from the North Sea. German fighters no longer haunt him.

But the clouds are now solid and even navigation estimates impossible. The Mustang whines on through the sky, westward bound . . . now over the North Sea. Brown looks for contrails. Surely some of the returning bombers would have left visible contrails. But the sky is unmarked. He begins to worry about course. He reaches down to number-two push button on his four-button radio, Air-Sea Rescue—guarded constantly by radar stations on the English coast—and calls for help: "Can you pick me up on radar?" he asks. Moments of waiting seem an eternity. Then a distant voice breaks the silence: "Continue on your present course. I think I have you." Then again: "Make a ninety-degree turn to the left." Brown swings *Hun Hunter* ninety degrees left and waits.

"Roger," comes the answer, "I have you, positive radar identification. Make a timing turn to the left." This completed, the voice replied: "We still have you. It looks like you're on the right heading for England. Give me a call in another five minutes."

For five more minutes the lone Mustang flies on. Then Brown calls Air-Sea Rescue again. "Your heading is very good," comes the confident voice from England. "Correct five degrees to the left." Brown completes the slight left correction. "Very good. You'll make landfall in near Dunwich. To what base are you going?" "Steeple Morden," Brown answers. The radar direction finder operator vectors him in, clouds now covering the North Sea solidly.

For what seems a long time Brown flies on, losing altitude slowly, until the RDF operator breaks in: "You're over the coast. Correct several degrees to the left for Steeple Morden." With that the operator says he will be unable to give further fixes. Then a familiar voice comes in over the radio. It is Steeple Morden tower, which has learned that he is headed in with a damaged aircraft.

"How badly are you shot up?" comes the query. "Just a few holes and my compass," Brown replies. Nevertheless, the tower maintains contact, offers assistance. For the first time, Brown notices other aircraft heading in his direction. Could they be other 355th fighters? . . . He keeps an eye on some on an identical course. From their markings he identifies them as from the group, also returning after the long mission. Brown glances at the clock on his instrument panel; it reads 3:15. He has been airborne six hours and fifteen minutes, an exceptional span for a fighter.

Lowering his nose steeper and steeper, and keeping the other fighters in sight, he nears Steeple Morden. Now holes conveniently appear in

the cloud layer below once again. Brown recognizes the countryside
below. At several thousand feet altitude the familiar dark runways and
Nissen huts of Steeple Morden come into view. He pulls back throttle
and lines up the runway. Would flaps and landing gear operate? Or
have they been damaged? The tower calls and suggests he park his
plane in front of squadron headquarters, rather than taxi it to the revetment. There repair mechanics will take over.

He flashes over the end of the runway at five hundred feet and curves
up into a tight left landing pattern. He pulls the landing-gear lever.
The hydraulic system functions; a thump tells him his wheels are
locked down—the last major worry. He slices lower and lower through
the spring air, at 120 m.p.h, and touches England at 3:20—six hours
and twenty minutes from take-off that morning! Since take-off he has
added two enemy aircraft and probably a third to his string of victories.

Holed *Hun Hunter* growls along the taxiway until it reaches 354th
Squadron headquarters. Then the big four-bladed prop whirls out, and
Brown slides the canopy back. A large crowd is on hand to survey damage and ask questions. Wearily, Brown answers them all. There is one
question he has been waiting to ask. Who were the pilots in the group
who left him in the lurch, without ammunition, engaging four enemy
fighters? No one knows.

The group commander recommended Brown for a cluster to his Silver
Star for this mission. But Wing decided the Distinguished Service
Cross would be more appropriate, giving the American ace an imposing
array of awards—among them the Air Medal with eighteen clusters, the
Distinguished Flying Cross with four clusters, the Silver Star, and the
DSC. The citation on the order from Wing Headquarters, awarding
him the Distinguished Service Cross read as follows:

For extraordinary heroism in action with the enemy, 11 April 1944: On
this date Lieut. Brown, while flying a fighter (airplane) over enemy-occupied territory, destroyed one enemy plane and damaged another by a strafing
attack against a well-defended airdrome. While regaining altitude he saw
an enemy fighter a short distance away. Without hesitation he attacked and
destroyed it. Although Lieut. Brown had expended all ammunition during
this action, when he observed four enemy fighters attacking two friendly
fighters, he, with complete disregard for his own safety, at once flew in to
assist the friendly fighters. His determination and boldness forced the enemy
to break off the fight. The outstanding heroism displayed by Lieut. Brown,
although completely defenseless, and his determination to assist his com-

rades, reflects the highest credit upon himself and the Armed Forces of the
United States.

The attack on Sorau had not been carried out without painful losses.
As final reports came in, it was discovered that sixty-four bombers had
been lost on the mission. The heaviest enemy attacks, obviously, had
been made on boxes other than those protected by Brown and 355th
Group.

The main thought in Brown's mind for several hours after the mission concerned the identity of the two pilots who had hastened away
from an unequal battle he joined to save their lives. That same night
he got the answer. The pilots were identified in one of the other squadrons. Confronting them at the bar, Brown raged: "What the hell are
you guys doing running off and leaving me?" The answer was ironical:
"Heck, we were out of ammunition," came the reply.

10 Clash Over Leyte's Ormoc Bay

DECEMBER 7, 1944:

Colonel CHARLES H. MacDONALD

Air Force Photo

WHILE the war in Europe was marching toward a climax and the inevitable defeat of Nazi Germany, events in the Pacific foreshadowed the eventual crushing of Japan. Here, as in Europe, the Army Air Corps and its fighter pilots were doing their share toward ultimate victory.

In October, 1944, two powerful United States military forces which had been advancing toward Japan converged in the Philippines. The pincer movement joined the forces of General Douglas MacArthur, which had advanced northward from Australia, and those of Admiral Chester W. Nimitz, which had thrust westward from Pearl Harbor.

The road to the Philippines and Leyte, where American Rangers landed (on the offshore islands) October 17, 1944, followed three days later by four divisions assaulting the east coast itself, had been long. The huge island complex, stretching more than a thousand miles from the South China Sea to the Celebes Sea, had been under Japanese control since June 9, 1942, when the last U.S. forces in the southern islands capitulated, more than a month after General Jonathan Wainwright surrendered Corregidor.

Since the United States had won the strategic island empire from Spain, at the turn of the century, the Rising Sun had been the only foreign flag to challenge the Stars and Stripes.

Japanese conquests continued unchecked throughout much of the Pacific until well into 1942 and the major task of the United States at this stage of the war was to maintain a lifeline to Australia which could be used to build up supplies and strength for a counter-offensive. The lifeline was maintained by successful naval battles in the Coral Sea and at Midway (in May and June) and by a victory over Japanese troops attempting to capture Port Moresby. The enemy was checked thirty-two miles from that city on September 17, 1942.

A Japanese landing force of 1,900 troops was also defeated in its attempt to capture Milne Bay and outflank Port Moresby during the same month, by the 7th and 18th Australian infantry brigades and U.S. Army engineers. The eventually successful struggle at Guadalcanal began August 7, 1942, when the 1st Marine division went ashore on several islands in the Solomons, which were finally secured in 1943— safeguarding the lines of communication between the United States and Australia.

In 1943 the giant Allied pincer movement toward the Philippines got under way. General MacArthur's forces began their push up the northern coast of New Guinea and Admiral Nimitz advanced against the Gilbert and Marshall Islands.

MacArthur's forces captured Salamaua, Lae, and, moving northward, jumped several Japanese strongholds into Dutch New Guinea, took Biak, Sansapor, and finally Morotai Island, which lies about three hundred miles from the southern tip of the Philippines. These campaigns consumed 1943 and most of 1944—it was September 15, 1944, when U.S. troops went ashore at Morotai.

Nimitz's forces took Makin Island and landed at Tarawa, in the Gilberts, on November 30, 1943. In 1944 Kwajalein and Majuro, in the Marshalls, were assaulted, and then Eniwetok, also in the Marshalls. Nimitz moved on the Marianas, landing Marines on Saipan June 15, 1944. In July of 1944 Guam was invaded and Tinian fell. Next, Marines pushed ashore at Peleliu in the Palau Islands, of the western Carolines, on September 15. Admiral Nimitz's forces had a base only five hundred miles due east of Mindanao.

Thus the two great converging American forces had pushed to within three hundred miles south, and five hundred miles east, of the Philippines by September of 1944. Plans had called for a landing on the southernmost of the major Philippine islands, Mindanao, by MacArthur's forces, but the U.S. Third Fleet, striking in support of the Morotai and Palau operations, found Japanese forces in the middle Philippines unprepared. Seizing the opportunity, American commanders canceled proposed assaults at Sarangani Bay (Mindanao) and Yap Island. Nimitz released to MacArthur three infantry divisions scheduled to capture Yap, under his authority, and General MacArthur laid plans to land on Leyte, in the central Philippines October 20, 1944.

On that date, four divisions, 1st Cavalry and 7th, 24th, and 96th Infantry, waded ashore on the eastern beaches of Leyte. Three days earlier the 6th Infantry Ranger battalion had begun occupying offshore islands. Twenty-nine months after the final American surrender in the Philippines, U.S. troops were ashore on Leyte. They were to provoke a desperate land battle and the greatest naval engagement of World War II—and several of the decisive aerial battles of the war.

For a time the invasion of Leyte encountered only moderate opposition; only one of the assault divisions initially encountered bitter resistance. But the Japanese command decided to stake everything on an effort to hold Leyte and cut off American troops landed there. Reinforcements, in the form of fighter aircraft, began to pour into the area. The combined Japanese fleet sailed for the area and troop reinforcements were rushed to the contested island.

The fleet was divided into three strong striking forces. One, approaching the landing area from the south, through Surigao Strait, was met and defeated by surface ships of the U.S. Seventh Fleet in an early-morning engagement on October 25. The most northerly Japanese fleet consisted of a carrier force and other warships and was defeated by the U.S. Third Fleet the same day.

The center Japanese fleet, which approached the landing area through San Bernardino Strait, ran into weaker opposition, sank several escort carriers and destroyers, and threatened to cause havoc along the landing beaches and among relatively unprotected supply ships exposed to attack from the best and fastest Japanese battleships, cruisers and destroyers.

Had the enemy admiral pressed his advantage, spectacular results might have been his, but, evidently doubtful of the whereabouts of the powerful U.S. Third Fleet, which contained enough carrier-based air power to destroy his surface force, he turned back after causing quite a flap on American beaches and sinking several small carriers and destroyers.

As the three Japanese fleets retreated, American ground and carrier-based planes pursued and attacked with telling effect. In all, the enemy lost three battleships, one large and three small carriers, ten cruisers and many other ships in the greatest sea action of the war, known as the Second Battle of the Philippines.

Fighting ashore then mounted in intensity and by November the Japanese had brought in tens of thousands of reinforcements to bolster the defense of Leyte. American troops pushed the enemy back but the battle widened and the Japanese clung to the northwestern area of the island with tenacity.

One of the requirements of the tactical situation was to bring in strong Army fighter forces, since the Japanese had available to them many fields, especially on Negros to the west, and many aircraft, and were preparing to throw everything into the Leyte struggle. Before the battle was over they would even employ Kamikaze attacks—which were to become much more frequent in the months ahead. Several Fifth Air Force fighter groups, among them the 49th and 475th, were established on hastily improvised fields on Leyte. These, and the Naval air arm, constituted American air strength in the battle for Leyte.

Ground fighting became more involved and during November General MacArthur brought in the 11th Airborne and 32nd Infantry divisions and the 112th Cavalry Regimental Combat Team to support the four divisions already engaged. The Japanese, however, maintained their hold at Ormoc, on the northwest coast, and continued to bring in reinforcements, though American air and naval forces exacted a heavy toll of enemy ships and men dispatched to reinforce Leyte.

The Japanese were determined to hold Leyte at all costs, and employed strong air forces and even airborne attacks on U.S. positions. The enemy's high command realized if the Philippines fell the Japanese lifeline to the Indies would be severed. Continuing the war for any length of time would be difficult because of the loss of precious oil.

For this reason, even after their fleet had been defeated, the Japanese made several major efforts to reinforce their troops. Their aircraft strafed the primitive fighter strips of the 475th and 49th Groups almost every morning.

When Japanese troop reinforcements continued to reach northwest

Leyte late in November, General MacArthur decided to bring in another division, and to land it on northwest Leyte, in the face of Japanese troops, at Ormoc Bay. For this job he called on 77th Infantry, which had just reached Leyte, and scheduled the landings for December 7, 1944—three years to the day after the enemy bombing of Pearl Harbor.

MacArthur's headquarters asked all-out fighter support from American squadrons on eastern Leyte in behalf of the task force which would steam into Ormoc Bay and discharge 77th. If the invasion of northwest Leyte was a success, enemy forces would be doomed, and the arrival

P-38's bombing near Ipo Dam in the Philippines.

of enemy reinforcements—which had been slipping in along the coast at night—could be brought to a halt.

The Japanese, fighting desperately to hold their positions around Ormoc, and trying to reinforce them for a future counter-attack, could be counted on to offer bitter aerial resistance to this sudden-death amphibious operation. Air battles, and perhaps a surface attack on the American force, could be expected.

Therefore, the Army's fighter groups on eastern Leyte were ordered to put aloft maximum strength to cover the landing at Ormoc Bay. These orders went out on the night of December 6.

Colonel Charles MacDonald, commanding officer of the 475th Group, and one of the group's three P–38 squadrons were stationed at Dulag airstrip on Leyte, on December 6, 1944. The group's three squadrons were the 431st, 432nd, and 433rd.

Pilots of all three squadrons lived at Dulag, located not far from where U.S. troops had first gone ashore on Leyte's eastern beaches, near Tacloban. A few miles to the north lay the planes of the 49th Fighter Group, commanded by Colonel Jerry Johnson. The two groups had been on Leyte only a short time. Operations were sometimes conducted in a sea of mud, and living and working quarters consisted of tents and partially framed structures covered with tents.

About eight o'clock on the night of the 6th an ops order clicked in on the teletype from Fighter Command near Burauen, giving co-ordinates at which the American convoy moving 77th Division would be found at dawn next morning. 475th was ordered to be over the convoy at first light. Certain attack by Japanese fighters and bombers awaited the ships of the amphibious force.

MacDonald, one of the top aces of the war at this time, with over a dozen kills to his credit, scheduled a briefing for nine o'clock. The dead-serious, stern-faced St. Petersburg, Florida, ace (MacDonald is a native of Dubois, Pennsylvania) would outline the mission to his pilots without delay since take-off next morning would be early, and because the Japanese might interrupt a morning briefing with one of their almost daily strafing attacks.

Flying officers, clad in tan khaki, filed into the group operations room at the appointed hour. A portable electric system lighted the tent-topped room and a big map of the Philippine area. After the group had assembled, MacDonald was summoned and began the briefing. He would fly with 432nd Squadron, which would take position low on the north side of the convoy, which would be traveling in a general northeast direction as it aimed for the northwestern shores of Leyte.

The 431st Squadron would be on the opposite side, to the south, also relatively low. The 433rd Squadron would fly high, as top cover. The group would pick up the convoy as it turned into Ormoc Bay, shortly after 6 A.M. MacDonald told squadron commanders to set up a flying schedule with all available planes so that some of the group's strength could be kept over the convoy at all times during the day.

To enable the group to achieve a sustained effort, squadrons would take off in twelve-plane formations. Since each squadron had approximately twenty aircraft, a small number would be ready to relieve the main force at any time, though some of the aircraft in each squadron were inoperational for various reasons. Thus original mission strength would be thirty-six fighters, plus a similar number from 49th Group.

With this short talk, a few words about the weather, which looked promising, and the warning that strong enemy aerial forces were sure to be encountered, MacDonald ended briefing. He told the orderly to wake him at four-thirty next morning and walked to a small tent where he and two others slept—on cots covered with mosquito net. He hoped to get as much rest as possible, knowing he would probably fly more than one mission before the sun set on the 7th.

At 4:30 A.M. on December 7 an orderly entered MacDonald's tent in pitch-black darkness. He nudged the C.O. and apologetically but firmly said: "You have to get up, sir." In response to MacDonald's half-audible dissertations, the orderly stood patiently by the cot and held his ground. He had orders to remain until the C.O.'s feet were on the floor; Mac-Donald was a good sleeper. But finally he surrendered to the inevitable, sat up in bed. The orderly departed.

MacDonald quickly dressed and hastened off to the mess tent, where a miserable breakfast awaited pilots. His consisted of peanut butter and bread and coffee. Few of the pilots could go the powdered eggs. Soon they were ready to head for aircraft. Piling into jeeps and weapons carriers, the three squadrons split and proceeded to their fighters.

Loaded down with parachutes and other flying gear, the men bumped along in the darkness until they reached a small clearing near their Lightnings, where final squadron briefing was held. Then pilots walked out to their silver fighters. The yellow spinners, official markings of 432nd, weren't visible in the December darkness. Spinners on 431st Lightnings were red, on 433rd planes blue.

Pilots climbed into their aircraft after greeting ground crewmen and waited for the first sign of light. After a few minutes MacDonald, noting first streaks in the eastern sky, pressed the energizer button. Engines—the P–38 had two 1,275-horsepower Allisons—began to whirl props and MacDonald taxied toward the end of the steel mat runway. Hesitating a moment at the end, to allow other pilots to pull in behind, MacDonald checked instruments, controls, and engines.

Ready to go, he waved a hand and eased throttle forward. To the west, keen eyes aboard ships in the convoy, about to make the turn into Ormoc Bay, searched the sky with care. They were forty miles away.

MacDonald could not take up position too soon as far as the convoy was concerned.

Putt-Putt-Maru, MacDonald's P–38, dipped and bumped down the runway, gathering speed. Near the end he hauled back on the wheel, the yellow spinners pointed upward, and the heavily loaded twin-fuselaged fighter lifted itself out of the mud. It was 6 A.M. MacDonald circled the field as the other fighters roared off the strip and closed in behind, one by one.

With the 431st and 433rd joined behind, MacDonald, at full strength, set course for the convoy, ten minutes away by air, almost due west.

The thirty-six Lightnings, climbing into the western sky, keep close formation. Altimeters register steady gains, 2,000, 3,000, 4,000 feet. To their left pilots of the 475th make out the dim outline of towering cumulus clouds. Then, in a few minutes, the shoreline ahead comes into view. Ormoc Bay. By now the Lightnings are at 6,000 feet. The sky is lighting up and the tall cloud formations to the left are clearly visible. The shoreline passes underneath. Eyes stare ahead to pick out the convoy, which should be just ahead.

The twelve fighters of lead squadron are followed, to the right, by 431st, and then, to the left, behind, comes the 433rd. Gun switches are on. Pilots are burning fuel in drop tanks, to use as much of it as possible before releasing them. Now the group is over the bay . . . eyes search out every corner of the sky and the water ahead. Then, up ahead, MacDonald makes out ships. He flies toward them, scanning the sky and studying the silhouettes of the vessels below.

The American fleet is almost directly beneath him . . . ships dot the water for miles . . . large ones and small ones. A line of destroyers is patrolling the northern edge of the convoy. MacDonald leads his squadron right in over the shipping concentration. The ships below appear to be in good order and unharmed.

The 432nd Squadron circles and weaves above the convoy. It is now daylight and the sight of all these ships is impressive. For some time the Lightnings patrol the air over the fleet below. The operation is proceeding in quiet and orderly manner. The routine patrol continues. No action.

And then, to his disgust, MacDonald's fuel gauges show tanks about empty. How can that be? His aircraft must not have been fully gassed up for the mission. He curses to himself. Without delay he picks up the mike and calls Captain Perry Dahl—Second Flight Leader: "Pee Wee, take over. I'm going back to get gas." Dahl acknowledges. *Putt-Putt* banks sharply out of formation and sets course eastward. MacDonald heads for Dulag, where he will be quickly refueled. Anxiously watching his gauges and hoping to avoid encounters with the enemy until refueled, he rotates his head constantly to spot bogies that might be encountered by the lone Lightning.

In a few minutes he is nearing Dulag. He approaches the runway, lowers wheels and noses downward toward the muddy palm-circled strip. *Putt-Putt* touches down and sloshes forward, finally coming to a slow roll. MacDonald taxies briskly along to his revetment. There he yells for the gas trucks. He waits impatiently for fuel. The trucks finally arrive and *Putt-Putt* begins to take on high octane. As the tanks are topped, at last, and he is about ready to go, the sound of approaching planes catches his attention. MacDonald looks up into the western sky . . . the steady roar . . . they're American planes. Then ahead some Lightnings come into view. It's the squadron coming back : . . he hadn't realized he had been on the ground so long.

One by one the silver fighters come down, their devil's face insignia and yellow spinners identifying them positively as the 432nd. As soon as he talks to the pilots, MacDonald learns the squadron engaged a number of Zekes minutes after he departed. Pee Wee had been shot down . . . he jumped out over the bay . . . it was a hot fight.

MacDonald orders planes refueled at once. Several are unable to return immediately for various reasons. He will take off again nevertheless. Minutes drag by. Meanwhile one flight has taken off to patrol the bay. Finally two other P–38's are ready to go, MacDonald's and his exec's (Lieutenant Colonel Meyrl Smith). *Putt-Putt's* props turn and soon they are lining up on the end of the runway again. MacDonald leads the two fighters off the strip and points his nose west. The Lightnings climb out on the same course followed on the first mission. The clock on MacDonald's instrument panel reads 11:18.

Ormoc Bay appears ahead . . . at the same time the radio comes to life: "Bandits—twelve o'clock high!" The call sends a chill of excitement up and down MacDonald's spine . . . nerves tighten and the anticipation of battle grips both pilots. MacDonald takes a long look ahead and above . . . he spots three Jack II's approching American ships. He immediately hits the "panic button"—full throttles—and eases the wheel into his stomach. The engines are wide open, every part in the Lightning shudders. The altimeter needle starts to climb rapidly.

The Jacks are now turning slightly to the left. MacDonald locks them in view. His engines are pulling 45 inches, turning at 2,700 r.p.m.'s. *Putt-Putt-Maru* knifes up through the sky at a fast clip . . . the outlines of the bandits ahead get bigger and bigger. MacDonald and Smith race on ahead and upward . . . the three Jacks they're closing are now approaching the cumulus clouds. MacDonald banks left. The tall clouds are almost straight ahead now . . . suddenly the Japanese part company . . . split into singles. MacDonald must pick one . . . he chooses one dead ahead.

The Jap ahead reaches the clouds and disappears before MacDonald's eyes. *Putt-Putt-Maru* flashes in behind him, blinded for a moment, then out again into the light, then in again, as the cumulus tops and cloud formations are interspersed by breaks of sunlight.

MacDonald knows it's difficult to follow an enemy through clouds. And almost always the fleeing fighter escapes his pursuer, since his turns cannot be seen by the hunter behind. In the seconds he is between cloud tops he scans all directions ahead. The chase through the clouds goes on, the P–38 pulling maximum power.

Then, a break! MacDonald's eye catches sight of the enemy out to his right . . . he's turned out of the clouds. Does he think he's shaken the two Americans? *Putt-Putt* leans right into a steep bank. MacDonald flashes out of the clouds and follows the Jap. The enemy pilot isn't asleep . . . he sees the Lightning come out of the clouds behind him. He wheels left, and streaks once again into the milky gray. MacDonald turns wheel hard left and kicks rudder. He curves back toward the clouds. The Jap is now out of sight, swallowed up in the unknown. MacDonald barrels in right behind him, and everything turns gray again.

As he roars through cloud, he keeps an eye peeled to the right. Then, between two cloud tops, for a second time, he spots the Jack trying to sneak off to his right. *Putt-Putt* stands on its right wing and belts out of the milky stuff . . . this time a little closer. The enemy pilot could probably get away if he stayed in the clouds long enough, and changed direction, but for some reason he is desperately trying to break away to the right.

Now he reverses course . . . left turn. MacDonald cuts him off more this time. *Putt-Putt* is getting closer and closer. As the Jack plows into the cumulus once more MacDonald holds on behind . . . his altimeter, steadily climbing throughout the chase, reads 10,000 feet. Grimly he holds course in the murk. In every split second available in cloud breaks he covers his right. . . . Then he sees him! The Jap now has banked out of the clouds again. Wheel hard right, *Putt-Putt* streaks out into the sunshine, left wing high—banking into pursuit at six o'clock.

This time the enemy pilot doesn't turn back. MacDonald is directly behind, moving up fast. He's in a blind spot for the enemy pilot, slightly below and immediately behind. Now the wingspan of the gray bandit grows larger . . . the P–38 is walking up behind him . . MacDonald glances through his fixed sight ring. In the yellow light circle the Jack ahead is squarely bracketed . . . and coming within range. MacDonald needs only a second or two . . . if the enemy pilot doesn't wise up . . . on and on him he comes.

At once he's on target . . . 700 feet, 600 feet, 500 . . . fire! *Putt-Putt's* twenty-millimeter cannon thunder and the four fifties roar . . . the Lightning shudders and leaves a trail of light smoke. Shells converge on the Jack . . . armor piercing and incendiary. MacDonald uses no tracers. The Jack is overlapping the edges of the sight circle . . . metal slams into him . . . he's being torn apart . . . but no fire. MacDonald keeps firing until he's almost running into the enemy tail . . . he notices the prop slow down . . . it whirls slower and slower . . . he's right on him. Suddenly he must haul wheel back to miss the enemy. *Putt-Putt* swishes up over the victim, just missing him . . . MacDonald looks back on his foe as he banks sharply to the left . . . the Jap is bailing out! His propeller has stopped turning altogether. Over the side the enemy pilot hurtles . . . the gray fighter falls off into an uncontrolled spiral to the right . . . the enemy pilot's chute opens. The Jack doesn't burn, spirals down and down toward the bay.

Meanwhile, Smith has attacked and set fire to another one of the Jacks, which spirals toward the bay below. The third Jack has pulled in behind MacDonald, who sees him in time and hauls *Putt-Putt* around in a tight turn.

But the enemy pilot is capable, and MacDonald can't maneuver onto his tail. Each time he tries, the Jap outturns him. Locked in a deadly dogfight over the bay, each pilot turning to close the other's rear, MacDonald is relieved at the sight of Smith coming to the rescue.

Flashing in behind the unsuspecting Jack, he quickly opens fire and his hits register immediately. The Jack begins to disintegrate and then a bright flame erupts, trailing backward in the slipstream. In seconds he is spiraling down toward the water below, goes in with a splash of foam and fire. Three out of three.

MacDonald scans the sky. No enemy planes are in view. The two-plane flight heads for the American ships to the north.

Take off and landing times given in ACTION data below.

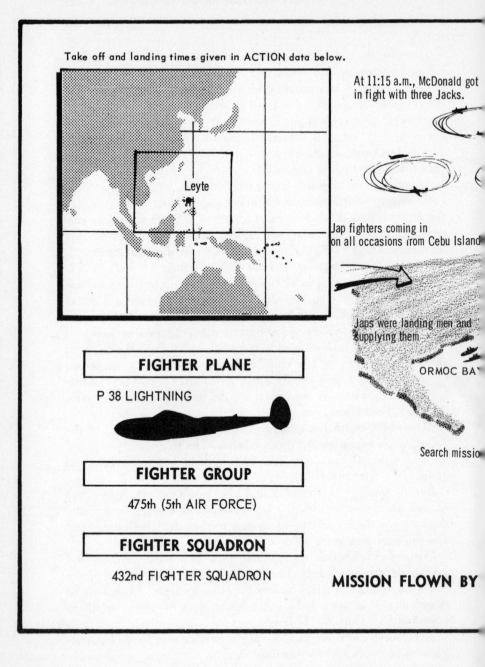

Leyte

At 11:15 a.m., McDonald got in fight with three Jacks.

Jap fighters coming in on all occasions from Cebu Island

Japs were landing men and supplying them.

ORMOC BAY

Search missio

FIGHTER PLANE

P 38 LIGHTNING

FIGHTER GROUP

475th (5th AIR FORCE)

FIGHTER SQUADRON

432nd FIGHTER SQUADRON

MISSION FLOWN BY

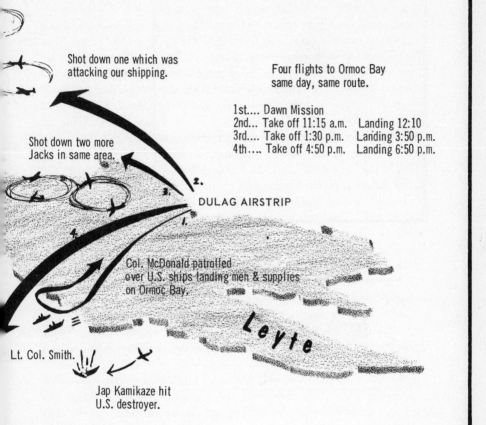

Shot down one which was attacking our shipping.

Shot down two more Jacks in same area.

Four flights to Ormoc Bay same day, same route.

1st.... Dawn Mission
2nd... Take off 11:15 a.m.   Landing 12:10
3rd.... Take off 1:30 p.m.   Landing 3:50 p.m.
4th.... Take off 4:50 p.m.   Landing 6:50 p.m.

DULAG AIRSTRIP

Col. McDonald patrolled over U.S. ships landing men & supplies on Ormoc Bay.

Leyte

Lt. Col. Smith.

Jap Kamikaze hit U.S. destroyer.

COLONEL CHARLES H. MACDONALD - DECEMBER 7, 1944

MacDonald weaves above the ships below at high throttle setting. Despite many calls about bogies, the enemy has apparently vacated the immediate area. The patrol goes on. The enemy doesn't return for the moment. Activity below progresses according to plan. Despite some damage, the big American armada below discharges supplies and equip ment and men. Everything remains quiet. After a few minutes more, MacDonald decides to return to Dulag. He will refuel and come back.

Twenty minutes later he is landing at Dulag. It is only 12:10. Mac-Donald checks with other pilots. Some are fatigued. Some of the air-craft need maintenance. The next mission will be flown in greatly reduced strength. For one reason or another only four pilots are ready to go at 1:30 P.M.—take-off time for the third mission. MacDonald leads the flight off . . . with Lieutenant Colonel Smith flying as element leader. As soon as the four Lightnings are airborne, they begin climbing into the west. But MacDonald decides not to patrol high this time. If Jap kamikazes attack, he wants to be low enough to bounce the Zekes before they reach the ships.

The Lightnings level off at 4,000 feet and pass over Ormoc Bay at this altitude. The American convoy lies straight ahead, apparently un-molested since the last attack, ships clearly visible at the low height. MacDonald and the other Americans know by this time that a group of Japanese ships is just a few miles to the north—to their right as they whistle in over the American convoy. The Japanese convoy includes warships, and apparently is a reinforcement for Japanese troops holding on a few miles up the coast from where American troops are now pour-ing ashore. The Ormoc Bay landing is certainly a daring one, for not far apart are two opposing convoys and U.S. troops are going ashore almost under the noses of the Japanese.

Now MacDonald's four twin-fuselaged Lightnings circles the Ameri-can convoy. The flight flies along the southern edge of the ships and studies the scene below. Everything apparently in order. Small boats are plying to and from the beaches and larger ships stand offshore. As MacDonald reaches the western end of the array of shipping, he banks right. Soon the four fighters are northwest of the American convoy—still no enemy is sighted.

Japanese shipping is not too far away . . . MacDonald decides to have a look. Things are quiet over the American convoy . . . he will keep it in sight, monitor the controller. *Putt-Putt* lifts a wing and points nose northward. Soon 432nd's flight is streaking toward the enemy

concentration just a few miles away. Pilots become more alert . . .
they must watch for anti-aircraft fire and fighters when nearing Japanese ships . . . MacDonald checks gun switches . . . on. The sun
shines brightly over the bay . . . no enemy fighters can be seen up
ahead, though the enemy's ships come into view.

Just then earphones vibrate: "Bandits—behind!" He snaps head back
. . . a gaggle of eight enemy fighters is almost on top of the four
Americans . . . diving at great speed. They must have started down
from a high altitude. Instinctively, desperately, MacDonald slams the
wheel left and back. *Putt-Putt* lurches hard left. He pulls the tightest
turn he can wring out of the Lightning . . . but not in time.

The four Lightnings are breaking in various directions as the Jacks
and Zekes flash down on them, from behind, opening fire. MacDonald's
quick left turn is not completed before the enemy fighters are among
the Lightnings, or where the Lightnings were a second ago. They
swish past and around him as he struggles to bring *Putt-Putt's* nose all
the way around and roll out in the same direction, this time behind the
Japs instead of in front of them. Then he and his wing man turn into
one Jack, who quickly breaks away. Now he's cutting in on one of the
last of the eight enemy planes from a forty-five-degree angle off the
enemy's rear. Holding wheel back and lining up the enemy in his sight
at the same time, straining through the pull of a tight turn, MacDonald
finds time to open fire from a slight angle astern.

The cannon and fifties shake the Lightning . . . but aim is good
. . . shells tear into the unsuspecting Zeke out to the right, ahead.
The cannon is exacting a heavy price . . . huge chunks of the light
Zeke rip off and sail backward through the air. The right wing comes
on up . . . the nose of the enemy fighter drops . . . it peels off into
a straight-away dive. Vertically the green-gray Zeke, streaking the sky
with white smoke and vapor, plunges downward. MacDonald watches
the show for a moment . . . the enemy pilot doesn't get out. The
Zeke goes straight into the water below, with a splash. Victory number
two for the day.

Up front MacDonald sees a Lightning streaking away from one of
the Zekes, but the enemy pilot is right behind him, and with greater
speed, from diving, the Zeke should be able to stay there. MacDonald,
throttles full forward, points his nose at the Jap. The P–38 looks like
Smitty's, his exec, today his element leader. MacDonald strains every
ounce of power out of the engines . . . the Jap is squarely on the

Lightning's rear . . . they are three or four thousand feet ahead. Mac-Donald banks left to cut them off, sensing their slight left turn, and starts closing in from eight o'clock.

He narrows the gap rapidly coming on from the side . . . the Zeke has the Lightning cold . . . MacDonald keeps the enemy plane in view. The Jap doesn't see him, obviously intent on the victim ahead, even though MacDonald is pressing in hard from the enemy pilot's left rear. The greenish-gray Zeke grows larger and larger and Mac-Donald lines him up in his sight ring, maneuvering *Putt-Putt* in a smooth left bank, slicing in nicely for a deflection shot. He is on the Zeke, ready to fire . . . but where is the P–38? MacDonald can't see him. He opens fire.

By this time MacDonald's left bank makes his approach a forty-degree pass from behind, left, and his shells streak ahead into the surprised enemy pilot. Instantly the 38's fire begins to tell on the Zeke. MacDonald keeps firing. White smoke trails back from the enemy . . . vapor and smoke . . . then *Putt-Putt's* shells find their mark and a small white fire flashes up ahead . . . the Zeke is already fatally damaged . . . before the enemy pilot can turn away, out of the trap. The right wing of the enemy fighter lifts slowly . . . smoke still trailing backward. MacDonald is almost on him at point-blank range . . . black fragments and bits of his aircraft fly backward through the air amid the white smoke and vapor. Suddenly the enemy fighter separates. The tail section and part of the fuselage glide slowly off the right . . . the front end, with cockpit and wings, goes into a forward tumble . . . there is no big burst of fire . . . the Zeke disintegrates! The two pieces of plane falling at different angles fascinate MacDonald for a split second . . . he notices the faded reddish-orange suns painted on the Zeke's wings, on the forward end of the fighter, as it tumbles down. The enemy pilot doesn't get out this time . . . either he can't get out of the tumble or he has been hit. Victory number three for the day! This one was fast.

But where is Smitty? MacDonald calls him on the radio. No answer. Did he get to the enemy fighter in time to save Smitty? MacDonald wonders. He searches the sky for the missing Lightning. He spots the other two from the flight . . . and a lone Zeke! The enemy planes have dwindled to one! The three Lightnings take after the lone bandit, who is full throttling it to the west . . . obviously headed for his base on Negros. The Lightnings follow on a westward course. Slowly they close from behind on the Zeke, which suddenly pulls up into a cloud.

The Lightnings come on, and reach the top of the small cloud. The Jap flashes out, ahead.

MacDonald is closest to the enemy. The two Lightnings with him are coming on behind, but not close enough to attack with him. *Putt-Putt*, still full throttle, roars on behind the low-wing silhouette ahead. Mac-Donald watches the range close . . . the enemy is being overhauled. He feels the excitement of battle once again and he gets ready to open fire . . . he is almost in range.

The Zeke out front suddenly lifts a wing and whips sharply up into a turn . . . MacDonald slams the wheel right and pulls it in as tight as he can turn . . . but the Zeke completes the circle in a smaller arc, and pulls back out on a western heading. *Putt-Putt* levels out after the tight, blood-draining turn, MacDonald finding himself a little farther back than when it began. The enemy pilot is adept. He knows he can't outrun the Lightning, but he can outturn it, and he's using this advantage to gain enough ground, when caught, to get away again.

MacDonald's wide-open Lightning is cutting the gap down fast again. The enemy didn't gain very much in the circle. The two Lightnings behind MacDonald are now closer, having gained distance when the Zeke and MacDonald circled to the right. The enemy pilot may not see the two support Lightnings. If he continues to circle when MacDonald pulls into range, sooner or later one of the other Lighnings will be waiting for him.

Now MacDonald watches the low-winged Zeke come into sight . . . into range. As he is about to press the firing button, the enemy aircraft ahead zooms up and around in a maximum bank to the left. *Putt-Putt* stands on left wing and MacDonald hauls the wheel back with all he's got . . . the Zeke is a tight-turning fighter. Doing the best he can and feeling the weight of gravity pressing down hard on his shoulders, he sees the Zeke pull slightly away as he rolls out again, resuming his western heading. MacDonald rolls out behind him . . . a little out of range once more.

He notices two silver Lightnings abreast of him now, one off to the right, one off to the left. It's three Americans behind the wily enemy pilot. MacDonald is nearest, at the point of the triangle, but the other two are close enough to discourage any more circles from the enemy.

Slowly the distance closes as *Putt-Putt*, for the third time, eases up behind the homeward-bound enemy pilot. MacDonald fixes the enemy in his orange sight ring . . . still a little far ahead . . . but *Putt-Putt* closes. Seconds pass slowly; now . . . almost in range . . . MacDonald gets ready. He can clearly see the rudder and tail section of the Zeke straight ahead, sitting there as if it's standing still. In a second or two more he'll have him. Then the bandit's wing goes up again . . . he's trying another climbing circle! Doesn't he know the other two Lightnings have closed him from behind? The Zeke turns right . . . straight into the path of the P–38 piloted by Lieutenant Leo W. Blakely. Blakely fastens on his tail, opens fire.

MacDonald can see the Zeke taking hits . . . the enemy pilot flew into the trap . . . the Lightning hangs on him, firing away . . . in a short time it's all over . . . the Zeke is smoking and plunging toward the sea. The enemy pilot won't reach Negros to tell his story today.

Now thoughts return to Smitty. With the Zeke accounted for, MacDonald turns back toward the American convoy. He hears pilots of other squadrons shouting excitedly . . . someone on the radio describes a kamikaze attack on an American ship. Eyes cover the sky in all directions. MacDonald banks left and curves gracefully around the westernmost ships in the U.S. convoy below.

Almost straight ahead, three dots . . . eleven o'clock. They are slightly below . . . about 8,000 feet . . . MacDonald identifies them as Zekes. They're heading down on the convoy. He decides to give chase. Throttles open up and once again engines are wide open. The Japs split into a two-plane element and a single . . . the two Zekes are turning hard left, heading for the clouds. They are already close. The third Zeke continues down. MacDonald points his nose at the nearest Zeke, one of the two curving away. For a few moments he closes from behind. Then they reach the cloud bank—refuge for fleeing Jap pilots today.

MacDonald gives up the chase, takes his eye off the clouds. The lone Zeke is almost directly below and heading down, low, for the convoy. He stands *Putt-Putt* on left wing and peels off downward after the single. His flight stays in position, in spite of the sudden maneuver. The Zeke is getting dangerously close to the U.S. ships. Now MacDonald sees another Lightning out front . . . closer on the Jap's tail than he is.

Suddenly the ships' guns belch flame and smoke. A barrage of heavy and light fire streaks toward the Zeke, who gamely comes on . . . toward one of the warships. It looks like a destroyer or light cruiser. MacDonald recognizes the Lightning following the daring enemy pilot in . . . it is "Andy" Anderson's plane. He picks up the mike and tells

Andy to break off the engagement. He pulls out of his own dive and turns away. The Jap is already down to 2,000 feet, moving at top speed. Anderson will never catch him in time and anti-aircraft fire is decorating the sky through which he must fly. Down and down the enemy pilot continues. Anderson doesn't break. He stays on the enemy's tail. The Zeke flashes over the one warship and heads for another . . . Anderson is flying through heavy anti-aircraft fire.

Spellbound by the spectacle unfolding below, MacDonald watches as the Zeke screams down on the second U.S. warship. He holds his breath . . . the Jap is a kamikaze . . . he's going to crash into the ship. Helpless, he watches the low-winged, single-engine Zeke, firing with everything it has. Then there's a flash below. The ship is hit. The Zeke flew straight into it. Fire and black boiling smoke rise from the stricken ship. MacDonald scans the sky, but sees no more enemy planes. He sees Anderson pulling up again, roaring over the warship just after it took the crash of the enemy plane. Anderson is lucky to be alive. Despite his daring chase the Zeke broke through.

MacDonald calls the controller below . . . he learns Smitty is missing. The American convoy is no longer under attack . . . other fighters are circling above it to defend against further attacks. So MacDonald eases back on the throttles and noses down . . . heads for the area where he shot the Zeke off Smitty's tail. The three Lightnings slant steadily downward . . . 3,000, 2,000, 1,000 feet. Down MacDonald goes . . . until only a few hundred feet over the bay. Then he and the two Lightning pilots behind search the waters below and around. They continue the search until gas tanks are about empty. Still MacDonald is not satisfied. He heads for home, heart heavy. If Smitty is down there in the water, he wants to spot him before the Japanese do.

In fifteen minutes the three 432nd Lightnings are approaching Dulag once again. It is late afternoon. MacDonald comes straight in and lands without losing a minute. Behind him the other two Lightnings touch down. As soon as he taxies to his revetment, MacDonald orders *Putt-Putt* refueled. He will go back one more time—to search for Smitty. Though having flown three missions already, and thoroughly whipped down from the excitement and strain of combat, MacDonald will take off again.

From among the other pilots three volunteer to accompany him back to Ormoc Bay. Two are the pilots who flew the last mission, on which Smitty was lost. In a few minutes four Lightnings are gassed up and ready to go. For the fourth time today, with the sun now lowering in the west over the palm trees, MacDonald pushes black-knobbed throttles to the stop. *Putt-Putt* howls down the sloppy runway. Three yellow-spinnered Lightnings follow him off. Turning immediately into the west, MacDonald pours on power to reach the bay as soon as possible.

The bay comes into view ahead and MacDonald starts out to the area where the Zekes and Japs jumped his flight earlier in the afternoon. Down low, throttles eased back, the Lightnings circle and weave above the waves. Each of the four pilots continuously covers the surface of the water around them . . . they hope to spot a dinghy bobbing atop the choppy surf. But the search goes on in vain. The Lightnings find no sign of life. The December sky grows dimmer and dimmer. There's not much time left. Until the last minute MacDonald continues the futile search. Then, at last, reluctantly, he calls the three Lightnings and tells them the flight will go home.

Darkness is falling as the four Lightnings arrive over Dulag for the last time December 7. Wearily, MacDonald sits *Putt-Putt* down on the muddy strip and rolls to the turn-off. Stars are already out in the Philippine sky . . . it has been a long day.

Several minutes later at group operations, discussing with intelligence officers the hectic battles of the day, MacDonald is called to the telephone. It is Fighter Command . . . General Paul "Squeeze" Wurtsmith. How did the 475th Group do today? MacDonald says the count isn't completed, but that 475th did well. Wurtsmith is elated. Many enemy planes were destroyed during the day, he says. He tells MacDonald other U.S. outfits did themselves proud. "Wasn't that something about Jerry Johnson?" he asks. "He got three today!" Then Wurtsmith asks MacDonald: "How many did you get?"

"I got three, too," MacDonald replies.

Final figures showed Fifth Air Force pilots shot down sixty-four Japanese planes on the 7th. The 475th Group accounted for twenty-eight of these. In addition, a number of ships in the Japanese convoy were sunk with an estimated loss of 4,000 Japanese troops—sent to reinforce the enemy's positions on the northwest coast of Leyte. Japanese interference with the American convoy was beaten back with surprisingly low losses. One American destroyer had been sunk, and one small transport. The 77th Division was safely ashore and fighting.

Despite the victory, MacDonald was depressed over the loss of Smitty and Captain "Pee Wee" Dahl, whom he had ordered to take over the squadron early that morning when he found himself low on gas and had to go home early. Dahl had been shot down in the fight which developed after MacDonald departed.

He had bailed out and landed in Ormoc Bay, with hands and hair burned badly from fire which enveloped his plane as he jumped out, in the middle of four enemy destroyers. The Japs on the nearest ship began to shout excitedly, and then a machine gun opened fire on him. Dahl played dead. The destroyer came closer and stopped engines to look him over at close range.

One bullet had creased his head and Dahl had concluded he was done for when the sound of approaching B–25's frightened the Japanese. The destroyer suddenly steamed off . . . leaving him five hundred yards from shore. At dusk a strong wind blew him toward shore. As he approached he noticed two patrols . . . one to his right and one to the left. He headed for a spot between them. Reaching shore, exhausted, he nevertheless ran up into the woods about a hundred feet from the beach. He crouched in some thick bushes.

Soon he heard approaching feet. He pulled out his forty-five and held it up in front of him. Then two feet stopped beside him. A face parted the bushes . . . a brown face. He pulled the trigger. Click! Wet powder! Lucky for him, for these were Philippine scouts, who took him to a guerrilla hideout. Many Japs were still in the area. The Filipinos applied coconut oil to his burns and two weeks later Pee Wee walked into the American fighter base—with a monkey on his shoulder!

MacDonald and other pilots of the 475th and 432nd Squadron were elated to see him.

Smitty wasn't so lucky. He was never heard from again.

For courageous leadership on December 7, and for the destruction of three enemy fighters, personally, and twenty-eight by squadrons under his command, MacDonald was awarded the Distinguished Flying Cross.

When he totaled his awards and decorations after the war, it was one of many. He had won the Distinguished Service Cross and cluster, the Silver Star with cluster, the Distinguished Flying Cross, with five clusters, numerous Air Medals and many other decorations. Moreover, he ended the war as the third highest-scoring fighter ace in the Far East and the fifth highest, in aerial kills, in all theaters, with twenty-seven victories.

11 *Surprise at Asch*

JANUARY 1, 1945:

Colonel J. C. MEYER

THE last German offensive, in late 1944, known as the Battle of the Bulge, was also the last big offensive on the part of the Luftwaffe aimed at knocking out Allied air power.

This Luftwaffe operation was carried out on the morning of January 1, 1945, when German fliers strafed and bombed Allied airfields in France, Belgium, and Holland, destroying 156 planes.

Air Force Photo

Losses suffered by the Luftwaffe were also high. After this gasp, the Luftwaffe never again assumed the offensive on such a scale and with such results. Nevertheless, the attack of January 1 took the Allies by surprise, and cost them dearly.

Preparations leading up to the effort included the greatest Luftwaffe concentration of fighters during the war. Throughout the late summer and fall months of 1944 the German Fighter Command steadily assembled a reserve for what was secretly called the "Great Blow." At this time German fighter production was higher than it had ever been before. The idea was to strike the U.S. Eighth Air Force a crippling blow with overwhelming strength—employing a force of more than

2,500 fighters. The Germans were prepared to accept the loss of 400 fighters in an effort to bring down at least 400 heavy bombers.

By November 12, 1944, the Luftwaffe had eighteen fighter wings and 3,700 aircraft ready. A few days later an order from Adolf Hitler changed the plan. Fighter reserves were to prepare to move to the western front, where they would take part in a great land battle—the Battle of the Bulge. On November 20 this transfer was ordered.

On December 16 Hitler surprised the world by launching a twenty-nine division onslaught against a thinly-held part of the American line in Belgium. The Nazi push for a time threatened to disrupt Allied lines and turn into a major American defeat. In seven days the Germans advanced fifty miles, having broken up or routed four U.S. divisions holding the line in the Ardennes—where the wallop of the German offensive was received.

Considerable confusion developed during the second and third days of the German offensive. Intolerable weather played its part. No Allied soldier or airman who fought through that winter will ever forget the cold, ice, snow, and fog—and stiff German opposition—which were constant companions. In the first uncertain days of the Nazi push, the 352nd Fighter Group of the English-based Eighth Air Force was suddenly ordered to move from its home to a new one, near Asch, Belgium, in the proximity of the front.

The fighter strength of the Eighth—a heavy-bomber organization—was primarily used to protect bombers assaulting German targets. The Ninth Tactical Air Force, in France, was used primarily to provide ground support and tactical assistance to the armies. The 352nd's orders were to support Ninth—which was soon to enter the raging ground battle with decisive results.

In the first days of the German offensive, however, foul weather—worst in years on the Continent—grounded Ninth Air Force. The German command had carefully waited for such conditions to launch its last great attack.

During this period of foul weather and military crisis the 352nd's planes and pilots were ordered to move. Within seventy-two hours after receiving the order, the group was ready for operations at Asch, in time to take advantage of clearing weather, which was to decide the fate of the German offensive. The redeployment of an air echelon in bad weather in seventy-two hours is a feat in itself, apart from the combat record the 352nd was to establish at Asch.

Pilots who had slept in comfortable quarters, at a permanent base in

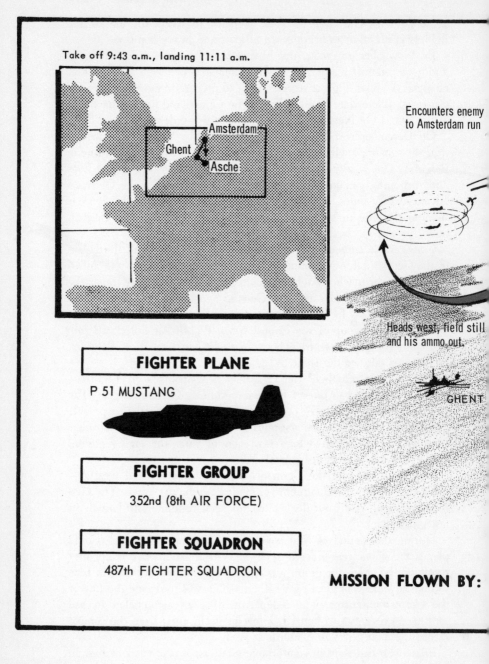

Take off 9:43 a.m., landing 11:11 a.m.

Amsterdam
Ghent
Asche

Encounters enemy
to Amsterdam run

Heads west, field still
and his ammo out.

GHENT

FIGHTER PLANE

P 51 MUSTANG

FIGHTER GROUP

352nd (8th AIR FORCE)

FIGHTER SQUADRON

487th FIGHTER SQUADRON

MISSION FLOWN BY:

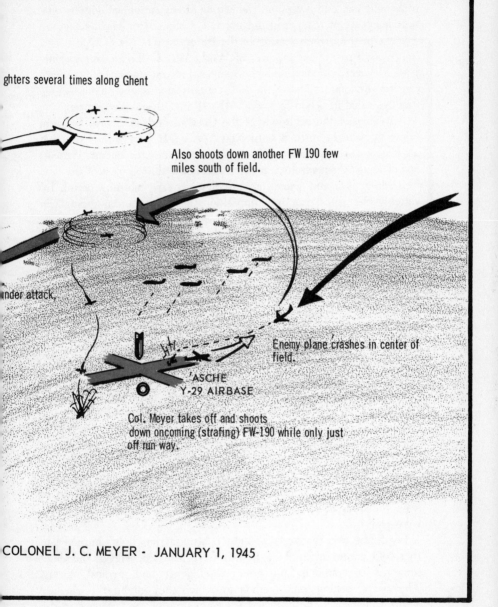

ghters several times along Ghent

Also shoots down another FW 190 few
miles south of field.

nder attack,

Enemy plane crashes in center of
field.

'ASCHE
Y-29 AIRBASE

Col. Meyer takes off and shoots
down oncoming (strafing) FW-190 while only just
off run way.

COLONEL J. C. MEYER - JANUARY 1, 1945

England, suddenly found themselves pitched in tents surrounded by snow and ice, and swept by the winds of an Ardennes winter. The superb morale of the 352nd did not fail. Colonel Jim Mayden's group was one of the highest scoring in the European Theater of Operations. It produced two of the top aces of World War II—Lieutenant Colonel J. C. Meyer, who today holds the unofficial record among living Americans for the total number of air and ground victories, and Major George Preddy, killed in action in World War II after thirty-one victories.

A week after the beginning of the German push skies over Belgium began to clear. From then until New Year's Day, except for December 28, the 352nd maintained daily operations against the enemy. At least one of its three squadrons was usually airborne during most of the day. Between twelve and sixteen aircraft flew an early-morning patrol. Invariably the patrol ran into opposition, and competition grew keen among pilots eager to be assigned to the first mission. The Germans were committing their carefully built-up fighter reserve, and for the first time in months the Luftwaffe was meeting the American and British air forces in equal numbers over the battle area.

In a frenzied first week of operations the 352nd destroyed an impressive number of German aircraft, playing a vital role in decimating the fighter force Hitler had thrown into the Battle of the Bulge, along with twenty-nine ground divisions. Pilots were seeing more combat with enemy fighters, and scoring more victories, than ever before.

Therefore, at midnight at the turn of the year, December 31, 1944, when orders reached the group outlining a maximum-effort escort mission for the next morning, Mayden, Deputy Commander Meyer, and the three squadron commanders were dismayed. The order meant no early-morning patrol next morning, consequently less chance to engage the enemy in combat. The bomber mission, which the 352nd was to escort, would take the group deep into Germany and consume most of the day. Since the greatest part of the Luftwaffe's fighter activity was concentrated in the battle area, pilots felt they were being ordered to leave the scene of active aerial warfare just when combat and victories were plentiful.

Inside the tent that served as group headquarters lights burned late that cold winter night. In a huddle were Mayden, Meyer, the three squadron commanders, and group intelligence and medical officers. They were seeking some method by which they might still schedule a patrol next morning. But careful examination of the language in the order, and consideration of every angle, failed to produce a solution.

At this moment, on German fields not too far away, pilots who were to fly every available Luftwaffe aircraft planned the morning's mission. Various wings and squadrons were assigned various Allied fields and one of the American fighter bases to be strafed was Y-29—home of the 352nd. Had pilots of the 352nd known of the German plan they would have been even more eager to withhold some of their fighters from the escort mission.

Meyer, deputy commander of the 352nd, unaware of the impending German fighter attack, nevertheless would not accept the decision to send all fighters on the bombing show. The heavy-featured, crisp-tongued New Yorker's final instructions to Otto Zeibell, Group Intelligence Officer, as the strategy council broke up on the night of the 31st, were that he be waked up early next morning, in time for a patrol, anyhow.

So at 7 A.M. on the first day of 1945, in fog and darkness of a memorable European winter, Zeibell shook Meyer out of his dreams in a sleeping bag, turned up the light in the tent. Meyer donned heavy socks, battle shoes, heavy underwear and the sweat suit and tank suit he wore on winter missions. Picking up heavy parka and hat, he hurried out to a waiting jeep, which carried him to group operations. It was 7:15 A.M. when he arrived.

Inside he got the weather report . . . not encouraging. The field was to be socked in for several hours. Maybe all the planning the night before had been in vain. Certainly there was no chance of a patrol until later in the morning. It was too early to call "Football" to get last night's orders changed. "Football" was the code name of TAC headquarters, which would have to give its approval if patrol or local tactical mission were flown by the 352nd that day. Meyer headed for the mess tent and breakfast. Outside he noticed an awful fog over Y-29.

Not too many miles to the east hundreds of German fighter pilots peered into the sky, also waiting for the heavy fog to disperse and permit take-off. ME-109's, FW-190's and other Luftwaffe types were armed and ready to go. Morale of German pilots had been buoyed by the apparent success of Von Rundstedt's offensive. Now they hoped to surprise unsuspecting Allied airfields as rudely as Rundstedt's divisions surprised outnumbered American troops in the Ardennes two weeks earlier. They did not fully appreciate of course, that the German attack had stalled, and that German troops were already falling back from advanced positions.

Fresh eggs were not available at mess for Meyer and other pilots of the 352nd that morning. As they sweated out the weather, and their orders, they downed canned grapefruit juice, French toast, salty bacon, and coffee. But at 8 A.M. Meyer was back at group headquarters putting in a call to TAC. He made his request straight and simple: "Can't we get the orders changed? We're missing a good chance for kills. Couldn't we run both a patrol and the escort's missions?" The answer—negative.

"Can we use only thirty-six aircraft for the maximum effort?" TAC would call back in twenty minutes. Meyer and other 352nd pilots hung in suspense. Twenty minutes later the call came in. General Elwood Quesada had made the decision. The answer—still no. Meyer, it seemed, had risen early that morning in vain. But the high-scoring, freckled, fair-haired deputy commander was not easily dissuaded. He would give it one more try. Again he called TAC. This time they put him through to Quesada.

"Can't we justify this on the basis that an enemy effort in the area is a threat . . . especially to so many heavily loaded P–51's taking off at the same time?" Quesada hedged. Neither he nor Meyer knew then what prophetic words had been uttered. He put Meyer on the spot. If he would state categorically the 352nd actually needed fighters for local operations, because of the enemy threat, he would approve the request. But Meyer had to take the responsibility.

Accepting it, Meyer said he thought a thirty-six-plane escort, with some fighters available for other duties, was proper. "We shouldn't take the chance," he said—referring to the dispatch of the group's full complement on an escort mission. Quesada approved the change over the phone. It was 8:45.

Without pause, replacing the receiver, Meyer blurted orders to operations personnel to find the commanding officer of the 487th Squadron, Bill Halton, and tell him to get to the briefing room with other pilots of his squadron. Then he called engineering and armament, telling them to get aircraft of the 487th ready. Ground crews had sweated through the night fitting extra tanks on the squadron's planes, preparing for a long mission. Now they went to work to get them off in a hurry.

Meanwhile, pilots of the 487th hustled to briefing. Twelve 487th aircraft would fly patrol, four less than normal squadron strength. The other four, plus thirty-two fighters from the 486th and 328th squadrons would give the group thirty-six fighters (three squadrons of twelve planes each) for the escort mission. Happiest among the base's flying personnel that morning were the dozen pilots of 487th's White, Red, and Blue Flights, assembled in the group briefing room by 9:05. They would fly the patrol.

Meyer let Halton outline the mission. Meyer would lead White Flight and be Transport White Leader. Halton would lead Red Flight. Bill Whisner would lead Blue. "Transport" was the code name of the 487th Squadron.

The patrol would fly to the St. Vith area. (St. Vith, having been the scene of bitter fighting, was taken by the Germans December 21 after a gallant defense by Brigadier General R. W. Hasbrouck and the 7th Armored Division.) Through St. Vith passed one of the main routes feeding the Nazi drive west, and ground targets were usually plentiful, air encounters with German defenders frequent. (Several German airfields were operating in the salient.)

St. Vith was one of the two most important transportation hubs in the Bulge. Hasbrouck's 7th Division had set out for it hurriedly on the second day of the raging battle, from the Aachen area, and by nightfall was in position, having covered a distance of fifty miles and having been forced to detour on several occasions to escape the onrushing columns of Sixth S.S. Panzer Army. Hasbrouck held out for four days, meanwhile being relieved by tough 82nd Paratroop Division, only to be pushed back by half a dozen German divisions on the 21st. The Germans poured reinforcements through St. Vith thereafter and its roadways became a scene of slaughter as Allied fighters and fighter bombers mercilessly strafed German mechanized equipment. It was to this area of activity and action that Halton proposed to go—and for good reason.

Meyer told pilots of the 487th the squadron would have to be back at Y–29 in time to provide protection for the thirty-six heavily loaded fighters taking off on the escort mission. He had stuck his neck out, he said, and if the squadron ran into something he wanted to make it pay more than usual. There would be no start-engine time, as was usual on fighter missions. Meyer would wait in his cockpit until weather permitted take-off. Then he would wave his hand and the eleven other fighters would follow him to the runway. The group filed out of the tent.

As pilots stepped outside they noticed an improvement in the weather. The base was still socked in but fog was burning off. Meyer, in a jeep, hurried to the parachute tent, donned flying gear. From there he drove out to *Petie*, his silver-billed Mustang, which reposed majestically in its revetment. Not far away were a number of P–47's—from another group. Armorers and ground crewmen had done a fast job on *Petie*. The fighter was ready to go, with drop tanks removed, fully loaded and checked. Already Meyer had scored twenty-two aerial kills. He wondered if this was the beginning of the mission that would raise his total to twenty-three. He wiggled into the cockpit and glanced up at

P–38's armed with bomb taxi for take-off from a Belgian airfield on a dive-bombing mission during the Battle of the Bulge. (Air Force Photo)

the gray sky. He would have to wait a little longer. At 9:40, the fog beginning to lift, he made the decision to go, waved his arm and started engine. Other Mustangs coughed and turned over. The squadron fell into line for one-at-a-time take-off. Meyer reached the end of the west-east runway, and flicked on gun and gunsight switches.

It is time to go. He rams the throttle handle all the way forward and the Mustang roars and rattles, lunging off. He begins to roll faster. In seconds he will be airborne. Then something strange up ahead catches his eye. Black puffs on the eastern edge of the field! Also . . . tracers from machine guns! The black puffs are all over the sky . . . as if anti-aircraft guns are firing at enemy planes. He presses the transmitter button of his radio, meanwhile keeping the growling fighter centered in the runway: "Marmite Control, Marmite Transport Leader . . . do you have anything in the area?" The reply comes back: "Negative." "Marmite" is the code name for Y–29's control tower.

What can it mean? *Petie* is rumbling down the runway in the direction of the flak bursts . . . base radar has nothing on its scopes. The sky at the eastern end of the field is now filled with anti-aircraft fire. The Germans have been bombing the field frequently at night, but not this time of day. Meyer keeps working rudders and feeling the stick. Then, up front . . . on the edge of the field . . . low . . . a bandit! An FW–190 straight ahead, just over the trees, racing around in a turn that will put him on a converging course.

His heart jumps! He will be a sitting target. He notices other German fighters circling the edges of the field, very low. Y–29 is coming under enemy strafing attack at the moment of take-off! The FW banks left and puts its nose down dead ahead for a strafing run, its blunt radial-engine nose now clearly identifiable. The two fighters are on converging courses. The German can take advantage of Meyer's plight and pour his fire into *Petie* before the Mustang gains sufficient speed to be maneuverable, even if airborne. Meyer watches the oncoming FW, paralyzed. To his side, off the runway, sits a parked C–47 transport.

The German aims at the larger target! The Mustang is making 100 m.p.h. Meyer, eyes locked on the ever-enlarging, fast-approaching enemy fighter, hauls stick back. He must get into the air. As soon as *Petie* is off, he retracts wheels. The nose points up . . . so quickly he almost loses sight of the German ahead. He pushes stick forward, to keep the FW in view. It is almost on him, firing away at the C–47. Meyer reacts instinctively as the oncoming silhouette grows larger and fills the gunsight ring. It's like a dream . . . the 190 is on him before he can think. His reaction is automatic; he pulls the trigger. Seconds only are available for the head-on pass.

Petie shudders at the recoil of six simultaneous guns . . . the sight circle is accurate . . . a stream of armor-piercing and incendiary shells slams into fuselage and engine of the low-winged enemy. The enemy fighter comes on, taking hits, more hits. Point-blank range! Meyer can see the effect of his guns, which surprised the German pilot. They rake the sky-blue fuselage and tear up wings . . . holes and chunks are torn out of the belly . . . it is an unbelievably short fight.

Frozen, Meyer watches the FW nose down. The enemy pilot can't go under him! The 190 inclines downward at the field . . . straight in! Meyer whistles by so fast the kill hardly registers. He has scored a victory almost before getting airborne! The FW–190 does not burn. It crashes not far from the olive-green C–47. Meyer doesn't have time to look back. He is climbing out of the field . . . there are other bandits in the area.

He trims slightly and leans into a left turn, to clear the area, searching out the gray sky in every direction. All over the field anti-aircraft fire is bursting, high and low. The scene is one of complete confusion. Meyer, already victorious, is still in a dangerous tactical situation. He wonders if other Mustangs, now getting off the field, are going to escape being strafed on take-off and how they will fare in a battle with the enemy, outnumbered and caught low and slow.

The roaring Rolls-Merlin steadily pushes airspeed needle forward and *Petie* gracefully slices upward in the turn out of the field. Now Meyer hears personnel in the tower below, and other Mustangs: "They're Germans! Jesus Christ!" And: "They're bandits; they're all over the place!" They are. Ground guns rattle away and German fighters plow troughs along the surface of the field, through planes and buildings—whatever lies in the path of the stream of shells. But the attack has not halted take-off. Some of the P–47's Meyer had seen parked nearby also scramble into the air.

The fog, some of it still not dissipated, obscures parts of the field and makes recognition of aircraft difficult. Meyer, eyes straining to find a target and keep from being one, continues climbing . . . 800 feet, 900 . . . 1,000. He sees no enemy plane trailing him at the moment. The altimeter registers 1,500, 1,600, 1,700 . . . 2,000 feet. He doesn't know what's happening below. But . . . out front, off to the right . . . two specks. Now they become dots. Meyer toes rudder and eases stick right. The right wing dips and he curves in behind.

Now at 3,000, Meyer levels off . . . speed advances to cruising . . . the gap between *Petie* and the two bogies ahead closes slowly. Meyer is following at six o'clock . . . he can't make positive identification yet. They must be bandits. He glances behind . . . nothing on his tail. He strains to get a good look, a sharp silhouette outline. Gradually the dark figures grow larger . . . Meyer is closing in . . . he shoves the throttle handle forward. The fighters aren't Mustangs . . . the nose is too blunt. P–47's? Maybe . . . maybe not. Now the aircraft are quite close, one just ahead of the other. Bandits! FW–190's! Beyond a doubt.

Meyer nervously feels the trigger . . . he's moving in steadily from dead astern. Already his sight ring is enclosing the wingspan of the trailing 190 . . . as soon as the enemy's wings reach from side to side in the yellow light circle he'll be in range. Seconds drag. Will the enemy pilot clear his rear in time to break right or left? Too absorbed with the strafing, perhaps unaware Meyer got off the field at the beginning of the attack, the gray 190's continue on course. *Petie* pulls up behind, and into range. The Germans have relaxed too long. The wingspan of the second 190 is now wide enough to fill the sight. White-bordered crosses became visible on the wings.

Fire! The moment he pulls the trigger he feels *Petie* dip and bounce . . . turbulence . . . he's in the propwash of his victim. He holds the nose in place as well as possible . . . his fire seems to find the mark . . . hits register. Then, up high . . . off left rear . . . light flashes. Meyer's head snaps left, looks up. Curving down from above, to get on his tail, he sees a sharp-nosed fighter . . . winking wing guns . . . obviously trying to save the 190's caught from behind. An ME–109!

It's a critical moment. Shall he break off the attack? The attacking enemy fighter is too far out to register . . . evidently he hopes to distract Meyer with his fire. *Petie's* guns keep firing. Meyer decides he has time to shoot down the trailing 190 before the 109 can line him up . . . in range. Seconds are tense. The 190 is taking hits, but in propwash Meyer can't concentrate his fire. Still, other bandits have gone down after fewer hits than this. Can he knock him down before the 109 is on him?

Now the 190 solves the problem. The enemy pilot suddenly rolls over on his back and split-S's, highly dangerous at low altitude. Meyer can't follow . . . the enemy pilots should go straight in . . . his chances of pulling out, missing the trees below, are slim. Also, he has taken hits . . . controls may not be working properly. Meyer breaks sharply left, now concerned with the 109 pulling into range. He loses sight of the remaining 190 ahead and feels the strain of a sharp left turn . . . blood rushes from his head.

The maximum turn takes him out of the 109's path of fire momentarily, but Meyer is caught in a delicate situation, enemy aircraft all around. He has lost sight of the 109 and the 109 pilot has the advantage —he may be turning in behind him! The damaged 190 is heading straight down . . . now he begins to pull nose up . . . dangerously low. Meyer glances behind for the 109 . . . nowhere in sight! He looks for the other 190 . . . in vain. Then he sees the 109 . . . fully occupied, a Mustang on his tail! The Mustang pilot arrived in the nick of time . . . for Meyer was within range of three enemy pilots. Off to his right he sees the Mustang scoring hits. The American pilot sneaked in from behind, taking advantage of the German's preoccupation with *Petie*—just what the 109 pilot had tried on Meyer! The 109 flames. Meyer breaks his glance. He looks back at the daring 190 pilot below, trying to split-S from 3,000 feet.

Pulling streamers and apparently headed for the trees, the 190's nose slowly comes up. From above it looks as if the enemy fighter is already in the trees . . . certainly he is going in . . . then the 190 cuts through the tops, chews up leaves and small branches . . . but makes it! He has split-Sed from 3,000—and shaken his tormentor! Incredible, and though the maneuver cost him a victory, at least momentarily, Meyer admires the ability of the German pilot. Not enough to leave him alone. Instantly he leans left and points his nose at the fleeing enemy below . . . this time he intends to finish the job.

Petie starts down from 3,000 . . . picking up speed . . . 300 m.p.h., 320 . . . 340. The 190 is also making good speed after its sensational dive. The Mustang whistles lower and lower, Meyer keeping his eye on the enemy below, now flat-out on the deck, weaving right and left slowly, and heading again toward Y–29. But Meyer closes the gap . . . the Mustang is faster . . . the sight ring begins to fill up . . . he gets ready to open fire once more.

Thump! Thump! *Petie* gives a lurch . . . Meyer glances behind . . . clear! Then he sees the puffs . . . black puffs and tracers . . . he's under fire . . . fire from the ground! American gunners at Y–29 are aiming at both Meyer and the 190 ahead . . . obviously think two bandits are making a pass at the field. Shall he leave the 190, let him get away again? Already hit, bursts all around him, he decides to hang on behind through the ground fire. He wants this victory. The 190 is almost in range . . . he cuts him off a little in each turn. A hail of fire comes up from below. Thump! Thump! Thump!

Meyer suddenly notices a hole in his wing . . . he is taking more hits . . . *Petie* shudders as ground gunners register . . . the hole is six inches long, several inches wide . . . but *Petie* flies on. Luckily, the shell didn't penetrate his wing tank. At last, Meyer banks sharply right . . . the sight of a hole in his wing brings him to his senses. No good shooting down an enemy plane and losing your own. *Petie* streaks right, to escape the defense barrage below . . . dern those gunners—don't they know a Mustang from a blunt-nosed 190? Meyer now notices several other holes in his wing . . . he wonders if the engine is hit . . . if coolant or oil is leaking. Loss of either would force him down.

Out of the path of fire, Meyer banks back left, keeping the fleeing 190 in view. Anti-aircraft gunners haven't been able to bring the German down . . . he hugs the deck and S-turns constantly. Meyer follows him, off to the right . . . the Mustang has speed on the 190. Meyer aims his nose left, angling back in again. Fire from the ground now is sporadic. He fires again. Thump! *Petie* takes another hit, probably from a machine gun. But Meyer strikes pay dirt too . . . his shells reach the enemy fighter. Encouraged, he continues to fire . . . the enemy's wingspan is full in the gunsight ring.

The gray fighter ahead, desperately turning, takes strikes in its engine . . . Meyer sees pieces fly off the engine cowl . . . has he got him at last? The 190's propeller seems to turn slower . . . definitely slower . . . it begins to windmill. Meyer races up on him, closing the gap faster. The German noses down . . . Meyer is on him, and then over and past him, before he can check speed. He banks sharply to the right to come around for another pass. The stricken enemy aircraft is trying a belly landing. The German has to aim for an open field just ahead . . . with no altitude to pick his spot. Just clearing some trees, he smacks the ground and bounces up . . . again he hits . . . and bounces. The third time the 190 flips over, end over end . . . it breaks up under the impact . . . a splash of fire! There was no bail-out. The enemy pilot had only a few feet when he took the fatal hits. A bright fire burns and a black curl of smoke reaches up for the sky. Victory number two for the first mission of 1945—aerial victory twenty-four for Meyer!

With other enemy fighters in the area, and knowing his ammunition must be all but expended, Meyer knows he must land as soon as possible. Having drifted away from the field, and lost all sense of direction, Meyer presses the mike button and calls Marmite Tower. He asks for a fix, which would bring him to the field in minutes. "Y–29 is still under attack," the tower reports. Unsafe for landing! The Jerries are really working it over today. Meyer decides to take up a compass heading west . . . the enemy homeland is east. He won't risk flying over an enemy field or getting involved over enemy territory. He'll wait it out.

For the first time in the day's battle he has time to take stock. His engine is running smoothly . . . he has enough gas to find a friendly field if he has to. He looks at the large hole in his wing, and the smaller ones. *Petie* can take it . . . the engine escaped the shells of friend and foe. He flies along, scanning the countryside. Up ahead he spots a large clearing . . . an airfield.

He glances around as a precaution. His head stops, eyes fixed on his right rear. Just off the rear, at five o'clock, three ME–109's are bearing down on him at top speed! Break left! *Petie* roars as he calls for power, and excitement of battle grips him again. He carves out a maximum vertical left turn, anxiously watching the bandits behind. They turn left to maneuver into position at six o'clock. But Meyer has begun his turn just in time. Now the four aircraft make up a big circle . . . Meyer trying to turn in on the tail of the third enemy fighter . . . the lead bandit attempting to get into firing position directly behind Meyer. Suddenly other fighters flash into view. Meyer spots 51's . . . this field is also under attack! But he must concentrate on the 109's; he banks as tight as *Petie* will turn without spinning, which might prove fatal.

The grim circular maneuver continues. Meyer gains on the third German . . . he fires a burst . . . then silence . . . out of ammo! Just then other P–51's sweep into the act. Meyer welcomes their appearance . . . they fly in from various directions. He has scored no hits on the third enemy fighter and would like to break off the battle. The area becomes filled with fighters . . . everyone milling around like mad. Meyer, out of ammo, decides to break out of the turning maneuver. Abruptly he banks right, again setting course generally west, full speed. Glancing back to see if the 109's follow, bending on all power for the getaway, he streaks away into the west. The 109's do not follow. Other Mustangs have occupied the Germans. Relieved, Meyer realizes he has escaped from a tight situation.

For ten minutes he flies on . . . the Germans can't be everywhere . . . he pulls stick back. He will gain altitude to improve vision and to avoid being caught low by the enemy, so often an insurmountable disadvantage in combat. *Petie* lifts his nose and the altimeter climbs . . . roads, rivers and streams grow smaller below. Meyer studies the terrain for a recognizable sign. Today is not a day for toothless fighters in the cold, pallid skies of Belgium. The minutes tick by . . . fuel is steadily consumed.

Then, up ahead, a city comes into view. The city might be Ghent. Something is moving in the sky above. He takes a longer look . . . fighters! Bandits! The sight sends a chill down his spine. Perhaps he has seen too many in one day . . . or maybe it's because he's unarmed. Meyer eases stick back and turns away, still high enough to get out

of the area before being seen. He flies northwest for several minutes
. . . fuel gauges gradually flickering nearer the empty mark, but still
enough left. He decides to call Marmite Control again, to ask what he
should do. The tower comes in immediately . . . there are still bandits
in the Y–29 area. No one knows what to tell him to do. Meyer pulls
back on the stick and resumes climb. He reverses course and flies back
toward the east. He will get higher.

Minute after minute passes. *Petie* drones upward to higher altitude.
Meyer begins to wonder when he'll get down . . . for the first time in
many missions his main concern is avoiding the enemy until he can
land. The Rolls-Merlin is still smooth. He wonders about the escort
mission—whether it got off. For some time he flies on alone, failing to
spot a bogy.

Meyer sees the mass of another city ahead. Airfields are certain to be
located nearby. It's a very large city . . . plenty of water around. The
closer he approaches the more puzzled he is . . . the city is quite big
. . . a port city. Amsterdam! Impossible. How did he get so far north?
But it is. Surprise is followed by surprise. He should have expected it
. . . black forms moving around and over the city and airfield! More
German fighters! Definitely bandits. A sense of frustration grips him.

Another shock . . . black puffs dot the sky out front . . . anti-aircraft fire. Below, they're shooting at him. Meyer instantly pulls up and
turns away . . . he banks right 150 degrees, points south . . . he will
head back toward Y–29, since the Luftwaffe seems to be everywhere.
But uncertainty creeps over him. An awful thought flashes through his
mind. Was that Hamburg? Was that why they fired on him? Is his
compass off . . . has he been flying north? He tries to put the uncertainty out of his mind.

Meyer glances over the earth below frantically . . . for some reason
he recognizes nothing. The clock on the panel tells him it's nearing
eleven o'clock. He wonders how much damage the Jerries did to Y–29,
how many pilots the 487th lost in the morning fight? Reflections are
brief . . . he must find a way out of his own dilemma. Still no landmark, no identification below . . . fields and forests and roads pass
beneath . . . paths of snow are everywhere, like the Luftwaffe. If he
were not both alone and out of ammunition, the flight would cause
little anxiety.

Five minutes pass . . . Meyer leans toward the glass in front of his
head. He sees an open field ahead . . . a grass airfield.

Meyer stares down . . . still not a sign of activity . . . only a few shabby buildings and no aircraft . . . maybe it's an auxiliary field. The surface is all grass and snow.

Then he sees three aircraft . . . not on the field . . . at twelve o'clock high. He can recognize the low wings, single engines . . . they're fighters . . . now the old shock again . . . ME–109's! They're about 1,500 feet higher than he is. Meyer's heart races . . . will he ever see the last of German fighters today—alone with empty guns? He anxiously watches the 109's grow larger . . . they're on a converging course. They seem to be heading slightly to his right . . . he eases the stick left, he'll bank slowly away and under . . . if they let him.

He can see the nose spinners now . . . yellow and red . . . the 109's themselves are gray-black. On they come silently overhead . . . no change in direction . . . *Petie* is curving gracefully to the left . . . now almost under them. Meyer's head is straight up . . . can they miss him? The 109's pass overhead . . . still no sign they see him . . . now he looks back, overhead . . . the bandits are flying on.

The fuel gauges are lapping nearer empty . . . Meyer realizes he must soon find Y–29. If he doesn't get back soon he risks running out of gas. The enemy must have departed by now.

In spite of holes, *Petie* is flight-worthy, and it can't be too far to Y–29. The holes in the wing aren't too serious . . . he's flown with them for most of the mission.

Meyer calls Marmite Control. The tower comes in. The field is at last clear . . . he gets a course to fly and the green light to land! He sets course and checks the time—ten to eleven. In less than thirty minutes he will be home. Meyer keeps checking the sky, but sees no enemy planes . . . the fog which was so heavy in the morning is now largely burnt off.

The flight home is less exciting than the morning mission. The bandits have all gone home . . . those not shot down by anti-aircraft and American fighters. He begins to recognize landmarks as he approaches Y–29. None of the mystery and fear of the unknown, which only a short while back gripped him through and through, are present. And in a few more minutes he'll have the answers to many questions.

The tarmac runway looms ahead—Y–29! Meyer gets landing clearance and starts down. The field isn't a shambles after all. The C–47 that probably saved his life is wrecked . . . so are a couple of fighters caught parked by enemy strafers. But damage is surprisingly light, considering the length of the German attack that morning. *Petie* inclines gracefully in, off the end of the runway, touches down smoothly. Meyer pulls the canopy back and taxis in. As he approaches the parking area he can see a group of men awaiting his arrival . . . looking his way and talking excitedly. As he pulls in to park they stare long and hard at riddled *Petie*. Meyer switches off, raises up in the cockpit. It is 11:11 A.M. His ground crew rushes up, and a number of others, including Otto Zeibell and the I.O., all yelling greetings. Their questions are many . . . congratulations too. They had wondered what happened to him after his second call to Marmite Control in the morning, when Marmite reported the field still under attack.

As he tells his story, Meyer asks about the rest of the patrol. Did they get off? How many men were lost? Who were they? Zeibell tells him four aircraft are missing, but the patrol and several P–47's which also took off scored many victories. Moreover, the escort mission also got off—thirty-six planes. The Germans hit several buildings, some equipment and destroyed a few planes, but damage was lighter than might have been expected . . . and lighter, Zeibell tells him, than that suffered at several nearby fields, according to the reports.

Meyer feels good. He wonders what will be the reaction of General Quesada, and others, at TAC headquarters. He wearily climbs into the truck that is to take him to headquarters. It is still early and at headquarters he learns another patrol mission is to go off soon. He asks to fly on it.

Petie will have to be repaired. Meyer will fly another plane. But when *Petie* is ready again, there will be two more swastikas painted below the canopy, number 36 and 37! Meyer has twenty-four victories in the air (his twenty-third and twenty-fourth scored that morning), thirteen on the ground. The total of thirty-seven is the highest in the European Theater of Operations for an American fighter pilot.

That afternoon Meyer flew his last mission, with no inkling it was his finale. Next day the weather socked in again over Belgium. The 352nd Group was grounded for several days. Before he was able to fly again he was seriously injured in an automobile accident, which confined him to a hospital for three months. At the end of the convalescence period he was ordered to the United States.

The war was about over. In those three months the Allies crossed the Rhine and drove deep into Germany. American fighter groups enjoyed a heyday strafing German aircraft crowded into a steadily dwindling number of fields available to the Luftwaffe, more about which

P–38's over France. Striped paint was D-Day recognition garb. (Air Force Photo)

we will learn in the next chapter. Meyer could not help thinking how many more chances he would have had, to score victories, had he been flying. But, on the other hand, his number might have come up. At least he lived through the accident, and the Germans never got a chance to even matters with him in the air.

He had the satisfaction of knowing his insistence on flying the patrol on the morning of January 1, 1945, was appreciated at TAC headquarters. And the fighters that escorted heavy bombers into Germany encountered no opposition. The bombers got through, bombed the target, and returned to bases in good order.

And the 352nd Group destroyed twenty-three German fighters, that day, final tabulations showed—an indication of the success of Meyer's strategy.

TAC headquarters thought so much of Meyer's performance, and that of the 487th, that the Commanding General, Army Air Forces, General Carl Spaatz, plus other top generals, paid Y–29 a congratulatory visit to express their appreciation. General Quesada was highly pleased that Meyer had talked him into permitting twelve 352nd fighters to fly patrol.

For gallantry in action and foresight in planning, Meyer was awarded the second Oak Leaf Cluster to the Distinguished Service Cross. And best of all, the four pilots reported missing when he landed at Y–29 the afternoon of 487th's patrol survived the mission. One reported in shortly after Meyer. Another, shot up by an enemy fighter, bailed out successfully, straggled in a few hours later. The third missing 487th pilot showed up next—having lived to tell his tale, which included the destruction of three German fighters before he, himself, went down.

And last, some time later, the fourth missing pilot—who had also taken to parachute—appeared at the base. The reception for all, especially the last, was warm. The 487th had unexpectedly flown one of the great patrol missions of the war, having lost planes but no pilots. The squadron had blunted the effect of the German attack on Y–29. This accomplishment required take-off in the face of a strong enemy air attack, and combat under the disadvantages of insufficient speed or altitude to meet the enemy on anything like equal terms.

The mission would never have been flown had not Meyer insisted on holding back some of 352nd's planes from the bomber escort mission. True to the traditions of the fighter pilot, Meyer was looking for a fight. On January 1, 1945, he found a good one—and more than an ample number of opponents.

12 *Death of the Luftwaffe*

APRIL 17, 1945:

Lieutenant Colonel JOSEPH L. THURY

Simon's Studio

THE last fifteen months of the war produced the climax of the greatest sustained aerial assault in history, that of the Allied air forces against Germany.

The Royal Air Force began the campaign with limited forces in 1939 and was joined by the U.S.A.A.F. in 1942. By 1944 U.S. fighters at last possessed the range to penetrate the deepest strongholds of the Reich, previously immune from all-out low-altitude fighter strafing attacks.

When these fighters began to roam the faraway corners of southeast Germany, all the enemy homeland became a combat theater. As the Luftwaffe's Commander, Hermann Goering, watched U.S. fighters over Berlin in daylight for the first time (March, 1944), protecting bombers unloading thousands of tons of explosives, he is said to have admitted the war was lost—unless the Luftwaffe could somehow halt the expanding assault from the air.

U.S. fighters appeared in growing numbers in all sections of Germany, strafing airfields, shooting up trains and other targets, and left behind a steadily widening trail of destruction. The Luftwaffe realized

1944 was the crisis year. Accordingly, top priority was given aircraft production.

German output rose swiftly the first nine months of the year. By September monthly production had reached its wartime peak—4,103 planes. The German aircraft industry that year produced 40,593 planes, by far the greatest number of aircraft it assembled in any year of the war.

This was accomplished despite heavy Allied bombing of strategic targets, including the aircraft factories, by a herculean effort, one phase of which was a dispersal of the German aircraft industry—which spread into more than five hundred small centers assembly work formerly done in several dozen factories.

Inevitably, as the aerial battle increased in tempo and size, losses became heavier. In December of 1943 the United States introduced its best long-range fighter, the P–51, and during 1944 and 1945 it became a well-known and dreaded sight in areas of Germany that had seldom suffered from enemy fighters before. And to add to the pressure, growing numbers of B–17's and B–24's were put into action each month.

The Germans attempted to upset the developing pattern of Allied superiority with a jet fighter capable of a performance far surpassing that of any Allied fighter. Fortunately Hitler delayed production of the ME–262 for almost a year, insisting it be developed as a bomber.

As a result, the ME–262 jet fighter was not available to the Luftwaffe until well into 1944, after the situation in the air had deteriorated to a point where a recovery was impossible. By this time sufficient airfields, gasoline, transportation and other essentials necessary for a major retraining program were unavailable to the Luftwaffe. Germany did not have the time, the uninterrupted production or the facilities and organization to re-equip and retrain her squadrons with what was then the finest fighting plane in the world.

The aim of the Eighth U.S. Air Force was to make certain the Luftwaffe had no breathing spell in which to recover the initiative. The Eighth was the larger of the American heavy bomber air forces attacking Germany. It was scattered throughout southeast England and its bases included a number of fighter groups—which carried in the B–17's and B–24's, and escorted them out again, after which the fighters sometimes went back into Germany to select targets of opportunity for strafing.

The other U.S. heavy bomber air force assaulting Germany was the

Fifteenth, based in Italy. The Ninth Air Force, a tactical aerial arm, was based in England until shortly after the invasion of Europe, in June, 1944, and then moved to France. It was equipped with medium bombers and fighters, which were often employed as fighter bombers. The Twelfth Air Force fulfilled a similar mission in Italy.

The first jet aircraft, a Messerschmitt 262A-1. (Air Force Photo)

The Eighth Air Force was the biggest U.S. aerial force in Europe, dropped the greatest tonnage of bombs and suffered the greatest number of casualties. It produced ten of the fifteen top-scoring American fighter aces of the war. One of the "hot" groups in the Eighth Air Force was the 339th. It arrived in the ETO late in 1944, but in one year of operations claimed 691 victories. It was commanded by Colonel John P. Henry.

It is to the 339th Fighter Group, stationed at Fowlmere, in Cambridge, that we now turn our attention, as of April, 1945—a month before V-Day in Europe.

On the warm sunny morning of April 16, 1945, eight Mustangs, half the 505th Squadron (the 339th consisted of three squadrons) cut gracefully through the skies of southern Germany. They were scanning the countryside between Munich and Chiem Lake.

Leading the eight silver-bodied fighters was Major Joseph Thury, of St. Paul, Minnesota, now a resident of Tampa, Florida. He searched out the countryside below for targets. Already the fighters had escorted heavy bombers to their target in Germany, and, following orders, they were now out to strafe enemy airdromes. They had separated from the main force after the bombers headed home to England and descended to 10,000 feet. With visibility good, sixteen eyes looked over a brilliant German countryside for prey.

Suddenly, a voice broke radio silence—reporting something moving below. On the autobahn! Thury strained his eyes. He couldn't make it out . . . though it looked like a tractor towing something. He dipped the nose of his fighter and began a slow turn. Seven Mustangs followed.

He descended, watching. The tractor was towing a large object with wings! Now thoroughly interested, Thury scanned the surrounding area.

His curiosity was aroused by a large open space near the autobahn, not too far from the tractor. A closer look penetrated impressions of camouflage. The large area was an airfield.

Thury flushed with excitement. He spiraled down . . . 6,000 feet, 5,000, still looking. A small road connecting the airfield and the autobahn came into view. The tractor was nearing the road. Thury looked again at the winged object behind the tractor.

It was an aircraft, but not a very familiar one. He looked again, and it came to him. It must be Germany's sensational new jet fighter, the ME–262! The tractor was probably towing it to the camouflaged airfield. Thury was getting close, down to 4,000 feet. He could distinguish two runways forming a cross, one longer than the other.

Now he looked over the edges of the field. Shadows . . . shapes . . . in the high trees surrounding the airfield. Pretty large. Aircraft! More aircraft, hidden in the edges of forest! The tractor undoubtedly was used to tow jets to the autobahn, which was being utilized as a runway when needed. Numerous shell holes were visible on the runways of the field.

It was a juicy target. Intelligence had long reported the Germans building jet fighters in this area. It was thought the Nazi factory producing these aircraft was located near Munich. Here was an opportunity to destroy a number of the enemy's best.

Thury pressed the mike button. "We'll go down and hit the field," he said. The eight Mustangs steepened dives. Gun switches flicked on and nerves tightened. The fighters, down to 3,000 feet, had not yet drawn a burst of anti-aircraft fire. Thury could see other Luftwaffe fighters on the field, mainly ME–109's and FW–190's. It was loaded. He estimated over two hundred enemy aircraft were on it or nearby in the edges of the woods.

Thury's Mustang, *Pauline,* named for his wife, sliced down to 1,000 feet and pointed its nose at the airfield. Four of the eight Americans broke off into a separate flight and pulled wide. Then they too pointed noses at targets on the field and began a long approach. All were making 400 m.p.h.

Thury lined up an ME–109 in his sight ring as he streaked down. No flak yet. The 109 got bigger and bigger. The trees on the edge of the field were racing under the wings nearer and nearer. The 109 was filling the sight ring. Thury pressed his right forefinger and six guns thundered.

Fifty-calibre shells spattered the ground in front of the enemy fighter, raced toward it, kicking up dust and dirt. The parked German fighter

An Eighth Air Force fighter pilot strafes a grounded Luftwaffe aircraft while another burns in the background. (Air Force Photo)

was struck by a concentrated barrage, and holes opened in the wings and fuselage instantly. Pieces flew off in all directions and almost simultaneously it burst into flame.

Pauline shot over the burning plane as black smoke began to curl upward—oil and gas burning. A burning plane was a kill and this thought flashed through Thury's mind. He looked back, pulling up, and saw his comrades giving the airfield a plastering. There was no enemy fire.

Several planes were burning. The four fighters which had been detached were hitting the opposite corner of the field. Thousands of fifties churned up dust and aircraft on that end. Thury banked to the left, to start round again.

Pauline, circling left, completed the turn around the field. Thury lined up for another pass . . . this time he spotted one of the new jets and got it in his sight. He pushed the stick forward, started down for a second pass. Three P–51's behind picked out other targets and headed down with him.

Suddenly the light reflected from the wings of Thury's fighters, sweeping in toward the field on the tops of the trees. They opened fire as they crossed the edge. Bullets kicked up earth on the field below. But there was something else . . . like tracers in the air. They were the orange golf balls of German anti-aircraft guns.

They flew through the air all around the eight attacking fighters. The enemy had only half a dozen guns in action, but they were a mortal danger, for one hit in the coolant, or another vital spot, and the liquid-cooled engine of the Mustang was finished.

Thury, down low, saw the flak too. He yelled into the microphone: "Get the guns first."

The 505th pilots turned their attention from the Luftwaffe's fighters. Every pilot searched out the edges of the field and any structure which might conceal an anti-aircraft gun. The orange balls from enemy guns gave the German positions away, as did the smoke from their rapid fire.

One by one German gun crews faced a swarm of hostile fighters, pouring forth concentrated fire. If the first Mustang missed, the next would zero in on the gun emplacement. It was a brief and bitter duel. The fighters, outnumbering the enemy guns, and with a five-to-one edge in firepower, silenced every anti-aircraft gun on the field in minutes. The Mustangs' decisive advantage had been mobility. The outnumbered enemy gunners fought and fell where discovered.

With the guns silent, Thury's 51's—some slightly damaged—resumed the attack. With forty-eight guns in action the enemy fighters parked on the field faced a hurricane of destruction. Thury started down on the ME–262 again.

From a thousand feet he opened fire. His fifties criss-crossed in front and scattered wildly over the field. Some struck the ME–262 almost immediately. *Pauline* kept firing, shuddering, and roared over the edge of the field. The ME–262 quivered in the agony of frequent hits.

Being smashed to pieces by hundreds of shells, the enemy plane finally began to burn. Victim number two. *Pauline* flashed over the wreck. The other Mustangs also did well on the pass. Fires popped out all over the field. It was ridiculously easy.

In rapid order enemy planes sprouted flame and smoke—ME–262's, FW–190's, ME–109's, and others. The eight U.S. pilots strung out in a left-turning gunnery pattern, each taking his turn as he came around to the field in the course of his circle. Twenty fires marked the death of German planes on the field!

Now the Mustangs were running out of ammunition. Thury decided to call it off. He ordered pilots to assemble behind him for the long flight back to England.

As the 505th climbed away from the airfield, dozens of burning Nazi aircraft sent smoke skyward. The 505th had suffered no losses. Back at the base, credit would be given for twenty German planes destroyed, many of them ME–262's. U.S. fighters were making a front line out of deepest Germany!

Two and a half hours after turning away from the carnage at Munich, Thury was landing at Fowlmere. Thirty minutes after landing he was accepting congratulations from Colonel Henry. The 339th was smashing up Goering's Luftwaffe as if it meant to do the job alone.

Thury was relaxing—draining tension as he related the highlights of the day's events to the C.O. The two were alone. Henry seemed highly pleased. Something in his attitude hinted he didn't consider the mission the final chapter.

At length he said: "Should the group hit the field again tomorrow?" Thury was surprised; he hesitated, thinking.

"I don't think that would be smart . . . but I'll go," Thury replied deliberately. He said it was logical to assume the Germans would move in strong anti-aircraft defenses—after suffering heavy losses on the field.

Henry exhibited mixed emotions. He didn't deny the logic. But he knew General Murray Woodbury planned to cut orders for another raid the next morning. Another successful action would probably mean a presidential unit citation for the group and a pleased wing commander. He told Thury as much, who replied: "Well, okay, I'll just tell everyone to be on guard for heavy flak."

Later that afternoon a field order clicked in on the teletype at Group Headquarters. One squadron of the 339th Group was to attack the same area next morning. Major Joseph Thury was assigned to lead the squadron—the 505th. As he read the order he wondered if the Germans, too, had guessed he'd come back one more time.

That night orders were posted in the 505th Squadron headquarters for the morning mission. Thury and his men talked it over in the black, Nissen-hut home of the squadron.

The bombers were going deep into Germany. The 505th would feint, going along with the big friends until the last minute, then turn south and streak toward Munich, two hundred miles south by southeast. Despite Thury's foreboding, morale was high. Pilots were eager to score another batch of kills, as they had on the first attack.

Victories were sweet, Thury knew, and the 339th had been late in going on operations: pilots were still hungry, having been stateside during most of the war, during the years when other groups were ringing up victory totals in combat.

Strafing enemy airfields was an unpredictable business. Sometimes an undefended or unorganized field was found, and a number of easy victories scored. But if the field was loaded with light and heavy anti-aircraft guns, these guns were a more formidable opponent than any enemy pilot.

Thury knew what some eager pilots didn't, or didn't care to think about. Many fighter groups in the Eighth Air Force were currently losing more aircraft and pilots trying to shoot up enemy planes on airfields than in aerial combat.

He thought about these things as they planned the morning mission. Talk and planning finally ended and everyone went to bed.

Perfect flying weather appeared when the sun rose next morning. Before the sun lit up the gently rolling countryside, however, a junior officer woke Thury, who pulled on his long flying suit, Army "slippers" and a green flying jacket, and headed for group operations. It was 5:15 A.M.

When the other pilots of the 505th, pedaling their bicycles, began arriving at the operations building, Thury had already been studying the weather, the map and the teletype reports. Sixteen pilots, plus a couple of spares, were to attend briefing.

At last everyone was in his seat, facing a huge wall map of Europe, on a slightly raised platform. There was good news from the weather officer. Nothing to worry about in the way of bad weather. A high overcast was predicted to extend all the way to the target, but would not

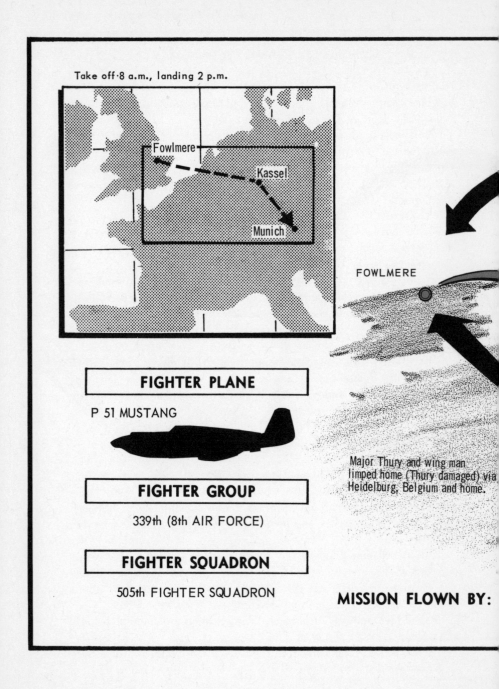

Take off 8 a.m., landing 2 p.m.

Fowlmere

Kassel

Munich

FOWLMERE

FIGHTER PLANE

P 51 MUSTANG

Major Thury and wing man
limped home (Thury damaged) via
Heidelburg, Belgium and home.

FIGHTER GROUP

339th (8th AIR FORCE)

FIGHTER SQUADRON

505th FIGHTER SQUADRON

MISSION FLOWN BY:

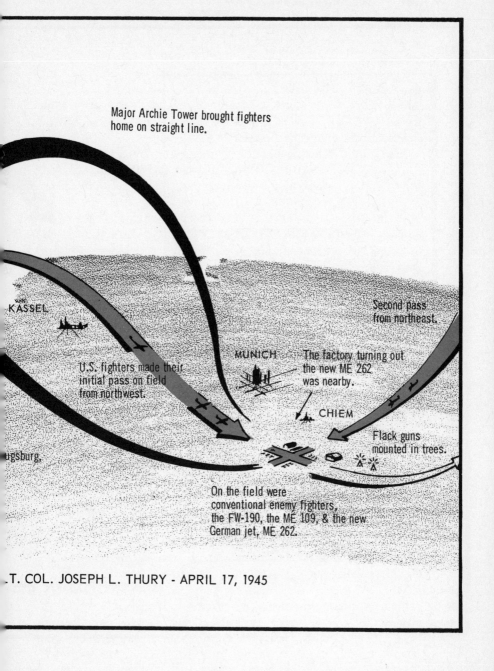

Major Archie Tower brought fighters
home on straight line.

KASSEL

Second pass
from northeast.

U.S. fighters made their
initial pass on field
from northwest.

MUNICH

The factory turning out
the new ME 262
was nearby.

CHIEM

Flack guns
mounted in trees.

ugsburg,

On the field were
conventional enemy fighters,
the FW-190, the ME 109, & the new
German jet, ME 262.

T. COL. JOSEPH L. THURY - APRIL 17, 1945

interfere with the fighters, which would remain below it. A few scattered lower clouds might be encountered along the route but could easily be avoided.

The assistant group operations officer called out compass course, the distress call in code, times and check points. Each pilot copied the information on plastic wood strapped to his leg, careful to write with special red crayon whose mark could be rubbed away quickly in case he was forced down in enemy territory.

Thury drew a chalk outline of the crossed-runway airfield. Most of the pilots listening had attacked the field the day before. Nevertheless, he carefully marked out the field and his proposed plan of attack. Today's attack would be different.

Of the fighters scheduled to take part, twelve or more would be assigned to top cover patrol on the initial pass. These were to circle the field and spot anti-aircraft fire when the other P–51's made the first pass. Thury didn't expect another pushover. If the four attackers drew too much fire, if the field was too heavily defended, the 505th would leave it alone. The 339th didn't want to trade planes and pilots for planes.

However, if enemy's fire was light, if it was such that the P–51's could silence it, Thury wanted the top-cover pilots to strafe the guns as soon as gunners gave their positions away. The fighters which had drawn initial fire would join the others and together the seventeen Mustangs would shoot it out with the guns, after which they would single out parked aircraft and strafe.

The 505th, Thury explained, would begin its flight on the tail-end of the bomber stream. Radio silence would be maintained until the squadron passed over Kassel, when it would turn right, following a 170-degree heading to Munich.

Take-off would be at 11:49 o'clock. Over the enemy field radio silence could be forgotten; targets and enemy fire could be called in by anyone.

"Synchronize your watches," Thury ordered. When this was done, he said: "This time let's clean things up—so we won't have to go back. Good luck." The pilots rose and filed out.

Breakfast was bolted down at squadron headquarters . . . canned orange juice, coffee, fresh eggs (black market, only for those flying), fried Spam, and toast. Breakfast finished, Thury gathered his men around him and gave them last-minute instructions on points not covered at group briefing.

Pilots were to kick a rudder when strafing gun emplacements, to scatter many shells over as wide an area as possible. This discouraged (and often killed) enemy gunners firing at U.S. planes, for fifty-calibre bullets struck such a wide area when rudder was intermittently applied no one was safe below.

Thury designated Major Archie Tower, operations officer, second in command, to take over if anything happened to *Pauline*. He said he would make the first pass at the field. It would be the test pass. If he was knocked down, the new squadron commander was to decide whether flak was too heavy to silence. If not, the remaining planes would immediately attack gun emplacements.

If flak was too heavy, the squadron would withdraw from the area and seek another target. Thury would make his initial pass over the center of the field, and if strafing were continued thereafter, the other flights would join him, one off his right and two off the left. All would make left-turning gunnery passes, to avoid accidents which might occur if some planes circled left and others right.

Pilots glanced at discs hanging on the wall, in the exact order of the morning's formation. A colored disc with each pilot's name and flight color hung in the exact position the formation was to fly. There was red flight—the lead flight, which Thury would head, and white, green and black flights, staggered in that order, and one spare.

The group dispersed; final huddling was over. Minutes dragged. It was unusual to have so much time. The 505th didn't have to worry about rendezvousing with a box of bombers today . . . it would take off at 11:49, long after the bomber stream had passed overhead, and fly along at the end until its departure from the long aerial line at Kassel.

Even after donning helmet and oxygen masks, G-suits, Mae Wests and parachutes, there was more time to kill. Thury used some by walking outside to see his crew chief. *Pauline* was parked less than a hundred yards from squadron headquarters. He found his crew chief ready and waiting, with news that the crew had worked through the night on a special wax job, to increase *Pauline's* speed by ten miles an hour. Thury offered sincere thanks . . . ten miles an hour could mean his life in a jam.

Bombers had stopped roaring by overhead an hour earlier. The rear boxes of a long stream were now strung out over the North Sea. It was after 11 A.M. Thury walked back to the ready room and yelled: "Time to go!" Pilots streamed out.

He returned to *Pauline*, accompanied by Flight Surgeon Fred Scroggins. As he was strapping himself in and hurrying preparations to take off, Scroggins had a word of warning: "Be careful, Joe," he said. "It isn't that important." Thury smiled and acknowledged the sentiment. He was ready to go.

"Clear!" he yelled to his crew chief.

"Clear!" came the reply, and then the whining sound of the energizer. When the Rolls-Merlin spit and caught, and the four-bladed Hamilton-Standard turned smoothly, the clock read 11:45. The crew chief removed chocks and *Pauline* roared slowly off, leaving dusty blasts from the sixteen-foot prop.

At the end of the runway Thury hesitated, until the rest of his squadron, taxiing behind him, could get in take-off position. Then he closed his canopy and spun his right hand round and round, pushing throttle forward with his left. Off to his right, his wing man was ready to take off abreast. Thury brought his spiraling right hand forward and down. Soon the two silver fighters were lumbering down the runway, gaining speed, and after a few moments Thury pulled back the stick to make *Pauline* fly. Her wheels lifted off prefabricated matting at 11:49 A.M. The mission was under way.

In a few minutes the 505th's Mustangs were all airborne, without mishap, having taken off two abreast and circled left until all were joined up. When the last element had cut inside the wide-turning squadron to catch up, Thury swung *Pauline's* nose to a southeastern heading, following the course of the bombers.

At 160 m.p.h. climbing speed, the heavily-loaded checker-nosed Mustangs cut slowly upward into the hazy sky. Soon the coast of England faded. Oxygen began to flow through mouthpieces. At 18,000 feet superchargers cut in with a roar. Silently the squadron continued on, caught up with and passed one bomber box after another.

It crossed in over the Dutch coast, still climbing, near the rear end of the bomber stream, over 20,000 feet up. Shortly after landfall in the squadron reached assigned altitude, 27,000 feet, and leveled off. Speed increased and Thury started checking geographical points below. He noticed the brilliant multicolored tulip fields of Holland, a panorama of spring beauty. In minutes Holland was behind and Germany underneath. Heads began to turn and eyes strained as the squadron crossed the Rhine.

No radio chatter marred the peaceful scene. The bombers created long vapor trails. Thury ordered the 505th to spread out, into wide combat formation. His fighters were steadily overtaking bomber boxes. Then he saw Kassel ahead. Minutes later he gave the signal . . . the seventeen silver Mustangs (one of the spares had won permission to go all the way) banked sharply away from the long bomber stream, right . . . their spinners aimed south. It was 1:45.

Pilots checked gun switches and extra gas tanks and made ready in every way possible. Thury ordered a slow descent. Speed increased. Ahead, right, Munich appeared . . . twenty-five miles distant! "This is Upper Leader," Thury said over the mike. "Drop tanks."

"Upper" was the code name for the squadron. Seventeen Mustangs released two silver 110-gallon wing tanks . . . fuel remained in most of them. As they tumble-plunged Thury ordered top-cover flights to increase throttle. He increased the rate of descent of his flight, which began edging ahead of the higher flights. The twelve top Mustangs not diving steeply strained to keep up. Thury's lead flight, which would make the initial pass, roared down faster and faster.

Munich was passed off to the right. A few minutes later, fifteen miles away, Thury picked out the field, a familiar sight. He turned left to follow the big west-east autobahn for the last few miles to the field. The flight reached 4,000 feet. The field ahead loomed larger and larger. The four silver fighters raced over the autobahn at 400 m.p.h. The thirteen above were at 10,000 feet, trailing slightly, throttles wide open.

Thury turned off the highway, forty-five degrees left, and aimed for the left edge of the field, avoiding its center. He flashed across the nearby trees and over the edge, opening up on an FW–190 at the far left corner.

Shells walked across the turf, ripped into the enemy fighter. Aim was so accurate the FW–190, at the edge of the far woods, blew up in a white flash in Thury's face! He streaked over it, through the smoke, stayed low. Not an enemy gun fired. A heavy black column reached higher and higher where the FW–190 burned. It was unexpectedly easy.

The three top-cover flights, seeing this, hastened down, peeling off and lining up for passes of their own. Thury circled to the left, intrigued that defenses were so feeble. Four of the top-cover fighters fell in behind him and the others stayed together. Thury had now completed his turn, lost some of his great speed, and was coming in again—this time over the center of the field. The nine other fighters roared toward the left edge, over which Thury had just flown.

The four fighters joining him had greater speed, having dived rapidly, and pulled even, in spite of everything pilots could do, including chopping throttles. So eight line-abreast Mustangs whistled down toward the field leading a second pass. Thury aimed at a plane parked on the distant edge.

Pauline flashed low over the hilltops and trees and burst over the field —seven other fighters on her sides. This pass was westerly. The enemy plane expanded in Thury's sight.

A flare arched up in the center of the field. On that signal, a number of anti-aircraft guns opened up simultaneously! Heavy defensive fire shocked Thury, even though he had taken it into consideration planning the mission.

The air filled with red balls, orange balls, smoke, dust. Then, right, Thury saw his number-two man in trouble. Holes opened in his wing. But he flew on. Thury now saw enemy gun emplacements ahead, and pointed six guns at the smoke puffs and open fire.

Thump! He looked at his right wing and saw a small hole. It was a confusing moment. Thury had seconds to decide what to do. He pressed the mike button and yelled: "Hit nothing but guns!" It was a gamble. If the guns were too numerous or if the fighters couldn't find them, losses could become prohibitive. Thury flashed over the far edge of the field, firing until the last second.

Pauline flew on despite the hole in her wing, several inches in diameter. Thury looked back at the field, staying low, away from flak.

There was somthing strange about the enemy's anti-aircraft guns . . . the smoke . . . it didn't start at the ground . . . he strained his eyes. Then he saw them . . . in trees! The Germans had built high gun platforms in the fir trees around the airdrome, hoping to escape the murderous ricocheting of the 30,000 shells the Mustangs had brought from England!

The Germans on these platforms were getting set to take a toll on the next pass. *Pauline* chandelled and Thury shouted excitedly: "They've got guns on platforms in the trees!"

The nature of the battle changed. Every Mustang pilot, alerted, searched the trees. Some, like Thury, had taken hits. On the third pass it would be enemy gunners on the receiving end. *Pauline* headed east:

Thury dropped his nose. Other fighters dipped and enemy gunners got set.

Thury kept his eyes focused on the rapidly nearing gun platforms in the trees, lined them up in the yellow sight ring of his sight. In range, he pressed the stick button, alternating rudder. Six guns scattered metal through the trees like hail. Other 505th attackers followed suit.

Thury estimated 20 German guns were firing. The P–51's were replying with 102. Some of the German guns were bigger but American fifties flashed through the skies at several hundred miles an hour while the enemy was immobile.

Havoc on the field was indescribable. German gunners, expecting the Mustangs to hit aircraft, were suddenly caught in a well-aimed barrage. Shells ripped up dust, almost obscuring the field. The Mustangs pressed their attack. One by one, gun crews were wiped out or forced to flee in a shower of shell.

Pauline whipped around, staying low, and led her section back for pass four. Once again Thury concentrated on the guns. The third pass had reduced enemy fire. As the Americans screamed down for the fourth time it was obvious the fight was being won.

On the fifth pass, *Pauline* opened on aircraft, the guns apparently squelched. This time he hit and set afire an ME–262. Two sections of fighters swarmed over the enemy field, up and down, down and around. More and more fires lit the scene. Thury came in for another pass and exploded his third victim of the day in the center of the field, an ME–109!

Eventually the enemy began to recover, though somewhat weakly, from the savage attack. Rifle fire from the ground became steady. Several Mustangs were hit. A few orange balls reappeared . . . a sign of twenty millimeters.

At that moment Thury was scoring kills. Catching two Focke-Wulfs together, camouflaged near tall trees, he set both afire with a telling burst, touching off a yellow splash of flame and fast-billowing, angry black smoke. Victims number four and five!

The rest of the pilots were scoring hits too. Thury watched them work over the airdrome as he pulled up, and then down, for pass number nine. After the first pass, the Mustangs had lost their great speed, which had made them difficult targets for flak. From 450 m.p.h., they were now down to less than 300. Doing close to 300, *Pauline* pointed her nose earthward. She had ammo for only one more pass. The field rose up fast . . . Thury sighted a target . . . ready to pull the trigger.

Pauline staggered. Crump! Then a number of lesser thuds. A big hole opened in the leading edge of the right wing . . . made by a twenty millimeter! *Pauline* lost airspeed fast. Thury kicked left rudder desperately as his fighter swerved down and right, managed to hold her straight and get to the trees. But *Pauline* had taken twenty millimeter and rifle fire on the ninth pass.

Thury picked up the mike: "I'm hit. Can't get any speed." He asked someone to follow him. Lieutenant James Starnes was nearby; he pulled in beside *Pauline*. The first thing he noticed was a foot-long hole near the landing light in Thury's right wing. *Pauline* was down to 130 m.p.h. Thury yelled to Archie Tower to take over, to leave the field alone if flak got heavier, and turned his nose northwest, toward England, as the Rolls out front labored heavily.

Starnes stuck close. He had to S-turn to keep from running away from damaged *Pauline*. Thury knew he had to climb. He gave *Pauline* full throttle. Slowly she pulled away from the Bavarian countryside below. As she rose, Thury looked back for a fleeting glimpse of the battle scene. Orange fires and tall black smoke columns. The spectacle could be seen for many miles!

Pauline finally reached 3,000 feet . . . still dangerously low, a perfect flak target. Down below Thury recognized Augsburg . . . sixty miles northwest of Munich. The tense flight continued. Beautiful Heidelberg at last appeared, two hundred miles from Munich. He was up to 5,000. *Pauline* flew on. Thury kept the left rudder pedal jammed and continuously applied left stick. His right arm ached and his left leg cramped. He couldn't relax either. *Pauline* roared on. Starnes stuck faithfully by her side.

Thury had reached Belgium, having skirted the guns of the Ruhr, when the engine began to run hot. Temperature soared. Though nearing the North Sea and close to home, Thury became anxious . . . safety just a short flight away and now engine trouble!

He opened mixture to full rich. Raw gasoline would act as a coolant. Still temperature moved up. Desperate, he cracked cowl flaps, though it slowed airspeed, of which *Pauline* had precious little. The cool air rushing into the engine finally began to check overheating. *Pauline* droned on. By now Thury's left leg, holding hard left rudder, was numb.

The North Sea was beautiful . . . but it passed under the wings and the hot engine ever so slowly. But at long last he saw the cliffs of Dover

. . . ahead, the green hills of England! *Pauline* flew on. Now Thury's hopes soared. Starnes radioed Fowlmere . . . "Emergency landing." Action was immediate.

Crash trucks, emergency equipment of all kinds and ambulances raced into position. All eyes at Fowlmere searched the sky. From the southeast, grinding along slowly, two red-checker-nosed fighters changed from specks to dots to aircraft. Thury knew he would have to come in at full speed . . . 130 m.p.h. He wouldn't use flaps or fly a tight landing pattern. He spotted the runway and made a slight left turn, lined up. Starnes flew his side.

Pauline's engine, rough but finishing the race, pulled the injured fighter the last mile. The runway got larger and larger, now came rushing up. Thury nosed *Pauline* down and headed for the near end. Thump! She hit the metal prefab. Thury pulled the throttle handle back. As soon as speed slowed to a moderate roll, his left leg collapsed from fatigue. It was 5:52 P.M. He had made it.

He managed to rumble into his revetment. Some fifty crewmen and base personnel crowded around. His crew chief looked at his shot-up aircraft in amazement. He crossed his arms in the cut-engine signal. Thury switched off.

A dozen men jumped on *Pauline's* wing. Among them was Flight Surgeon Scroggins and Intelligence Officer Charles Hammond. When Thury climbed out amid congratulations, Scroggins put his arm around him. "You boys sure did good, Joe."

Thury downed two swigs of rye. He never drank, though pilots were allowed two ounces of whiskey after missions. But on this occasion he took two. Hammond supplied the rye. The toast was not inappropriate. Another thirty-nine enemy aircraft had been destroyed! That was fifty-nine in two days for the 505th—many of them ME–262's. Thury had destroyed two the first day and five the next—seven in two days!

The 505th was on its way, in claiming more victories in a year than any other squadron in the Eighth Air Force. For the missions to the Munich–Chiem Lake area, the 339th received the presidential unit citation. For leading the attacks, Thury was awarded the Silver Star.

Next day the flight surgeon and Thury left on three-day leave to London. *Pauline* was junked. Besides the bigger holes, she took more than her share of smaller ones. The crew chief, in fact, counted more than a hundred of them—memoirs of one of the great strafing attacks of World War II.

By the end of the war, Thury had been credited with the destruction of twenty-five German aircraft in strafing attacks, in addition to several aerial kills, adding up to one of the great combat records of World War II.

INDEX

Rouen, 69
Rouen-St. Otterville, 149
Ruhr, 128, 246
Russia, 5, 23, 66

Saffron Walden, Essex, 62, 80
Sagan (now Zagan), 80
Sakai, Saburo, 43
Saipan, Marianas, 190
Salamaua, 83, 89, 190
San Bernardino Strait, 191
Sansapor, 190
Sarangani Bay, Mindanao, 191
Schilling, Lieutenant Colonel
   Dave, 157
Schweinfurt, 148, 149
Scott, Colonel Robert L., 43
Scroggins, Flight Surgeon Fred,
   242, 247
Sells, Lieutenant William O., 41
Shanghai, 3
Shaoyang, 43
Siang River, 8, 16, 17, 20
Smith, Lieutenant Colonel Meyrl,
   197, 198, 199, 202, 203, 204,
   206, 207, 208, 209
Solomon Islands, 22, 190
Somme River, 69
Sorau, 170, 171, 174, 188
Spaatz, General Carl, Command-
   ing General, A.A.F., 229
Spain, 190
Spanish Civil War, 9, 147
Split-S, 184
Stalingrad, 42
Starnes, Lieutenant James, 246,
   247
Steeple Morden, 171, 172, 185,
   186, 187
Stettin (now Szcecin), 180
Stewart, Group Leader Everett W.,
   171, 172, 176
Strausberg Airdrome, 176

Strauss, Lieutenant Andrew B.,
   167
St. Omer, 66, 67
St. Paul, Minnesota, 232
St. Petersburg, Florida, 194
St. Vith, 217
Suichwan, 43
Surigao Strait, 191

TAC (Tactical Air Command),
   215, 216, 227, 229
Tacloban, Leyte, 194
Tampa, Florida, 232
Tarawa, Gilbert Islands, 190
Thury, Lieutenant Colonel Joseph
   L., Chapter 12, 230–248
Tinian, 190
Tokyo, 4
Tower, Major Archie, 241, 246
Tunis, 116

United States, 3, 4, 22, 23, 43, 54,
   155, 169, 190, 227, 231
U.S.A.F., 4, 231
U.S. Army Air Corps, 5, 57, 62,
   128, 189
U.S.A.A.F., 4, 21, 22, 26, 47, 61,
   64, 66, 82, 93, 107, 109, 149,
   153, 230
U.S. Navy, 21, 22, 99

Von Rundstedt, 215

Wainwright, General Jonathan,
   190
Walcheren Island, 160
Wash, The, 141
Watkins, Lieutenant James A., 41
Wattisham, 67
Wehrmacht, 64, 147

Set in Linotype Fairfield
Format by Norma Stahl
Manufactured by The Haddon Craftsmen, Inc.
Published by HARPER & BROTHERS, New York